"And now I'm afraid we must get on with the more regrettable stage of our brief acquaintance." Captain Feeny

"Well, even if we found nothing, it's an effective discovery." William XU

"Free cable is the ultimate aphrodisiac." Chip Douglas

"... cause as we sit here chatting, there are important papers flying rampant around my apartment cause I don't have anything to hold them down with." Paul Hackett

"Greetings Earthlings. I am the Bishop of Battle, master of all I survey. I have 13 progressively harder levels. Try me...if you dare." The Bishop of Battle

"God, this is my man, and you better take care of him, or I'm gonna wax your ass." King Blues

"Hey, Hey! Let's go to McDonald's!" Black Belt Jones

"Billups Allen is my kind of film writer and *101 Films You Could See Before You Die* is my kind of book: a user guide for the infinitely curious; a beginner's mindset for the trenches-dwelling buff. I discovered movies that felt like they'd been waiting for me all along and was reminded of ones I loved that had been sacrificed to time and a crumbling memory. In Billups's world, there's only one bar to talk turkey when the movie is over, and you leave your brows—highs, lows, and in-betweens—at the door." – **Nate K., host of Burn It Down!, WFMU**

"His taste is wide-ranging—that is to say, all over the map. He reviews everything from *Kind Hearts* and *Coronets* to *The Cable Guy*; *Angel Heart* to *Zodiac*. He finds an interesting angle on all of them, invariably rooting out what good he can find in even the worst movies..." – **Mike Stax, Ugly Things**

"Billups not only sneaks you into amazing films you might not have heard of, he gives you a fresh perspective on what you already saw. Reading *101 Films You Could See Before You Die* feels like you are hanging out early at the theater together with a soda and candy, learning about absolute gems. The book has that genuine excitement to see what trailers are going to come up before the movie you've been waiting so long for. Movie reviews are better with Billups' enthusiasm." – **Mike Plante, director of *We Were There to Be There* (2021)/programmer at Sundance Film Festival**

"- ...smart, unpretentious and entertaining writing." – **Steven Puchalski, Shock Cinema**

"A no-nonsense film guide written with candor and charm, full of a passion that decries pretension. This book is for people who want to experience a true smorgasbord of cinema curated with an informed, often funny and refreshingly unique voice." – **Josh Schafer, Editor-in-Chief, Lunchmeat Magazine**

"*101 Movies You Could See Before You Die* isn't a definitive list of what a film fan should see. It's a reflection on what a fan has seen. Reading the impressions of other fans is what fanzines are all about. I'm a fan too. That's how I know this book is a fanzine in disguise." – **Greg Cartwright, Reigning Sound**

"If you've never had a friend who always has a movie you've never heard of to recommend, who has a thought-through opinion on every DVD in the dollar bin, who knows exactly who that actor you vaguely recognize is AND what band they were in in the '70s AND why the band broke up AND what '90s CD compilation their only single was re-released on—this book could be that friend." – **Dorothy Gambrell, Cat and Girl Comics**

"If someone's gonna talk movies to me, I want it to be Billups Allen." – **Bloodshot Bill**

101 Films You Could See Before You Die
a film guide for the disenchanted

By Billups Allen

First published in the U.S. in 2022 by
Goner Records
2152 Young Avenue
Memphis, TN 38104
Layout by Jen House
Edited by Andria Lisle
© Billups Allen, 2022
ISBN 9-780999-540046

*This book is dedicated to anyone who ever bought a ticket
for whatever movie starts next.*

101 Films You Could See Before You Die
a film guide for the disenchanted

Table of Contents

Introduction 13

Chapter 1: Adrienne Shelly 18
Trust (1990) 20
Hold Me, Thrill Me, Kiss Me (1992) 21
Sudden Manhattan (1996) 23

Chapter 2: Americana 25
The Apostle (1997) 26
Bamboozled (2000) 27
Ragtime (1981) 30
The Swimmer (1968) 31
Zodiac (2007) 33

Chapter 3: The Blame Game 35
The Cable Guy (1996) 36
Ishtar (1987) 38
Neighbors (1981) 40

Chapter 4: Dangers on a Train 43
Midnight Meat Train (2008) 44
Runaway Train (1985) 45
Train to Busan (2016) 47
Transsiberian (2008) 48

Chapter 5: Detective Perspective 51
Gorky Park (1984) 52
High Heels (1991) 53
The Secret In Their Eyes (2009) 55
Sharky's Machine (1981) 56

Chapter 6: Documentaries 60
Jimi Hendrix (1973) 61
Louie Bluie (1985) 62
Marlene (1984) 64

Chapter 7: Farnsworthy 67
The Grey Fox (1982) 68
The Straight Story (1999) 69

Chapter 8: The Final Frontier 72
Europa Report (2013) 73
Event Horizon (1997) 75
The Green Slime (1968) 77
Outland (1981) 78
Planet of the Vampires (1965) 79
Sunshine (2007) 81

Chapter 9: Franchiseus Interruptus 83
Superman Returns (2006) 84
The Thing (2011) 86
Wes Craven's New Nightmare (1994) 88

Chapter 10: H.G. Wells 91
Time After Time (1979) 92
The Time Machine (1960) 94

Chapter 11: Hi, Karate? 96
Black Belt Jones (1974) 97
The Octagon (1980) 98
Timecop (1994) 100

Chapter 12: Horror 102

Body Snatchers (1993) 103
Calvaire (2004) 104
Candyman (1992) 106
Christmas Evil (1980) 107
Dead and Buried (1981) 109
Def By Temptation (1990) 110
Evilspeak (1981) 112
Eyes Without a Face (1960) 113
Lair of the White Worm (1988) 115
Nightmares (1983) 116
Possession (1981) 118
Resolution (2012) 120
Severance (2006) 121
The Shrine (2010) 123
Starry Eyes (2014) 125
Trick or Treat (1986) 126

Chapter 13: Just for Laughs 129

Brain Candy (1996) 130
Cedar Rapids (2011) 131
Four Lions (2010) 133
Hamlet 2 (2008) 134
In a World (2013) 136
Kind Hearts and Coronets (1949) 137
King of Hearts (1966) 139
Lust in the Dust (1985) 140
Safe Men (1998) 142
Three O'Clock High (1987) 144

Chapter 14: Loose Can[n]ons 146

Dredd (2012) 147
The Punisher (1989) 149

Chapter 15: Michael Mann 151

Thief (1981) 152

The Keep (1983) 154
Manhunter (1986) 155

Chapter 16: Monster Mash 157

The Blob (1988) 158
Crawl (2019) 159
Dagon (2001) 162

Chapter 17: Music be the Food of Love 164

32 Short Films About Glenn Gould (1993) 165
Get Crazy (1983) 167
Nico 1988 (2017) 169
Phantom of the Paradise (1974) 170
Rockers (1978) 172
Round Midnight (1986) 174
Tender Mercies (1983) 177
Wattstax (1973) 179
Wild Style (1983) 180
Wild Zero (1999) 183

Chapter 18: Nostalgia-rama 185

Cooley High (1975) 186
Matinee (1993) 187
The Wanderers (1979) 189

Chapter 19: Sci-Fi 191

Attack the Block (2011) 192
The Lawnmower Man (1992) 193
Miracle Mile (1988) 195

Chapter 20: Serrated Edges 197

God Told Me To (1976) 198
Lifeforce (1985) 199
Session 9 (2001) 200
Timecrimes (2007) 202

Chapter 21: Speak of the Devil 204

Angel Heart (1987) 204

Devil (2010) 206
Mr. Frost (1990) 208
Prince of Darkness (1987) 210

Chapter 22: Stepchildren 212

After Hours (1985) 213
Barry Lyndon (1975) 214
Trafic (1971) 216

Chapter 23: Threes 218

Alien 3 (1992) 219
Exorcist III (1990) 221
Halloween III: Season of the Witch (1982) 222

Chapter 24: And ten more 225

Bad Influence (1990) 226
Diamond Men (2000) 227
The Duellists (1977) 229
In Bruges (2008) 231
The Last Days of Disco (1998) 233
One False Move (1992) 235
Take Shelter (2011) 236
Vanya on 42nd Street (1994) 238
The White Ribbon (2009) 240
World's Greatest Dad (2009) 241

Three Interviews 245

Interview with Pleasant Gehman 246
Interview with Nick Prueher and Joe Pickett 253
Interview with Mary Woronov 264

Introduction

101 Films You Could See Before You Die: a film guide for those running out of things to talk about.

Expectation is the great killer of fun at the movies. Expectation is also the primary goal of movie marketing. If they can get us all expecting something, they've done their jobs. There was a time when the expectation was to buy a ticket and see a movie. It was a relatively simple equation. Now no movie comes to fruition without expectation. Expectation has gained importance exponentially since I became aware that I liked going to the movies. The best movies forever exist in your head. The more hype there is, the more let down you're inevitably going to be when the time comes to sit and pay attention to a movie.

I was eight when I saw *Star Wars* (1977) for the first time. I recall seeing it, but I don't recall having heard of it before we went. My parents took me because we were at a gas station and could see the line was shorter than it had been since it opened. That was at the DeVille Cinema in Jackson, Mississippi. The theater is long gone, but the building is still there. I still have a visceral reaction when passing the shopping center. I used to go to that theater with my grandfather. I wish I could see one more movie there in the same sort of way I wish I could hug my long gone dogs. I remember a lot about the night I saw *Star Wars*. I remember sitting to the left inside the theater. I remember being scared by a poster for *Alien* hanging on the wall. When I got home I put erasers on the arms of several chairs around the house and pretended they were buttons in the cockpit of a spaceship. That was probably more fun than I ever had collecting the action figures.

Star Wars was an immense cultural turn for me. All I ever wanted to do for years after was to go back and see that movie again. My grandparents sat through it several times. If VCRs existed then, I'd have probably watched it three or four times a day. What a left hook it was; one that I didn't see coming. Of course, I now realize *Star Wars* brought with it a lot of new problems to independent cinema, but I've always been grateful I saw it under the circumstances I did. I consider myself lucky for that. Another early memory is a dream in which, from the back window of our beige station wagon, I watched a shopping cart follow us home. I won't be attempting to write a book about that anytime soon.

My dad told me recently, very matter-of-factly as he does, that I was once dropped on my head when I was very young. My parents for some reason took me to the drive-in. They figured the volume would keep me awake and they could keep an eye on me. I was too young to remember that, but I like to think I've never looked back. I love movies. I love theaters. I loved when my mom would bring home a VHS tape from the grocery store without anyone asking, especially when I was sick. I still love going to the movies with someone when they want to see something and I don't know what it is, except that it did once lead me to a screening of *The Sisterhood of the Traveling Pants*. Don't ask me what I thought that movie was going to be about.

As much as I love going to movies, I love reading about movies. I love reading about what other people think is a good or bad movie. I love academic books about film. I love genre guides. The history of film is endlessly interesting to me. But lists mentioning death stress me out. The concept of having a hundred things to do before I die strains my sense of order somewhat. When I first saw *Star Wars*, I felt like I'd be seeing *Star Wars* forever. I don't have a list of a hundred things to do before I die, reminding me I have a limited number of *Star Wars* screenings left on this planet. I have to see these movies before I die? Or what? *He worked hard at being a good person, but alas, he never did get around to seeing The Deer Hunter (1978), sooooo.*

Firstly, I don't really want to die. Secondly, I hope near the end I have more to think about than if or not I've seen the exact hundred movies some list says I'm supposed to see. That means every time I watched *Dodgeball* (2004) or *Balls of Fury* (2007), I should have been watching Godard or I was wasting my time. Yes, that looks good on paper, but try it in practice. By my estimation, I was not wasting my time. But what if I die thinking about that? What if I see one of the hundred more than once? Does three viewings of *Clerks* (1994) negate the need to watch *The Apu Trilogy* (1955, 1956, 1959)? I don't think it does. This is a slippery slope for a neurotic. And they do this with everything: loads of things I don't care about have 100 lists. Every pizza slice is a distraction from the 100 restaurants we're meant to patronize. What if I like one of the hundred restaurants and go every night *until* I die? What if I go to one restaurant a hundred times and the waiter decides to kill me? There'll be ninety-nine restaurants I'll never get around to unless one of them happens to be Arby's. And Arby's wasn't my choice that time either. Neither was the Algonquin, where I actually have had dinner in spite of my station. But no one forced me to go to Arby's or the Algonquin. I still had a choice.

Maybe I'm getting off track, but it would be nice to get some help from other entities if society is meant to devolve into nothing but a series of lists. Maybe show the top hundred movies on airplanes. The FAA can make you sit and watch *400 Blows* (1959) and forbid you from getting up and roaming around the cabin during the boring parts while flight attendants monotonously croak pre-written cultural context into the PA microphone. In an emergency, they can quickly screen a hundred trailers of the hundred movies you're supposed to see before you die as the plane goes down. You ultimately die screaming, but also with a vague sense of what a hundred movies you were supposed to have watched were about. That would spare your mother or significant other an awkward last minute cell-phone call.

Yeah, yeah. I know. If you're reading up to this point you have dismissed me as a neurotic and/or contrarian. And I am. I enjoy it. But I don't think I'm better than you just because I know about a few movies. I'm not a monster. I'd be happy to look at *your* list. I love a good movie suggestion. I'd like to make a good movie recommendation to someone one day. More often than not, people don't seem to like the movies I recommend. I'm obsessed with movies people aren't that crazy about. Why? I don't really know. But it doesn't help my life much. I do think it's good to be aware of other's canons. It's good to cultivate this attitude in every aspect of your life. No matter where you live, someone does something well there, and you should be aware of it and want to write about it. It's good to have some respect for history and artistry. But I've seen *Ernest Goes to Jail* (1990) as an adult and enjoyed it. I'm not recommending you do the same.

There were circumstances. Contexts. Bonding. Other.

My point is, if you think I have bad taste, I'll take that. If you're interested enough to still be reading this, try not to think too much about the status of the films in this book. They're just movies I like and/or see some strange value in for various reasons, and for some reason I have a desire to point them out to you rather than live a regular life, a life that might end with me not having seen all the movies I was supposed to see, but might end with me recognizing the full breadth of Dolph Lundgren's performance as *The Punisher* (1989). These are movies I've seen that I enjoy and feel have slipped through the cracks of the annals of time for one reason or another. And if you think I'm a hack, read something else. No one is forcing your hand. I'm sincerely not claiming this to be an important list of movies. It's just some stuff that interests me. And you don't have to see all of these movies before you die. Or any of them for that matter. You will most certainly die anyway.

Chapter 1: Adrienne Shelly

A surge of independent films in the 1990s caused a collage of comedic voices to find their way out of the garage and congregate in the art house, second run, and occasionally part-time porno theaters across the country. Heavy dialogue, blunt observations, and the occasional absurdity took hold of a younger audience with an ironic sense of humor. Comedy inadvertently took on new responsibilities. Bill Murray's ironic swinging and Chevy Chase's deadpan carousing were becoming passé. Blossoming were low-budget films with a new comic sensibility. Kevin Smith's camera captured the everyday life of a gaggle of store clerks. Spike Lee's sense of humor gave us pause to consider what we were laughing about. Quentin Tarantino's ironic veneration of fading celebrity allowed some good actors to stay relevant.

There was a change of sense of humor coming out of the wild, cocaine-fueled 1980s. Actress/director/writer Adrienne Shelly and director Hal Hartley were among the shock troops of the new wave of '90s independent films. A carload of us went to see *Trust* when it played at Washington D.C. 's Dupont Circle 5. The Circle 5 would play a major role in my movie upbringing, not because it was such a great underground arthouse theater, but because you could see a film like *Trust* while explosions from big budget action movies bled through the walls. Shelly and her co-star Martin Donovan blew me away with their dark outlook and matter-of-fact delivery. That movie blew me away. Later, at a great arthouse theater called the Key, I didn't realize I was seeing Shelly on-screen again in a lesser movie called *Hold Me, Thrill Me, Kiss Me* that was billed as being suggested for people who enjoyed John Waters' sense of humor. *Hold Me, Thrill Me, Kiss Me* was a tamer and less subtle affair, but Shelly's smart sense of humor bled through a rough film that would become a loveable film to me anyway. Hal Hartley's first collaboration with Shelly, *The Unbelievable Truth* (1989) is a superior film to *Hold Me, Thrill Me, Kiss Me*, but I wanted to explore this brief period when the depth and richness of Shelly's role in independent film affected me greatly and in some ways kicked off an early version of a film checklist that would follow me ever since. Sadly, Shelly was murdered in a senseless crime in 2006. She left behind a legacy of uniquely funny films. Here are three films from the '90s illustrating the wide span of her talent from her collaborations with Hartley, to her writing and directing, and just plain putting in work when she was cast in a role.

Trust (1990)
Directed by Hal Hartley
U.S.A. 107 min.

Trust is Hal Hartley and Adrienne Shelly's second collaboration. Alongside Shelly, many of the same actors from Hartley's first film *The Unbelievable Truth* (1989) returned in *Trust*. In the film, Maria (Shelly) is a high school student quarreling with her father. After a fairly typical argument, she tells him she's pregnant. Shelly slaps her father and leaves the house. What she doesn't see on her way out the door is that her father is in such shock he drops dead. She goes about her business doing typical teenage stuff, including informing her boyfriend Anthony (Gary Sauer) of her pregnancy. This doesn't go well, and the situation leads Maria down a few dark alleys. Meanwhile, Matthew (Martin Donovan), an angry nihilist, is quitting his job. Matthew is a whiz with electronics but has trouble keeping work because he doesn't like television and refuses to fix T.V. sets. The local fix-it shops need people to work on televisions. Matthew is a no-nonsense nihilist who is able to aggressively stand up to anyone and everyone except his sadistic father Jim (John MacKay). Matthew and Maria meet and find meaning in the world defending each other. Although the idea of a working marriage comes up, the relationship is largely platonic. It makes for a touching partnership without the obligatory love scenes and tropes. Along the way, the two also set out to solve a mystery regarding a stolen baby. In the bleak exploration of the lurid side of Long Island created in the film, baby theft is played for comedy, a theme the Coen Brothers were not afraid of three years earlier in *Raising Arizona* (1987). *Raising Arizona* did an excellent job of creating a world in which a kidnapping could be construed as funny. Roger Ebert, though complimentary of aspects of *Trust*, complained the world created in this film is uneven. I disagree, because the world they exist in is a constrictive version of a suburb. Here the curtain is pulled away from two Long Island homes revealing despair, oppressive parental relationships, and boredom; inserted is a compelling love story that doesn't have anything to do with sex. The tone and setting work as a dissection of the romantic comedy genre.

Trust builds to a triumphantly melancholy ending. It's bleak in the sense that, of course, these people probably won't be okay in the grand scheme of events at play at the end of the story. But neither will the perfectly matched lovers in a similar film where you find satisfaction in their kissing and walking off into the sunset. There is a certain hopefulness rising among the chaos exploding from their logjam. Besides making a very blasé and funny film, Hartley created a relationship between two main characters you can root for without needing for them to be together. The finale creates unique homage to bittersweet partings like *The Umbrellas of Cherbourg* (1964) or *Casablanca* (1942). It is one of my favorite romantic movies because the romance is largely expunged and what's left is the reality that sometimes you don't know what you need, but you may get it when you need it.

Hold Me, Thrill Me, Kiss Me (1992)
Directed by Joel Hershman
U.S.A. 92 min.

After an auspicious start with lead roles in two Hal Hartley films, Adrienne Shelly appeared in the 1992 film *Hold Me, Thrill Me, Kiss Me*. There are better examples of Shelly's range as an actor. Shelly also had nothing to do with producing or directing the film, roles she would excel at later in her career as she made some interesting dark comedies of her own. But I enjoy the trash-cinema nature of *Hold Me, Thrill Me, Kiss Me*. The film is not as crass as John Waters' movies, but it exercises similar bones and muscles with black humor coming from loud characters living on the outskirts of society. Shelly plays a role in the main story, although the film occasionally breaks down into vignettes regarding the back-stories of the residents of a trailer park in Northern California. Lucille (Diane Ladd) portrays a lustful, slightly above middle-aged woman whose stories often reach into the too-much-information category. Olga (Ania Suli) and her porn-obsessed son Lazlo (Bela Lehoczky) live together in not-so-great harmony due to an incident in which Lazlo believes Olga owes him a large sum of money. Olga is an elderly woman claiming to have been an opera star in her home country of Hungary. Timothy Leary has a role as a criminal go-to type who is trying to help one of the main characters Bud (Max Parrish) flee the country. The mix of professional and non-professional actors often adds to the fun and realism of the conversations and creates humor in these absurd situations.

Shelly anchors the film in many ways, primarily due to her ability to act and cement some of these absurd scenes together. Shelly portrays Dannie, a naïve girl living in a trailer park that serves as the end of the road for the lively cast of characters. Her sister Sabra (Andrea Naschak) is a stripper and working porno actor. Sabra lords over Dannie since their parents died in a mysterious fire. Bud is a second-story man hiding out in the trailer park. This plot unfolds patiently as anecdotes and soliloquies from the other tenants of the trailer park paint pictures of life in a small Northern California town. Among several high points, the film can be occasionally uneven due to the variety of ensemble characters being introduced and left behind as the plot struggles to stay relevant. But there are some good laughs and crazy performances in tow. The earnestly amateurish feel fits the tone of some of the early made-to-be-cult movies like Paul Bartel's *Eating Raoul* (1982) and Alan Arkush's *Rock 'n' Roll High School* (1979). The film also has a solid rock'n'roll soundtrack featuring the Pixies, the Cramps, and the Violent Femmes. It's a fun movie and is another film that didn't get a home video release outside of VHS until 2018. Here is another of Shelly's performances available only to people who kept their VCRs.

Sudden Manhattan (1996)
Director: Adrienne Shelly
U.S.A. 80 min.

As a director and producer, Shelly wrote, directed, and starred in three films. Sudden Manhattan is her directorial debut. The plot is absurd to the point of surrealism, but it's a fun ride for those who believe people like Dali and Borges may have had a sense of humor. Shelly portrays Donna, a writing student who sometimes sees things that are not there. Donna witnesses a murder and believes her breakfast eggs are trying to tell her something about it. She gets involved with Adam (Tim Guinee), who slowly ingratiates himself to her as events in her life appear to repeat themselves around this murder she can't seem to navigate past. She then sees another murder very similar to the first one. She can't convince anyone she's seeing these things. She has no proof. She sees it again. Now she comes across as crazy. Adam enlists acquaintances to help set a trap to investigate. While this loosely connected group of people attempt to make sense of her experiences, the plot lines intertwine and involve her group. *Sudden Manhattan* is Shelly's most bizarre effort, one I recommend if you're into surreal plotlines intertwining. Much of the action in the film is unlikely, but it's a fun movie if you can push logic to the side.

Shelly's second directorial effort is another interesting dissection of genre. Shelly continues the deconstruction of the typical "woman comes in and changes a sad man's life" narrative in the 1999 film *I'll Take You There*, a horrible title as the implication that a pseudo-romantic comedy with this title opens the door for sadistic producers to create a trailer using the Staple Singers' song of the same name. Shelly appears in the film, but only briefly. The main character is portrayed by '80s actor Ally Sheedy. Sheedy portrays Bernice, a girl who agrees to go on a date with Lucy's (Shelly) brother Bill (Reg Rogers). Bill has been dumped recently. He isn't over his ex and can't get his life together. He agrees to drink with Bernice and lashes out at her, viciously calling her "desperate" and "ordinary." It's an obvious first-strike to shoo her away. Bernice is shocked. She leaves, but arrives back on the scene three days later. She's been wandering around. She hasn't bathed. She hasn't gone to work. Something about their encounter threw a switch. Bill and Bernice end up on a road trip together while Bernice slowly unravels. In one scene, Bernice acquires an antique pistol and tells Bill if he takes her to the store he can borrow her car. While Bill broods in the driving seat, Bernice is seen in the background robbing a dress shop of all the dresses off the mannequins in the window. She walks casually out of the store with the pistol in hand and the dresses folded in her arm. It's a funny film with Ally Sheedy off the leash as the Shelly character and Shelly's dark sense of humor informing the path of resistance against making a typical romantic comedy.

Chapter 2: Americana

I love a good slice of Americana. Some movies make great commentary about our Nation's institutions. *Mr. Smith Goes to Washington* (1939). *Meet Me in St. Louis* (1944). *The Natural* (1984). *The Right Stuff* (1983). *Team America: World Police* (2004). This section deals with movies with American-specific themes that stir my wonderment about our great country.

The Apostle (1997)
Director: Robert Duvall
U.S.A. 134 min.

The Apostle is a great film, but unusual in that it works best if thought of as a piece of fantasy Americana. Some of these scenes are said to have been from actual churches, which opens a load of questions I don't fully have time to go into in this writing. If I thought churches and church-related organizations like the radio station depicted in this movie really work as they're depicted on screen, I might have a better opinion of the role of religion as a practicality of everyday life. The plot of The Apostle requires you to make a leap of faith about the motivations of many of the characters involved. You're meant to like the main character, and he's likable to a point, so it works until you think too much about it. If you put aside what you know, or think you know, about religion you can enjoy an inspirational and well-developed story. If you think too much about the perpetration of religion by a con man on the citizens of a small town that could use help in other areas, you may lose the point in your own narrative. You might be thinking I need to lighten up, but in real life I would have trouble rooting for this man based on charisma alone.

Robert Duvall portrays a Pentecostal minister named "Sonny" Dewey, the head of a large church in Texas. He is a little crazy, but he is determined to spend his time on Earth preaching. I'll warn you: there is a lot of preaching in this film. Dewey preaches as a guest speaker in big churches. He preaches in tents in fields with Spanish interpreters relaying what he's saying. There is no place he won't take the Word of the Lord. Along the way, you learn that this schedule has worn down Dewey's relationship with his wife Jessie (Farrah Fawcett) who is also part of their established church. Jessie doesn't possess the same drive to follow the Word to the nth degree, and their divorce is imminent. For Jessie, it's a done deal. Even so, she isn't a monster. She engages patiently in the process of easing him into it. Dewey spends a lot of his alone time at night praying and talking to himself, even torturing himself as he hopes against hope that God will intervene and save his marriage. All of Dewey's praying reveals that he lacks the insight to wonder if he might be part of the problem. Dewey blames demons, etc... His alone time creates a creepy tone in the film. After a while, as Duvall and Fawcett beautifully set the stage for their failed marriage, you forget that you're watching two such iconic actors. There are moments where you feel something bad is going to happen, but the dread is pulled back for a later outcome. They dispense with active shouting matches and threats. Scenes unwind, like Jessie quietly seeking out and unloading a pistol. These activities do come to a head, and at this point it behooves me to stop talking about it, as the plot takes an unexpected turn aided by solid storytelling and great misdirection. You know something is coming because it's a movie, but they do a great job of not telegraphing the punch. It's impossible to get through this story without questioning the nature of forgiveness or where it fits as a concept, but there is a good story housed in the film. They pulled it off; the rest is up to you.

Bamboozled (2000)
Directed by Spike Lee
U.S.A. 135 min.

Pierre Delacroix (Damon Wayans) is an angry broadcast executive. His tenure at a large network has garnered lukewarm attention and has dulled his interest in creating programs. Delacroix is determined to be fired from his job as an executive programmer so he can move on. He devises a plan to create a show utilizing the dance prowess of a street performer named

Manray (later known as "Mantan") and building the show around him with the sets, clothes, and jokes of an old-time minstrel show. Manray (Savion Glover) is a terrific tap dancer aided on the street by his friend Womack (Tommy Davidson). Delacroix, Manray, and Womack create a minstrel show for broadcast television, with Delacroix expecting to be fired at the pitch meeting. But his boss Thomas Dunwitty (Michael Rapaport) is a loudmouth young executive who sees himself as someone who knows African Americans better than Delacroix. The plan to get fired backfires as Dunwitty buys hard into the idea of reviving the minstrel show. The concept is an instant hit, with fans arriving in black face and sparking protests and outrage in others. Instead of being fired, Delacroix becomes both the hero of the network and a lightning rod for backlash as the producer of the problematic television show. This situation causes him to further explore his feelings about what it means to be African American.

Others struggling with their reactions to the show are Delacroix's assistant Sloan (Jada Pinkett Smith) and her somewhat estranged brother Big Blak Afrika (Mos Def). The leader of a militantly pro-African hip hop band called The Mau Maus, Blak auditions for the show before knowing the full details of its content. He and his cohorts conspire to shut down the show, but often fail at rallying the troops. Meanwhile, tensions regarding the show escalate across the board. Reverend Al Sharpton and Johnny Cochran both make appearances in scenes protesting the network.

Aside from the hard political questions hard wired on the screen, *Bamboozled* is entertaining on multiple levels. Savion Glover is an excellent dancer. His dancing is a key element to the film, and sometimes the audience is forced to watch him perform in full minstrel regalia, which viscerally causes the type of confusion the film suggests. How can we watch this and enjoy it? Another strong point in the film is the relationship between Glover as Manray and Davidson as Womack. Their friendship is touching, furthered by Womack's awakening to the situation. Davidson is a criminally underutilized talent who deserves more screen time, and he's due for a reevaluation from filmmakers. Like many Spike Lee movies, there are interesting vignettes sewn around the main plot broadening the complication of the primary dilemma. One of the most interesting subplots is the visit Delacroix makes to his somewhat distant father Junebug (Paul Mooney). Junebug is a comedian who has kept his career in Afro-centric bars and audiences. Junebug has no desire to do material that would help him cross over to white audiences and doesn't do much to hide his disdain for Delacroix's network job.

Bamboozled was shocking in 2000 when it was released. One of the more interesting things about revisiting the film is how the scenes involving the production and broadcast of the show seem satirical to the point of surreal by 2020 standards. Or do they? Knee-jerk liberalism would certainly stop a show like this from getting past the pitch stages. On the other hand, in the age of post-Trump, there may be more people than ever who might greenlight a return of the black-faced minstrel show. Spike Lee is among the world's greatest living directors. This movie deserves to be discussed because, besides being a well-executed story with some truly great performances, there was a time I would have declared it too absurd for a story like this to ever happen. But as America races to trip over itself, particularly in the media, this movie could become too relevant sooner rather than later.

Ragtime (1981)
Directed by Miloš Forman
U.S.A. 155 min.

Ragtime, like many good historical dramas, is a great Sunday afternoon movie. It efficiently explores the boons and struggles of a wide swath of American society without insultingly cloying drama, and it allows the viewer time to ponder America's journey from a time before both world wars, accessible mass communication, and equal rights. The story is set near the end of the Industrial Revolution right before the declaration of World War I. The Edwardian period in England is winding down and America is coming into its own. Rather, this is America discovering its identity. Newsreel montages are interspersed throughout the stories setting a tone for the drama of the era. Real events are portrayed alongside fictional plots. Thinly connected arcs intersect to paint a picture of a moment in time in American history. *Ragtime* has the pace and scope of an iconic American film like *Nashville* (1975) where the minutiae unfolds in the lives of major and minor players exposing the culture in detail. A major launching point is the public shooting of industrialist Stanford White (Norman Mailer) and the very public "Trial of the Century" of his killer Robert Joy (Harry Kendall Thaw). Another chunk of the film is mapped through the life of Joy's wife Evelyn Nesbit (Elizabeth McGovern). Like many other characters in the film, Nesbit is loosely connected to many of the storylines. We also see the story through Coalhouse Walker Jr. (Howard Rollins), an African American pianist who fights back against an injustice dealt him by the local fire department and makes a stand against unfair treatment of African Americans during this time. The events in the film are also loosely seen or connected by a family living in upscale New Rochelle, where Walker has a child with the maid.

The family is known only as Mother (Mary Steenburgen), Father (James Olson), and so on. Younger Brother (Brad Dourif) becomes obsessed with Nesbit but is eventually rejected and eventually joins Coalhouse Walker Jr.'s fight for justice. Separately, Nesbit and Mother meet a toymaker named Tateh (Mandy Patinkin) who will become a major player in the upcoming silent film industry. Other interesting characters include Commissioner Rhinelander Waldo, who James Cagney came out of retirement to portray, Booker T. Washington as played by Moses Gunn, and early film appearances by Frankie Faison, Samuel L. Jackson, and Jeff Daniels. Various characters wind in and out of focus, but the plot never gets confusing or slow. The burden of this weighty cast interacting at different intervals of the story falls on director Milos Forman, who handles the glut of serendipitously bound characters well enough to leave the film with a sense of hope in tow. Although the nuts and bolts of the story are based in some fact, the story doesn't always go the direction you think it will. The connections are uncanny, but illuminating as a new vanguard of people discovers the struggle of the American dream.

The Swimmer (1968)
Director: Ellen Perry/Frank Perry
U.S.A. 95 min.

The Swimmer is a surreal romp based on a short story by the great American short story writer John Cheever, an author adept at peeling back the layers of the facade of the American dream. The film relies on the foundation that in an affluent Connecticut neighborhood, swimming pools are tucked away in many of the back yards. This realization comes to Ned Merrill (Burt Lancaster) at a pool party with friends during a pleasant, mid-morning gathering. A fit middle-aged man who likes to kid his friends about their weight and talk about his good old college days, Merrill is in unusually good spirits at the party. It's a nice day at a friend's pool. They are feasting on drinks, jokes, and stories. He makes an observation that there are enough swimming pools between the party and his home that he could swim to his house, and then just as arbitrarily, wanders off to jump in a neighbor's pool. He's decided he's going to swim home. It's the sort of thing the joker at a party might say. But Merrill is off pool jumping like a bored teenager. Residents come out to see what he's up to. Some are glad to see him. Some are not. Some of those chastising Merrill clearly have history with him. It becomes clear things are not going well for him, and he isn't acknowledging it. There's clearly something wrong with him.

Lancaster does an excellent job as the film's unreliable narrator. Merill seems mostly unaffected towards people's attitude towards him. The tone of his trip becomes creepier as he gets closer to his final destination and the frivolity of his decision to swim home takes on new realities. Along the way, he picks up his old babysitter Julie (Janet Landgard). She follows him for a while under the guise his plan is groovy, but soon detects something is off about him. Others are nonplussed and even hostile at the sight of him. He comes across a larger pool party where he is recognized by the host and barely tolerated until Merill had his first notable breakdown in the film. He believes a handmade hot dog cart at the party belongs to him. Does it? The audience can figure it out, but no one at the party is moved. Lancaster plays the role close to his chest. It's a blank but stunning performance, especially for someone with a reputation as such a lavishly brazen actor in other roles.

Merrill's breakdowns and confusion comes on slowly, keeping the journey something of a mystery and exponentially creepy. It's not all morbid either; there are moments of fun absurdism, like when Merill comes across his nudist neighbors. Why are there nudist neighbors? There is no direct explanation except that behind the tree-lined drives of America, you'll never know what you'll find. Perhaps it's an allegory of America being its own adventure.

Zodiac (2007)
Directed by David Fincher
U.S.A. 157 min.

Zodiac acts as a police procedural, a newspaper story, and a horror movie rolled into one compelling narrative. It's a police procedural void of clichés: no hero cop, no last minute confession, no unsupportive captain, no last minute hidden evidence that's been in plain sight the whole time, etc. It's a newspaper story that tells the unfortunate truth that after a certain time, the story doesn't matter much to the public. It's one of those hefty narratives that never get dull. There is something magical about a big film with loads of characters that can be woven into a plot that can hold your attention for as long as *Zodiac* does. Here, the audience watches the true story of the Zodiac killings and pieces together multiple theories through several main characters as weeks and months pass with little progress. It's a lot to ask from a movie, and *Zodiac* should be watched solely to study how this can be done. Paul Avery (Robert Downey Jr.) is a crime reporter following the Zodiac case closely, partially because the Zodiac Killer famously sent cryptic and taunting letters to San Francisco area newspapers during his primary killing spree. Avery's sidekick is the unlikely Robert Graysmith (Jake Gyllenhaal). Graysmith is the paper's cartoonist, but he ingratiates Avery with a penchant for puzzles and thinking outside the box. On the case for the police are homicide inspectors Bill Armstrong (Anthony Edwards) and David Toschi (Mark Ruffalo). Through these four characters, we see the ravages time takes on a case like this. The camera unapologetically regards people who, despite all their time and best efforts, are forced to live with an unrequited mystery and are further taunted by more murders over a long period of time. Wrapped inside the procedurals is stark horror tension, which is buried like an M&M floating in a bucket of popcorn. The portrayal of the second murder plays with sharp imagery as a couple lying in a park on a lovely day are causally terrorized by a man wearing a black hood and a large silver medallion with the Zodiac's symbol on it. Fincher uses innovative horror tropes to catch the audience by surprise. Even though the scene is master-level horror, it doesn't come across as egregious. It captures the sad, unnecessary nature of the murders without glorifying them. The film adroitly manages that fine line, not sensationalizing the Zodiac, but showing the hold he had on the Bay area at the time.

The film has an entire second half where the intrigue switches gears. It appears very purposeful when Anthony Edwards and Robert Downey Jr.'s characters leave the story. The film then engages Gyllenhaal's Graysmith to a new level and brings in big, fun guy actor John Carroll Lynch as Arthur Leigh Allen. Allen is the favorite subject on a lot of Zodiac theorist lists. Graysmith is the author of the book the movie is based on and, like the book, we see Graysmith chase down several theories including Allen. All of this is done with a solid attention span. It's a mystery without a conclusion, and *Zodiac* carries this out with dignity and satisfaction. It's an unusual film with terrific performances that serve as a lesson on how to tastefully handle a big subject as a narrative.

Chapter 3:
The Blame Game

Here, I'm going to go a little too far in defending three movies I enjoy that have been the butt of many jokes. You may just blow my opinions off as those of a contrarian, which I fully cop to being. And you may continue to hate these movies, but at the very least, I'm going to make a case for their reassessment.

The Cable Guy (1996)
Directed by Ben Stiller
U.S.A. 96 min.

A dark comedy, *The Cable Guy* is often criticized as being too dark for the audience it was meant for. I never understood this criticism. Are we to start measuring darkness levels in scripts? I get that it's because Jim Carrey was the star, and at the time he was popular for acting buffoonish. He certainly acted buffoonish and took a beating for how this film came out. Even so, I count it among his best performances. Sure, his silliness doesn't entirely project the weight of what is happening on screen, but that's what makes his performance so eerie and so great, whether intentional or not. Imagine someone so disconnected with reality that they can move around and function like "Chip," Carrey's character. *The Cable Guy* is a well-constructed story. It carries some insight into Ben Stiller's early humor. His TV show was not the best thing he ever did, but taken in the context of this movie, you can see that Stiller had a lot of commentary in him early on. So you have a smart director with his sights on the nature of media, and a loony comic actor in a starring role, and to boot, you've got a seasoned straight man in actor Matthew Broderick. I'm still confused as to what the lost expectation was?

Steven Kovacs (Matthew Broderick) is moving into a new apartment. Chip/ The Cable Guy (Jim Carrey) arrives to install the cable. Chip susses that Kovacs is depressed and makes a friendly gesture. It's a bizarre one, but friendly nonetheless. Kovacs reluctantly agrees to hang out. Chip pursues the friendship to unusual and varying degrees of success, alternately annoying and helping Kovacs with the minutiae of his problems. This is a completely reasonable first act. Everyone has had a friend who bothers him or her a little. A friend who calls you more than you answer. A friend you only invite to certain things. I've been that friend. As you might guess, Carrey's performance is over the top. Sure, in real life you could see yourself needing to avoid the sort of trouble he brings. But if Chip were only mildly annoying, there'd be no plot. Furthermore, Broderick plays a good mark as a person going through a breakup. Someone whose confidence is low and may be acting slightly passive in life just to avoid uncomfortable situations. The main characters are established and their relationship degrades due to a series of escalating events.

If you don't like Jim Carrey, then there's no need to watch this. That's fine. But his performance here is appropriate for the film. He is put into an existing story and his mannerisms

```
The Cable Guy
   Jackie Brown
   The Bounty

The Blob '88
After Hours
   Gorky Park

Midnight Meat Train
32 Short Films About Glen Gould
THE EXORCIST III

MANHUNTER
BARRY LYNDON
   Rick James Episode

Krush Groove
TRick or Treat
   GWAR on Joan Rivers
```

and misdirection make his next move hard to pin down. His erratic behavior and unusual plans are enough to provide comedy and entertain without letting you process the next situation. And some scenes just work to showcase Carrey's comedic style. If this were a Fred Astaire film, some of these segments would be designed to show off dancing prowess. Carrey's character is resourceful like a serial killer. There are likely people out there we're glad don't have the proclivity to kill, otherwise they might be good at it. Serendipity is occasionally too much on his side, but he carries the plot when you can't entirely guess what's coming or how it will arrive, and it provides laughs along the way. This would be too dark a movie, perhaps, if Kovacs had been left in a suitcase on the side of the road, like at the end of *Henry: Portrait of a Serial Killer* (1986). There's a dark movie for you. *The Cable Guy* is funny and smart and does a fine job of contextualizing a situation that would scare the shit out of the average person. What else do you want from it? Sure, it's not for everyone, but then again, nothing interesting is.

Ishtar (1987)
Directed by Elaine May
U.S.A. 107 min.

There is something about the bandwagon of a bomb at the box office that people love to jump on. For instance, I knew about the Michael Cimino film *Heaven's Gate* (1980) at an early age because Mad Magazine made regular references to its box office failure. Once some momentum gets going in that direction, people love the joke and have no qualms about piling on. Sometimes it's just circumstance and bad luck that drives the bad press avalanche phenomenon. Ishtar was the butt of many late-night monologue jokes upon its release. Ishtar was produced on a strained set. Director Elaine May clashed often with actor Warren Beatty and the cinematographer Vitorio Storaro. News of this got out, tainting the press's view on how the production was proceeding. Budgetary problems were also leaked to the public. In short, this film was tossed into the Coliseum to be torn apart by dogs before it had a chance to be fairly evaluated. Even the great cartoonist Gary Larson made a Far Side drawing about its failure. Being the great guy that he is, Larson later retracted his work and apologized.

Ishtar's plot follows two terrible songwriters who find each other and form a terrible duo. Chuck Clarke (Dustin Hoffman) and Lyle Rogers (Warren Beatty) find an agent named Marty Freed (Jack Weston). In these cynical times, a low-budget agent representing a struggling stable of mediocre performers is a trope Hollywood hasn't trotted out much since 1984's classic *Broadway Danny Rose*, or the pseudo-musical series *Road to...* produced between 1940 and 1962, which starred Bing Crosby, Dorothy Lamour, and Bob Hope. *The Road to...* series is what *Ishtar* is modeled after. Freed gets the two a gig at a hotel in Morocco, prompting the very funny line "A lot of acts would kill for a booking in North Africa." There's one laugh right there. The two run afoul of the CIA and unwittingly become involved in a plot to overthrow the current political regime.

The structure of *Ishtar* in its emulation to the *Road to...* movies is a bit corny and outdated, but the storyline patronizing political intrigue is relevant even today alongside other films about incompetent government operations gone wrong. Hoffman and Beatty are believable as a couple of guys so wrapped up in what they're doing that they are clueless as to what is happening to them. Beatty in particular plays a solid "dummy with a heart of gold" that keeps the duo's moral compass in check. The film has an old-style dynamic to its humor. There is one regrettable scenario where Clarke is trying to convince a third party that he is translating between two groups of Arabs speaking different dialects, of which Clarke speaks neither and is just connecting nonsense words. I'm going to warn you about that scene because it's not too cool. But there is a lot to like about *Ishtar* if you enjoy the old road/buddy-comedies to which it obviously pays homage.

Neighbors (1981)
Directed by John G. Avildsen
U.S.A. 94 min.

There are so many problems with this movie that it's hard to compartmentalize the arguments against it. Actors John Belushi and Dan Aykroyd didn't like director John Avildsen's vision for the film. The original soundtrack concept was deemed inappropriate and replaced with tone-bending, cartoonish riffing. Belushi was reported to be in a bit of a spiral in his personal life. And having read the excellent book by Thomas Berger that the film is based on, I agree that the movie does not do the novel justice. Berger's book is a dark comedy about paranoia challenging the reader with Jorge Luis Borges-inspired surrealism set in a familiar suburban landscape. It's an excellent novel. To enjoy the film, it is important first to divorce yourself from the source material, but then that could be said about a lot of adaptation projects. *Neighbors'* bad reviews are part of Belushi folklore. Roger Ebert defended it with remarks calling the movie "...hallucinatory black humor." He also said, "It grows on you." *Neighbors* has been with me for a long time, landing at a time in my life when I so blindly adored the Belushi/Akroyd pairing that I wouldn't have called anything they did a failure. But when I first saw *Neighbors*, I was steeped in the humor of the day. This comedy did, in fact, grow on me. For decades I've revisited this movie and found it to be worthy of mining for humor.

The most striking question about the plot is why do Earl

Keese (Belushi) and Vic Zeck (Aykroyd) go to such lengths to vex each other? Their clashes are anarchic in practice and futile in ambition. The consequences of their actions have no intellectual or financial payoff. They don't seem to care much even about winning. They seem to be motivated to foul each other. When push comes to shove, one will defend the other just to keep the rivalry going. You can talk that into a flaw, but combined with the absurd world they create between two suburban houses, the back and forth is oddly captivating. Their actions rarely have much effect on the next set of actions. It's as if Jean-Luc Godard had directed a series of Tom and Jerry cartoons. Fueling this is another idea that most movie theory books will tell you is a bad thing, but what endears *Neighbors* to me is the little motivation that the characters have to act the ways that they do. They are both enigmas in their own worlds. Keese is at base a boring, suburban office drone. But put into situations in which most people would just lock the front door and ignore, Keese takes the acid. He walks down the road to clash with his new neighbor.

That brings me to the most compelling argument for *Neighbors*: Aykroyd himself. Every review I've read mentions how Aykroyd and Belushi went against their usual character dynamics to make this movie. It's mentioned as a negative in bad reviews and occasionally as brave in better assessments of the movie. But I've never read a review that mentions Aykroyd's performance in the film, which I find sets the movie well beyond the standard comedy of the time. Aykroyd is often mentioned as a primary character in Belushi's career: a silent sidekick and nerd-driven intellectual. Aykroyd is most at home in roles like his sleazy con man Irwin Mainway from *Saturday Night Live*. He's as great as the spiv-inspired pitchman for a blender-turned-fish scaling device as he is as the unsavory TV presenter E. Buzz Miller, who delights in showing clips of animals having sex on his television show. Aykroyd's front-of-house characters may have been a bit overshadowed in the wake of Belushi's meteoric rise, but he is a comedic genius all his own. *Neighbors* is one of Aykroyd's best performances. He excels at hawking nonsense through cigar clenched gold teeth as the smoke rises into his dyed blonde curly locks. If Keese is an enigma in the film, Vic is impenetrable. You learn he was a nurse. That's about it. What motivates this man to do the things that he does?

Neither character makes total sense, and there is no time in the film that either one of them couldn't just walk away from the other. There's nothing at stake. You could pick out and champion several things I've said here and claim that's why *Neighbors* is a bad movie. But maybe even throwing out the rules isn't enough sometimes. Maybe you'll watch this and enjoy it and wonder: how did disgruntled stars, a frustrated director, a dislodged soundtrack, and a series of truncated and sewed together vignettes accidentally make a funny movie? Maybe I just like it and I've steered you wrong. But I agree very much with Ebert's assessment: the film grows on you.

Chapter 4:
Dangers on a Train

The 50-second film *L'Arrivée d'un train en gare de La Ciotat* had its first screening on December 28, 1895. As legend has it, frightened Parisians bolted to the back of the room in fear of the footage of a train arriving at the La Ciotat station. This account of people running from the film of a train barreling at the screen has been argued several times, but the idea of trains adding intrigue to a narrative holds true throughout the history of film. *L'Arrivée d'un train en gare de La Ciotat* wouldn't be the last film to utilize train travel as a setting for drama and intrigue. Even though train travel isn't as relevant in our everyday lives as it used to be, cinema continues to hold a place for it. Train travel has its own set of minutia and rules. The setting is slow going. The implication of falling off or being separated from your party in a strange place is inherently terrifying. And at the same time, train travel is romantic. It's close quarters. And no matter what you do, you're more or less at the mercy of more experienced travelers. These are some overlooked train-based narratives you may want to ignore for a bit if you're planning a romantic trip along the rails.

Midnight Meat Train (2008)
Directed by Ryuhei Kitamura
U.S.A./U.K. 98 Min.

Clive Barker can paint a dark, surrealist tale like no other horror writer. To follow him down his alleys of sensibility is to believe that demons operate by an arbitrary set of rules. *Midnight Meat Train* is adapted from a short story from the first volume of Barker's *Books of Blood* series, an absolute must read for fans of short horror fiction. But where Stephen King often puts his character's Maine-grown sensibilities to task in nuevo American gothic tropes, Barker connects to the demons and doesn't give his characters much time to consider the right thing to do. And they often pay in literal blood and guts. Barker's stories are ripe for the screen. He goes for the gore, but also tries to get his audience there in an intelligent and thoughtful manner. Your average spurned townie doesn't often come into play as the killer. Or so it may seem to Leon Kaufman (Bradley Cooper, a year before his massive breakthrough in *The Hangover* (2009). Kaufman is an art photographer who, in a strange confrontation on the subway, photographs a woman who is being harassed. The camera's presence scares the would-be attackers, and the photos attract the praise of high-end gallery director Susan Hoff (Brooke Shields). Hoff likes the pictures, but is nonplussed with the rest of Kaufman's work and encourages him to get more real. Kaufman then becomes obsessed with following a local butcher named Mahogany played by English footballer and actor Vinnie Jones. Mahogany's neat, conformist appearance reads suspiciously to Kaufman. He's an "imposing character" without subtext. Kaufman figures he's up to something and needs proof, but decided he better get a picture of it himself so as to grab a spot in Hoff's next gallery show. Kaufman begins following Mahogany much to the detriment of his health and well-being.

Meanwhile, Mahogany's methods and motivations are arbitrary, keeping the police and the audience in the dark about his background. The special effects and gore in this movie are a spectrum of low-budget fun and full-blown cinematic massacres. *Evil Dead* actor Ted Raimi lends a rather absurd death to the proceedings. I enjoy Barker's short stories because the scares and the scope of his ideas are often terrifyingly large, but they place the burden on the character who is opening the doors. They're often flawed, but not irredeemable. Cooper and Jones strike a strange balance in the film and it works. *Midnight Meat Train* is a small obsession that goes big. It works both as a Barker demon-tale and also as one of those strange New York City stories you might think of when riding alone on a subway car.

Runaway Train (1985)
Directed by Andrey Konchalovsky
U.S.A. 110 min.

If you've seen the anarchic documentary *Electric Boogaloo: The Wild, Untold Story of Cannon Films* you may remember *Runaway Train* mentioned as one of the lesser-known jewels produced during the reign of Golan Globus. Director Andrey

Konchalovskiy has a long filmography including films made in the Soviet Union, post-Soviet Russian films, and Hollywood productions including, stay with this, 1989's infamous buddy cop flop *Tango and Cash*. I'm not familiar with *Tango and Cash*, but it certainly must not have suffered from slow action. Konchalovsky can express a taut action sequence. *Runaway Train* is a tense movie involving characters you can't quite pin down in a situation you can't totally see happening, yet the situation becomes acceptable as the characters commit.

Oscar Manheim (Jon Voight) is a prison folk hero. He's been in the hole for three years. Amidst a prison riot, a court order releases him from solitary confinement. Oscar wastes no time executing half an escape plan he has been concocting. Throwing a wrench in the plan is a cheap hoodlum named Buck McGeehy (Eric Roberts). Buck tags along. In spite of Oscar not wanting Buck around much, Buck pulls his weight and the two make a daring escape from Stonehaven Prison Maximum Security Facility, only to hurl themselves into the Alaskan wild half-dressed, nearly freezing to death before arriving at a busy train station. Dressed in stolen work clothes, the two hop a freight train, presumably one that will carry them through the impenetrably frozen Alaskan tundra. But in a twist unknown to Oscar and Buck, the train conductor has a heart attack and drops dead. After a small collision, the two become wise of the situation and make their way to the engine room. They are able to circumvent a smashed walkway blocking the front of the train. By the time they discover the train has no conductor, the engine is unreachable. The train barrels across the cold Alaskan landscape.

By now you're thinking this coincidence is a bit outrageous, but the journey includes scrapes over icy ledges, trains hitting trains, blocked railway changers, and, believe it or not, a helicopter chase. You won't care if the premise is a little far fetched. The screenplay is based on an Akira Kurosawa screenplay, so you can set aside plausibility for a psychological complexity that keeps motivations shifting smoothly enough for a tense plot with an opaque ending. Voight and Roberts carry the narrative with excellent performances. *Runaway Train* is also beautifully filmed, with contemplative and terrific footage shot in Alaska and Montana. Perfect if you're looking for an intelligent and taut action movie.

Train to Busan (2016)
Directed by Yeon Sang-ho
South Korea 118 min.

The 2000s brought with it new interest in the zombie movie. After the success of a few stellar zombie narratives like *28 Days Later* (2002), *Shaun of the Dead* (2004), and a surprisingly fresh remake of *Dawn of the Dead* (2004), cinema was rife with dead bodies crawling out of graves and onto screens. For a while, everyone with a camera was making zombie movies, experimenting with zombie movies, or spoofing zombie movies. It didn't take long for zombie fatigue to set in. For those in doubt of the existence of fresh meat, 2016's *Train to Busan* is one of the tightest, most claustrophobic zombie movies ever made. Director Yeon Sang-ho presents the most unique zombie narrative in many years by setting all the action on a commuter train to, as the title suggests, Busan. Busan is a large city in South Korea, home to the sixth busiest port in the world. It's a two-and-a-half to three hour train trip for those traveling between Seoul to Busan, but for those making the commute on this particular morning, it's going to be a rough ride. Sang-ho utilizes the tropes of his predecessors nicely and adds a few new twists without changing the rules of the game significantly. It's a fun movie with excellent performances.

The story opens on financial worker Seok-woo (Gone Yoo).

Seok-woo is having trouble relating to his daughter Su-an (Kim Su-an). For her birthday, she wants to go to Busan to visit her mother. As the train pulls out of the station, a mysteriously injured person boards unnoticed. As people discover her hiding in the bathroom they try to help her, but I don't have to tell you that she has a quickly spreading disease and, yeah; you get the idea from there. Seok-woo is a straight-laced business type who finds an unlikely alliance with rough and ready passenger Sang-Hwa (Ma Dong-seok) and his pregnant wife Seong-kyeong (Jung Yu-mi). Sang-Hwa and Seok-woo don't get on well at first, but they'll soon have to pick a corner, nearly literally, as every section of the train becomes infested with flesh-eating zombies. They eventually unite and create a formidable fighting team: a great motif as characters are forced to make hard decisions about helping and/or teaming up with other passengers. They also face a pocket of passengers who feel they are safe and won't let others in their train car. For such a narrow setting, the scope of nooks and hideaways creating danger and redemption is excellent. The film is masterfully shot for maximum tension. The performances and scenarios are solid and create genuine fear and sadness as the protagonists are slowly culled. It's a great film with great scares and a surprisingly warm ending that leaves a little room to cheer.

Transsiberian (2008)
Directed by Brad Anderson
Germany/U.K./Spain 111 min.

The Trans-Siberian Railway is the longest railway line in the world. It's entirely likely there's a story or two riding those rails at any given time. Director Brad Anderson co-wrote and directed the labyrinthine horror movie *Session 9* (2001), also covered in this book, which was set at Danvers State Mental Hospital in Danvers, Massachusetts before it was torn down.

Such a scary place deserved to have a story written about it. I wonder if there was a similar approach here: the Trans Siberian being a setting so large and foreboding that a film had to be made. Elements of a typical "thriller on a train" narrative are in play, but the story deflects expectations and creates genuine suspense eschewing the common tropes.

Roy (Woody Harrelson) and Jessie (Emily Mortimer) are missionaries in Beijing. On their way home, the two decide to visit Moscow by way of the Trans Siberian. Roy is a train enthusiast and can't miss the opportunity. Jessie is a good sport. Within the confines of the train, Roy and Jessie make friends with fellow travelers Carlos (Edwardo Noresa) and Abby (Kate Mara). Carlos and Abby appear to be a little worldlier than Roy and Jessie until details about Jessie's past come out over drinks one night. Jessie appears corruptible. Carlos too appears up to no good. Roy is especially naive. Abby is the wild card. The train takes the group into rural areas where the government's hold on the populace is palpable. Abby sees people interrogated openly. Police need very little reason to get into people's business. A warm but cynical policeman named Grinko (Ben Kingsley) traveling to a conference enters the picture. Grinko appears trustworthy and reasonable, but to quote Max Cherry from *Jackie Brown* (1997): "... a good cop will never let you know he knows you're full of shit."

By now maybe you've imagined a film with loads of double crosses, and that's astute. But the screenplay creates tension by testing your faith in the character's loyalties with some unusual tests. The claustrophobia and minutiae of foreign travel amplify the fears and tension created for characters whose motivations are born out of circumstance. Even when escaping detection, there are shockingly futile moments of "what now?" It's a taut movie with great acting and an unusually satisfying plot for how many alleys these four encounter on a simple train ride.

Chapter 5:
Detective Perspective

Since there has been narrative cinema, there have been detective movies. Whether it's a pipe-smoking Englishman, a precocious high school girl poking her nose where it doesn't belong, a van load of unemployed kids and their dog, a society couple and their dog, a cartoon mouse, or a person who is just getting too old for this s%$t, detectives are necessary to wrap up our cinematic messes. These four detective stories resonate with me. Why? Why indeed? The game is afoot.

Gorky Park (1984)
Directed by Michael Apted
U.S.A. 123 min.

The film version of Martin Cruz Smith's best selling novel could fall into the category of an above average but somewhat forgettable thriller you might enjoy on a rainy day and forget soon after. But some movies possess an ethereal quality that elevates their historical worth. *Gorky Park's* tone, underlined by James Horner's bleak score, Ralf D. Bode's cold cinematography, and stand-out performances by William Hurt and Brian Dennehy, really captures America's fear of Russia during the 1980s. Russia was a primary diplomatic enemy to America in that decade, and nowhere were we reminded of that more than in American movies. But more than most of its cinematic competition, *Gorky Park* abandons stereotypes yet manages to create a bleak and paranoid entity behind the dark narrative of a KGB murder cover up. That and a hefty look into the unforgiving Russian black market will have your paranoia radar fully tuned.

William Hurt plays Arkady Renko, an orthodox cop in Moscow who is regularly forced to acquiesce on his hunches and good sense to stay on his team's good side. This time, on the case of three murdered students, Renko is urged to drop the case in no uncertain terms. But his sense of justice and the brutality of the slayings of the young, somewhat innocuous students compels him to investigate. Through an unlikely turn of events, Renko encounters William Kirwill (Dennehy), a New York City cop investigating the death of his brother in Moscow. While it seems Kirwill would have a hard time going unnoticed in Russia being an NYC detective, the chemistry between the two cagey cops is created through one of those magical duos born by pairing great character actors.

The film encapsulates a moment in time when Russia was America's sworn and mysterious enemy. Inherent fear of the ruthless and unforgiving KGB encourages dread and paranoia in the narrative. Not allowing much comfort are the dangerous, "nothing to lose" characters involved in the black market. Alexie Sayle (co-creator and author of British cult television program *The Young Ones*) makes a memorable appearance as a black market spiv, a role he has played several times for comedy. This role's move to a dramatic setting makes a quick case for sympathy for the character without giving away his fate. The supporting cast is a believable group of small-time criminals trying to sneak around a looming government that would show them little mercy were they caught.

The only telegraphed punch is Lee Marvin playing Jack Osborne, a suspicious merchant who quickly becomes the subject of Renko's attention. Just being Lee Marvin means he's up to something, but Marvin puts in a great performance while being a team player, allowing Hurt room to portray the problem that won't go away. The case finds Renko and Kirwill digging deeper into the connections given in the movie towards a slightly unlikely but entirely satisfying resolution.

High Heels (1991)
Directed by Pedro Almodóvar
Spain 112 min.

High Heels was released the year after of one of Almodóvar's more successful exports *Tie Me Up, Tie Me Down* (1990). *Tie Me Up, Tie Me Down* garnered some international success. In America, it joined films like *Henry: Portrait of a Serial Killer* (1986) and *The Cook, the Thief, His Wife and Her Lover* (1989) which were under discussion by the MPAA as to whether they needed an NC-17 rating to bridge the gap between R and X.

High Heels marked a bump in distribution for Almodóvar in the U.S. This unusual murder mystery/melodrama didn't rock the boat as much as *Tie Me Up, Tie Me Down*, but it's a great movie with some good laughs and a secret in tow.

Becky (Marisa Paredes) is a famous singer and actor. She's also the absent mother to Rebeca (Victoria Abril). The movie opens on a time when Becky lost track of Rebeca at an open-air market. Becky is focused on her career and decides to go to Mexico for a job. She leaves Rebeca behind in Madrid. Mexico consumes Becky for fifteen years. The two are reunited for a time when Becky returns to live in Madrid. Rebeca is grown and working as a newsreader. She is also dating an older man named Manuel (Féodor Atkine). Manuel owns the station where Rebeca works and is also an ex-lover of Becky's. Manuel doesn't take his marriage to Rebeca very seriously. In spite of his macho demeanor, he is threatened by Rebeca's friend, a mysterious drag show performer who imitates Becky's 60s songbook under the name Lethal. Manuel is having an affair with Isabel (Miriam Díaz Aroca), the station's sign language interpreter, who is after Rebeca's seat reading the TV news. Manuel also seduces Becky again in an attempt to relive the glory days. One night, after sleeping with both Becky and Isabel, Manuel is murdered. There are three suspects. Rebeca goes to jail after a dramatic and hilarious on air confession where she describes the murder in detail to her agape staff. But is she the real murderer? If this all sounds convoluted, wait until a detective named Eduardo Dominguez (Miguel Bosé) enters to investigate. Rebeca goes to jail for the crime. Inside she learns the ins and outs of prison life. She is also treated to an impromptu prison musical number. This story is ripe for Almodóvar's unique style of melodrama. His palate of bright primary colors, dark humor, and tales of tense family relationships frame the story.

The Secret In Their Eyes (2009)
Directed by Juan Campanella
Argentina/ Spain 129 min.

Benjamin Espósito (Ricardo Darin) is a retired Argentinian cop with a haunting memory of an old case he could not see to a conclusion weighing on him. He's writing a novel, but he can't even bring himself to write what he's thinking. In a flashback to 1976, we see he's recalling a brutal murder. The year this happened is also the year he fell in love with a colleague: Irene Menéndez Hastings (Soledad Villamil). Hastings is a judge now. Espósito visits her to get some perspective on the case. They sit and reminisce about the case and the year they met: 1976.

This was also the last year of the dictatorship of Isabel Martínez Perón. The political turmoil surrounding her reign and fall caused complication to the winding case. Espósito and Hastings continue to reminisce and the audience sees them snake through this inexplicably unwinnable case in key flashbacks, including government corruption and the general indifference of the police to the murder. There is some misdirection and the case is closed. People involved come into power quickly and squelch evidence and wield influence, only to lose their positions and disappear once again, as was the danger for many citizens at the time of the unrest.

The film contains excellent performances all around. Darin and Villamil as star-crossed do-gooders, Richard Morales as Pablo Rago, the grieving widower whose efforts cause the case to be reopened at an opportune moment, and Guillermo Francella as Pablo Sandoval, Espósito's intelligent but overdrinking sidekick. Argentina under the failing Perón administration is a dangerous enough place to be, let alone for people trying to solve a case no one wants solved. Moments of tension creep around every corner, especially as Espósito often does not know who's after him.

One stand out scene contains two minutes and thirty-three seconds of Espósito and Sandoval chasing a suspect through a crowded soccer stadium during a match. Handheld camera shots push through the crowded stands and labyrinthine halls of the stadium in one long take, creating a shaky and tense foot chase. The roar of the crowd intensifies the shaky the camera. It's one of the wildest chase scenes since Steve McQueen hit the accelerator as Lt. Frank Bullitt in the infamous car chase through San Francisco in *Bullitt* (1968). The soccer stadium chase is truly a very unique scene, one with such ingenuity you'll have the urge to wish you could show it to Hitchcock and ask him what he thinks of it. The case has a nice Serling-esque wrap up, so let's not divulge details of the case. You'll have to trust that the ending, performances, portrayal of Argentina during the fall of Perón, and the soccer chase scene are reasons enough to cherish this film. It won "Best Foreign Language Film" at the Academy Awards before they realized every film's language is foreign to someone. But it won nonetheless. You'll agree it deserved it.

Sharky's Machine (1981)
Directed by Burt Reynolds
U.S.A. 112 min.

For a movie star with 143 films listed on IMDB, Burt Reynolds acted in surprisingly few good movies if you really dig into his oeuvre. Some of his films are well-remembered. Some of his films probably hold on to the scent of nostalgia. Reynolds is undeniably fun to watch. But when you're counting "good" movies, it's a stretch to push the boundaries of qualifying films past much more than his cult of personality. An obvious high point is *Deliverance* (1972). Include *Smokey and the Ban-*

dit (1977) and that's two. Hitchcock reportedly liked *Smokey and the Bandit*, so you'd be in good company, although I don't recommend running out to prove me wrong and accidentally watching it sober. I'd make Burt Reynold's list of good cinema to include three if you count *Boogie Nights* (1997). *Boogie Nights* was a turning point into a second act in his career. But it didn't stick because Mr. Reynolds hated the movie and denounced the role. He left behind his persona of a low-brow, sleazy producer with a good heart, which for my money, had tread left on its tire for the remainder of his career. So the "good movie count" ends at three for me. A couple more of his movies are nostalgic to me personally,, but I don't widely recommend them. If you look at the rest of his career, he was in some pretty awful films. However, I am going to say he was in FOUR good movies. There is a gem that shines through like a shiny coin in the mud: *Sharky's Machine*. Reynolds delivers as both an actor and a director this noir-inspired thriller fusing a common Mickey Spillane-inspired cop drama trying to solve a mystery while dealing with ninjas, a government conspiracy, and an intense hit man on PCP. Yes, you read that right. PCP. I double checked. The hitman is portrayed by Henry Silva. Silva's character doesn't keep a little head stash with him. He's getting full-on wet before work.

 Tom Sharky (Reynolds) is a tough cop demoted from the Atlanta Police Department's narcotics department to the vice squad after being blamed for a drug deal gone wrong. This version of a big city vice squad is a haven for over-achieving, misunderstood super cops. Sharky's buddies operate at such a high level they all end up being busted back to the vice squad at some point. I don't know if that's how it works in real life, but I'm okay with it for now. Sharky's "machine" includes Papa (Brian Keith), an older cop keeping his head down in the vice squad so he can retire with his full benefits. Papa is capable of inspiring the gang to get involved in a case way above their head. Arch (Bernie Casey) is a laidback Zen master who comes in with necessary wisdom as the plot requires, but always with a little prompting from Sharky. Nosh (Richard Libertini) is a smarter-than-all-this technician who begrudgingly gets his hands dirty. The obligatory frustrated police chief is played by Charles Durning. Sadly, there's not much in the way of a strong female character in this film. Most of the women in the movie are hookers and exist in the short and long term only to be saved by our mustachioed hero. There's a scene where Sharky interacts with a partner's young daughter, but that only seems to be shoved in to indicate that he's capable of not killing something. As a side note, Reynolds often displays an indifferent interaction with children in his films. Pay attention to that sometime; it's interesting.

The movie serves well as a solid example of an eighties cop shoot-em-up before we worried too much about who was being shot at. At the same time, the hubris manages not to be excessively offensive to any particular race or creed. It might sound too much like a refuge for clichés, but the cast sells it. They play their roles aware of what they're involved in, and each actor helps to sell the ensemble as a solid group of flatfoot misfits working together. Reynolds is at the helm, both in the film and behind the camera, but steps aside enough in both duties to leave room for the rest of the cast. Reynolds' signature good 'ole boy arrogance takes a back seat, and he plays Sharky's flaws with grace. The plot has enough twists to keep it afloat between firefights. And a stunt in the film holds the world record for a 220-foot wireless jump from Atlanta's Hyatt Regency Hotel by legendary stuntman Dar Robinson.

The film also contains high-level tough guy dialogue like: "Somehow I get the feeling that your rear end is puckering up" and "You're fucking up my city 'cause you're walking all over people like you own them. And you wanna know the worst part: you're from out of state." Also, a hot tip for record collectors, the soundtrack is often found in dollar bins and includes an excellent version of The Crusaders' "Street Life" performed by Randy Crawford. This is the same version used in the opening of *Jackie Brown* (1997) if you're keeping up. If you enjoy narratives featuring flawed cops, it's a cut above the standard. If you like action movies but don't want to support Mel Gibson, *Sharky's Machine* will help fill the void.

Chapter 6: Documentaries

I don't have to spell out this category too much. A good documentary can be informative and entertaining. A bad one can be dull. Lately so many music documentaries are produced it's hard not to get doc fatigue, especially when excessive talking heads take over and/or a film needs to be stretched to a feature length run time. A documentary should know how long it's supposed to be. These three are a bit older and a bit less orthodox when it comes to style and storytelling. But primarily, these three subjects were fascinating characters and the directors of these films rose to the occasion when illuminating their vast accomplishments.

Jimi Hendrix (1973)
Directed by Joe Boyd
U.S.A. 98 min.

This film opens unceremoniously on footage of Pete Townsend speaking to a camera. His age and his checkered blazer indicate it's not too far into the 1970s. He's the first of a series of talking heads to speak about their experiences with the late guitarist Jimi Hendrix, a player who is credited with changing the face of rock 'n' roll in the late 1960s and sadly became one of the prototypes for rock stars dying young. Often filmmakers pad their films with a parade of celebrities, family, and the inner circle of a musician to fill time and raise the subject's god-like stature. But director Joe Boyd recognized something important in this bit of film. Townsend was reminiscing about coming from a place of fear. Fear that he was not the guitar player he thought he was after seeing Hendrix. These candid remarks set the tone for the film, which was made shortly after Hendrix's death in 1970. It is clear that Hendrix was still heavily on the minds of his friends and peers. Through Boyd's choice of interviewees, the deity, the human, and the guitar player all come out during the course of the film. Besides just saying how great Hendrix was, they tell how his life and death affected the world surrounding him. It wasn't always good. It wasn't always bad. And it wasn't always one or the other.

One great thing about interviews with Jimi's pre-fame cronies: the people he hung around with in Harlem paint a side portrait of the New York scene during that era when they were all kicking around and jamming in the same orbit of nightclubs and theaters. Hendrix's initial fame came in London after relocating there and getting the attention of Chaz Chandler from the Animals. But before Chaz, Hendrix played every soul circuit venue New York had to offer, gigging with the Isley Brothers, Curtis Knight, and many others. The stifling hierarchy of the club scene was an anathema to Hendrix who was very anxious and motivated to play. His Harlem friends describe these pre-fame years in stark and relatable terms.

Long portions of Hendrix's mid-career success are punctuated by segments of an interview taken from his appearance on *The Dick Cavett Show*. Cavett and Hendrix have a solid repartee. Chopped up through the middle of the documentary, the interview provides a nice touchstone and insight into Hendrix's personality. Also driving this movie are long segments showing performances during various stages of his short but meteoric career. Hendrix was a performer, and to watch long segments of his playing forces you to engage with the music and reflect on what you now know he is going through around that time. Not that it's a drag to sit through a whole Hendrix song, but the opportunity to linger for long sections of the film allows the viewer to ruminate on the interviews and conjecture about a musician whose life was in the limelight, whose legacy gained iconic status quickly, and who, at heart, was a shy and reserved artist.

Louie Bluie (1985)
Directed by Terry Zwigoff
U.S.A. 75 min.

Near the beginning of the film, blues and country musician and visual artist Howard Armstrong tells the story of how he got the nickname Louie Bluie. He tells a lot of stories in general. If he's not telling stories, he's telling jokes from what you can tell is a lifelong arsenal of collected gags. Armstrong tells stories on subjects ranging from the eating habits of his friends, to musicians he's known, his travels through the

American south, and, most relevantly, his memories of playing music in the 1920s and '30s when string bands and blues pickers ruled the land. Louie Bluie comes across larger than life, but is a somewhat clandestine character in the world of music. Much of what remains of his recorded output exists on other musicians' recordings for 78 rpm records collected by esoteric record collectors. Collecting "78s" is an obsession you get a feel for in Zwigoff's later and best known documentary, *Crumb* (1995) and, through Steve Buscemi's character Seymour, is expounded on a bit in his narrative film based on the comic book story, *Ghost World* (2001). Here, you get the origin story told by those left standing to tell it. Many of Armstrong's friends get together and still play for fun, or occasionally a few bucks. These seasoned musicians hang out and laugh playing for small audiences in small bars and venues. Zwigoff quietly follows Armstrong in the old style of documentary filming where the exposition is left in the characters you come across along the way. He only interferes occasionally to straighten out information lost in translation. From this distance, Zwigoff excavates the last remnants of a circuit of country and blues musicians via short treks through rural Tennessee and all the way up to Chicago. But this film doesn't come across like a funeral or eulogy. Most of the people who perform in the film look like they're still playing for the fun of it, and the lifelong lesson is if you have some friends and can raise your voice once in a while, you're doing what you're supposed to be doing while you're on this planet. Louie Bluie himself is a renaissance man in his own right. He draws in a similar style as cartoonist and future Zwigoff documentary subject Robert Crumb. These two practice a style of drawing that inherently evokes Americana. Various points in the film find Louie Bluie studying Italian, discussing Picasso, and railing on religion. *Louie Bluie* is a simple documentary by a great documentary director. It also serves as one of the most important music documentaries to come along. It tells the story of a microcosm of a scene in its early stages, at the time a fairly new arena of American pop music at its beginning. You see a scene in its decline, and understand there is still hope in creating as long as you keep grinning and strumming.

Marlene (1984)
Directed by Maximilian Schell
West Germany 94 min.

Marlene opens on a shot of a reel-to-reel tape recorder. Marlene Dietrich repeatedly thwarted director Maximilian Schell's attempts to make a documentary about her in the past. After much prodding from her *Judgment at Nuremberg* (1961) co-star, Dietrich finally acquiesced. The caveats for the making of *Marlene* are: 1) she will only allow Schell to record her voice and 2) she won't allow cameras in her apartment. Resigned to make the film, Schell films the tape recorder. It's an unusual solution.

As the tape recorder spins, Dietrich's voice is an indictment on Schell: "Do you think I'd go and sit in some sad, stuffy old cinema and watch an old film?" Dietrich makes it clear early and often throughout the film she doesn't share her fan's enthusiasm for film history. She never watches her films. They don't interest her. As with many of the statements aimed directly at Schell, she makes it clear with claws out. She does not appreciate sentimentality and doesn't play nice to be a good sport. Schell includes several audio clips of her bored defiance in the opening segment as the camera pans back slowly from the recorder. Covered is a range of topics Dietrich is going to discourage and scold Schell over. She answers questions with the venom and confidence of someone beating a congressional grilling.

The first shot eventually cuts to Dietrich talking to the crowd at her final concert appearance. Here she is more humble, exemplifying the grace you would expect her to have as she leaves the stage for a final time. After a few more clips, the film cuts to her in a scene in the western *Destry Rides Again* (1939). Here she's swinging a gun around a saloon threatening Jimmy Stewart. The whole saloon has to hit the deck as she waves the gun around. This is a glimpse of the fun and anarchy prevalent in a typical Dietrich performance. As the film continues, we see many clips of her oeuvre. But if Schell is enjoying anything too much, she'll shut it down with statements like "We (Germans) didn't have kitsch. We didn't have sentimental feelings." And so they dance, Schell trying to reason with Dietrich as she continues to put caveats on the project. He tries to appease her as best he can. Schell builds a set resembling her apartment, hires doubles of varying ages, and follows his staff around to use as second unit footage. There are also talking heads interviews with the few people close to her.

Dietrich begrudgingly opens up occasionally: not in a satisfyingly sentimental way, but more as if annoyed at Schell for being a fool for being interested. She doesn't seem to care about setting the record straight regarding the "fifty-five books" about her. She tells the story of the audition for what would inform her iconic performance of "Falling in Love Again" in her breakout film *The Blue Angel* (1930). Of course by her account, the books have it all wrong. It may sound like a documentary falling apart at the seams, but Schell works with what he has and Dietrich seems to occasionally let go of her inhibitions long enough to tell a story.

If the film sounds like little more than a grumpy rant by a Hollywood icon, her rapport with Schell and inclination to give praise where praise is due creates occasional warmth that drives the film forward. It becomes apparent some of her defensiveness has to do with her not wanting to appear to be pining for another time. You can't help but root for Schell as he dissects statements she makes when she refuses to answer his questions directly. Throughout the film, Schell tries to sell her on commenting directly on her films, but she will not allow herself to be filmed or watch any of her old films. "I've been photographed enough" is her mantra. After much pushing, she's convinced to have a video brought to her house to watch one movie and one movie only: *The Scarlet Empress* (1934). She insists they fast-forward to the end. The screening instigates a fight with Schell that leads her to denigrate his existence by calling him an "old film buff."

The film ends on an angry montage using clips from her films and look-alikes destroying the set while the audio plays out her excessive berating of Schell. The anger montage is an interesting document exposing the artistic frustration. Has Schell gone mad? Or has he accurately articulated artistic frustration? Before the argument, Schell explains under his breath how her agent slipped him a note with a quote from Dante Alighieri: "There is no greater pain than the recollection of past happiness in times of misery." The segment is a poignant wrap up towards the end of a challenging documentary and shines a vulnerable light on the aging star. Werner Herzog once said "There is never an excuse not to finish a film." Schell's *Marlene* is a glistening example of this advice. Against all odds, Schell created an excellent documentary and unwittingly captured a rare portrait of an enigmatic icon.

Chapter 7: Farnsworthy

Roger Ebert once said: "no movie featuring Harry Dean Stanton or M. Emmet Walsh can be altogether bad." I feel this sentiment could be stretched to include Richard Farnsworth. Farnsworth started his long career in film as a stuntman. As an actor he made unaccredited appearances in iconic films like *The Wild One* (1953), *The Ten Commandments* (1956), *Blazing Saddles* (1974) and the TV mini-series *Roots* (1977). Farnsworth proved he could carry a lead in two films I admire. The first is the excellent Canadian revisionist western *The Grey Fox* (1982) and also his last lead role in the unusual David Lynch (or unusually straightforward for Lynch) film *The Straight Story*. Both films are based on true stories.

The Grey Fox (1982)
Directed by Phillip Borsos
Canada 92 min.

This low-budget Canadian film covers a year or two after the third prison term of real-life stagecoach and later train robber Bill Miner. Miner was an actual cowboy criminal whose third strike led him to a long stay in San Quentin. He emerged at the turn of the century to find the stagecoach gone the way of the wooly mammoth and taught himself at a late age to rob trains. He got the nickname "The Gentleman Bandit" for being polite and patient with his partners, victims, and the authorities. He believed politeness and professionalism cut down on accidents and unwanted heroism. He is credited with inventing the phrase "hands up." His legend grew into a Robin Hood-like persona because he never stole from the passengers and only swiped property connected to the railroads. Who but Richard Farnsworth could fill the persona of such a gentleman bandit?

Farnsworth had a long career as a stuntman and character actor before taking leads in film. His warm but firmly butch disposition was notable as a supporting character in the Americana classic *The Natural* (1984). This story begins with Miner's release from San Quentin to discover a new world he doesn't understand. He is intrigued by a device that holds a blade against an apple and spins it to remove the peel. He takes this device to his daughter who is glad to see him. But her straight-laced husband is nonplussed to have Minor back in the mix and Minor gets the itch to rob again. After this false start to go legit, Miner travels to Canada where he settles and plots under the new name George Edwards. In a small town in British Columbia he makes friends with the intellectual and forward thinking members of the town including photographer Katherine Flynn (Jackie Burroughs). Time seems to soften

Miner, but it won't be long before both his past and his desire to ply his trade in the new world get the better of him.

The film is lavishly shot in British Columbia near where Miner actually set up shop in Canada during this time in his life. The film crew was allowed special access to the Fort Steele British Columbia heritage site and the natural backdrop of the forests and mountains in the area are worth the price of admission, as this allows for some astounding footage of Canada's reserved wilderness. One site where Miner actually tried to elude authorities is featured in the film. Even Miner's actual .41 Bisley Colt revolver was donated by a collector to be used for close ups with Farnsworth in certain scenes.

Miner is believed to have staged the very first train robbery ever in British Columbia. This crime is portrayed in the film with humor and irony; Farnsworth carries the gentlemen's moniker for Miner with as much sympathy as a train robber can be allowed. You can often find yourself rooting for the bad guys in movies, but Farnsworth's polite manner, wry smile, and muted humor brings Miner's legend to the screen so vividly it's agonizing to imagine he probably will not get out of the film unscathed. As a revisionist western, the movie removes a lot of the massive shootouts and violence from the train robbery scenario and replaces it with humor and a human face. *The Grey Fox* is a little-known film only recently released on DVD and Blu-ray. For western fans, it's worth searching out.

The Straight Story (1999)
Directed by David Lynch
U.S.A. 112 min.

Between the Ouroboros-inspired narrative of *Lost Highway* (1997) and the atmospheric Los Angeles epic *Mullholland Drive* (2001), director David Lynch took on a surprisingly conventional tale directing *The Straight Story*. And a straight story it mostly is, especially for Lynch. The title of the film is a reference to its real life subject, Alvin Straight. Straight accidentally accrued a few minutes of fame when he drove a riding lawnmower from Iowa to Wisconsin to visit his ailing brother in 1994. It was a 240-mile trip. Again, on a riding lawnmower. It sounds pretty insane, but I dare any real American not to dig deep and admire the bit of Lewis and Clark wedged into such an effort. *The Straight Story* conveys some of the details of the trip as Straight camped along highways and small roads on his way to Wisconsin.

For Lynch, *The Straight Story* is among the most innocent of his filmography, yet the Lynch stamp on this conventional story showcases his ability to tell an American yarn in all its glory and absurdity. Ironically, the movie opens very similarly to his 1986 noir oddity *Blue Velvet*. We see, in innate detail, a sunny day in small town America. The minutiae of small-town life. People are shuffling about. A woman prepares to lie out on a lawn chair in the yard. We're led from a quiet day to a dark window. We hear something unsettling.

But here, instead of uncovering a web of subversion, the film focuses on a nice guy living a simple life in a small town. He's fallen down. He is not a strong man. Straight exposes deep knowledge regarding the nature of existence from behind his ruggedly smiling eyes and mustachioed smile. He crawls down the highway on his riding lawn mower towing a small trailer with a mattress and a cooler on board dispensing life philosophy and sound advice to those he encounters: a teenage runaway, participants of a bicycle race, a frustrated woman who seems to habitually hit deer with her car, and various others. Lynchian watermarks show up throughout the movie in ways you might not expect in a story like this. The cinematography is excellent, presenting deep shots of endless strips of highway and long shots of Straight striking a charming silhouette as he putters along our God-given American highways. The score is also omnipresent, occasionally used to strike ominous tones that remind you Straight is engaged in dangerous activity, but more often evoke the wonder of being alone on an unusual journey. The sort of time taken to look out at a rainstorm from an office window or connect with an insect that isn't bothering you. It's the type of inspiring story rarely this well-executed without being corny.

Chapter 8:
The Final Frontier

    My grandmother was one of the first people I knew to have HBO back when it wasn't even a 24-hour channel. I saw *Alien* (1978) for the first time at her house. I remember it viscerally: sitting cross legged in front of her television with a Coke and probably a snack for comfort while she dozed in her chair behind me. She also had a load of sci-fi paperbacks from my father's childhood. She was pretty open minded about what we watched and read when we were together. I convinced her to take me to see *Cheech and Chong's Still Smokin'* (1983) when I was thirteen. She's gone now, and I still hear about it from beyond the grave because my mother won't let it go. Like Jason Voorhees, that screening haunts me. I also saw *Friday the 13th* (1980) sitting on her floor.

Europa Report (2013)
Directed by Sebastián Cordero
U.S.A. 97 min.

Found footage as a genre doesn't immediately evoke impressions of quality or high art. There are a lot of horror-themed cash grabs made by broke directors desperate to make a movie. I don't begrudge that. It's better than sitting around the house waiting for someone to recognize you. And, to be fair, the idea of found footage lends itself to horror. The very notion of "finding" a tape denotes the idea the footage was something you weren't meant to see in the first place. I found an unlabeled super 8 tape behind my radiator in a scuzzy apartment I rented for ages. I was feeling pious and broke it with a hammer. That story has become a curse. Every time I tell that story, someone yells: "How could you not watch it?" But I thought about how I would have liked to be treated in that situation and did what I thought was the right thing. I was a little suspicious of who had the apartment before me and, believe me, you didn't want to see that.

The template for horror as found footage exists in early examples of the horror genre like *Cannibal Holocaust* (1980) and *The Blair Witch Project* (1999) where footage is discovered during a search for missing people. Looking at the ever-growing list of found footage films, other genres are seeping in, including the love story. The found footage love story genre is going to have to become really sharp to get me interested in it, but I never say never when it comes to movies.

My interest will likely stay in the horror/sci-fi arena at least for the time being. As the list of found footage films continues to grow, many of us have presumably seen our share of bad ones. I don't mind the genre per se. I'm willing to give these films a hell of a lot of leeway for some reason. Some are effective if not great films by definition. I confess I enjoyed a silly horror film called *Grave Encounters* (2011) for all it had to offer. The story involved a crew of amateur filmmakers trying to make a film/TV show. The Spanish film *REC.* (2007) is a great zombie narrative, the starkness and immediacy of which flows decadently through the rough action of the hand held camera, a staple in the found footage filter. *REC.* uses the genre well by staying pretty soundly in the rulebook and kicking in some nice surprises. I forgot *District 9* (2009) is considered a found footage title the last time I watched it. Surely it must be the *Citizen Kane* of found footage films at this point. I even enjoyed the much-maligned *Apollo 18* (2011) for its creativity of thought. Of course, the very nature of *Apollo 18* negates the possibility of "finding" the footage, but to keep score in this genre is not accepting why you're likely watching the film in the first place.

Europa Report is a giant leap for the possibilities of found footage. Here's a piece of hard sci-fi in the ring with some legitimate science in its corner. The "found" footage is a narrative formed by transmissions from scientists on an exploratory mission to Europa, a moon of Jupiter we already suspect has oceans dwelling beneath its surface. This would mean a solid case for life existing under the surface. The crew is an affable bunch on a long mission to land on Europa, get some samples, and fly back. Along the way, the crew loses touch with Earth due to some irregular sun activity. They decide to press on even though it's dangerous to continue. There's little reason to be in danger if they can't send back information, but turning back may also be a mistake. The crew preserves in the hope that they're still relevant. At this point they're nearly two years in. And they've got to be able to contact Earth at some point. Right? Well not before a series of events messes up equipment, landings, strategies, etc... The chain of events puts a strain on the mission. There are not many specifics to give away without ruining the chain of events leading to a pretty exciting ending. The claustrophobic setting inside the ship and icy surface of Europa creates great tension and is terrifying at times. There are a lot of moments spent straddling the terror of being lost in space and lost at sea. These characters are put through the ringer, but the film also has moments of hope sewn into the bummers brought about by mission failures. These guys stick together. It's a well-done film for scares and rumination. If you've felt burned by found footage in the past, see this one and consider if the genre still has something to offer.

Event Horizon (1997)
Directed by Paul W.S. Anderson
U.K. 96 min.

Event Horizon is a great sci-fi story with solid special effects, a great cast, an unusually gruesome horror arc, and loads of demon/hell nonsense. It got bad reviews upon release and didn't do well at the box office. It endured because it was edged into cult status due to a successful home video release. But even the current Internet evaluations are still not very favorable. I can see maybe why it didn't initially perform well. It can be vague at times. I posit, other than being a little convoluted, *Event Horizon* belongs in the canon of great sci-fi, at least from the era.

The story opens on the Lewis and Clark, a rescue vessel with a crew trained at performing deep space extractions on a mysterious mission. The experienced crew get edgy when they discover their new mission is to rescue the Event Horizon, a ship that lost communication on its last mission, disappeared for a bit, and then mysteriously reappeared in a dead orbit around Neptune. The details of the malfunction of the Event Horizon are unknown, but the mystery causes most to say it should stay where it is and not be salvaged. That is not the opinion of Dr. William Weir (Sam Neill), the Event Horizon's chief designer who is along for the ride. He is there in hopes of restoring the derelict ship and getting some answers. Weir, like many of Sam Neill's characters in smaller films, is a rational, intelligent man who goes bananas and becomes a raging lunatic in full throttle. The Lewis and Clark's cool captain S.J. Miller (Laurence Fishburne) is not thrilled to be there at all, let alone have his ship and crew endangered for the sake of Weir's weird investigation. Once the Event Horizon is boarded, it's apparent something weird is going on. Evidence points to strange deaths from extreme torture and bodies mutilated for unknown reasons. There's a ship's log, but it's hard to decipher in that way all space ship logs are hard to understand at crucial times. But this log has a hell of a reach. Weir and the others begin having mild hallucinations. Weir's are making him particularly hard to cope with. He is sucked in quickly as his real motive for making the trip becomes apparent. The movie takes a horror genre turn as the translation of the log becomes more apparent and some of the Lewis and Clark's crew have accidents. All the while, Miller just wants to keep his ship afloat and his crew safe. Fishburne plays against Neill's nutzoid well as a compassionate and grizzled captain and a nice ensemble of character actors portrays the crew. Even Paul W.S. Anderson has said the ending is a bit confusing, but better that than no movie at all. *Event Horizon* is a fun and competent horror/sci-fi hybrid, and if you found the ending of *Aliens* (1986) where Ripley goes back into the nest after Newt when every other character was killed on sight, you should cut *Event Horizon* some slack and have a good time with it.

The Green Slime (1968)
Directed by Kinji Fukasaku
Japan 90 min.

1968 was a good year for gothic horror. It was also a transitional year for horror and sci-fi. *2001: A Space Odyssey* wowed the world with a new level of special effects. *Night of the Living Dead* upped the gore level and established some long-living tropes that would inform zombie narratives for decades. But there were loads of other sci-fi films released that year. Some are classics. Some are lost to time. *The Green Slime* is a stand out for a few reasons. The film opens out of the gate with a psychedelic rock theme song that can only rightly be described as groovy. It's a real '60s swinger written by Charles Fox, who also wrote the music for *Barbarella* (1968). This low budget Japanese/American co-production has a dark and stylish look. There are a few major plot points predating *Alien* (1979) and *Armageddon* (1998) that cause the picture to seem more mature than '68. Sure, space as a place often doesn't work like it's depicted in the film. Smoke doesn't burn off and rise in space. But this story works hard to entertain and has an interesting plot.

The movie opens on scientists and astronauts zooming headlong towards an asteroid they intend to land on and study. They're planning to blow it up before it hits Earth. And, wow, the mission goes pretty smoothly. Afterwards, the crew is relieved. There's a celebration. And with their guards down, people start disappearing. Where are they going? Of course, *The Green Slime's* special effects were trounced by *2001: A Space Odyssey* and the film is not as gory as *Night of the Living Dead*, but there are some good kills. Even if they aren't gross enough to satisfy a horror hound, they are unpleasant, and sometimes unpleasant is enough. The strange gore segments are fun and make up for having to look at a string or two when the spaceships and asteroids pass by. This movie has the distinction of having been used as the lesser-seen pilot for *Mystery Science Theater 3000*. Ex-Toho employees designed both the special effects and the monsters, so if you're into Godzilla-style entertainment, it's solid late-night viewing.

Outland (1981)
Directed by Peter Hyams
U.K. 109 min.

A lot is made of *Outland* being a fairly obvious remake of Stanley Kramer's *High Noon* (1952). The basic plot is very similar. Sean Connery portrays Federal Marshal William O'Niel in a role similar to Gary Cooper's Marshal Will Kane. *Outland* is cleverly set in the future on Jovian moon of IO. On IO there is a small mining town operating mostly under the rule of the parent company Conglomerates Amalgamated. The new marshal should be the law, but this is a company town, and he is mostly alone in his opinions regarding his importance to the community. Conglomerates Amalgamated is content to operate under its own boundaries. Past marshals assigned to the post have been content to toe the company line until their tour is complete. But when a string of suspicious deaths causes O'Niel to dig deeper than the company would like, the end result is a group of thugs are sent to deal with him on the next stagecoach. Excuse me, I mean, supply ship.

If you're profoundly attached to *High Noon*, *Outland* might seem like a weak interpretation, but fans of sci-fi can enjoy the story on several levels. The deaths in the camp are bizarre and creative. There is a short-lived mystery in play that cleverly fills the time before the obligatory showdown. Peter Boyle puts in a great performance as Mark Sheppard, the camp's manager and Connery's foil. Sheppard can't understand why O'Niel would put time into solving the case. You don't really have to see *High Noon* to guess how that goes over, but the story of the investigation leading up to the showdown is strong. From the confined space of the mining camp, O'Neil must take to the outside in a spacesuit to combat his attackers. The claustrophobia of the camp compared to the wide-open space of the surface of IO seen from the windows sets a nice contrast for a confrontation. Some of the situations during the space parts of the chase are a bit implausible, but they are fun, well-placed action sequences using analogue special effects. It's a quality film with good performances worth a watch if you tend to re-watch *Alien* (1979). Hyams went on to direct another solid sci-fi film time has brushed under the rug, the film version of Arther C. Clark's *2010: The Year We Make Contact* (1984). He has a penchant for making slightly harder sci-fi dangerous and entertaining.

Planet of the Vampires (1965)
Directed by Mario Bava
Italy/Spain 88 min.

1968 was a pretty pivotal year for sci-fi and horror films. The aforementioned *2001: A Space Odyssey* and *Night of the Living Dead* made it a big year, but there were also game-changing cult films like *Planet of the Apes, Barbarella, Rosemary's Baby,* and *The Green Slime* (also mentioned in this book). There is a load of influence in those titles. Many legendary writers and directors cop to watching *Planet of the Vampires* looking for style tips and borrowing ideas. An article in a 1979 issue of Cinefantastique notes how specifically the look and sequence of big ship search in *Alien* (1979) bears an uncanny resemblance to a sequence in *Planet of the Vampires*. The story follows the Galliott and the Argos, two deep space vessels lured to an uncharted planet by a distress signal. The Galliott tries to investigate and lands hard. While the crew of the Argos investigate the wreck, bodies from the Galliott begin coming to life and stalking the survivors. The bodies are being taken over by the Aurans, an ancient race of aliens that want to get off the planet. Their plan is to take over the Galliott's crew and ride off on the Argos.

Mario Bava shows what you can accomplish with a lot of style and not so many resources. This is a hip looking film. The sets appear ominous, even though many of them are created with cheap sets and forced perspective. Bava uses fog and unorthodox lighting to cover the inexpensive nature of the sets. His vision for the film is imaginative. The crew of the Galliott and Argos are adorned in swinging black leather motorcycle outfits. The gloomy setting of *Planet of the Vampires*, which predates Romero's 1968 classic *Night of the Living Dead* by a few months, is especially notable for the use of animated corpses. Romero's corpses were frightening in the world of black and white film. Here Bava uses space created between sparsely placed bright red, green, and purple lamps in the background to create pallor in his baddies. This is also an early look at how some later comic book films employed light to make sets. It's an influential picture for certain. Decades later, Dan O'Bannon, who wrote the screenplay for *Alien*, would admit he took the idea for an abandoned giant skeleton from *Planet of the Vampires*. But he certainly wasn't the only one with his eye on this film. It's a must see for sci-fi fans.

Sunshine (2007)
Directed by Danny Boyle
U.K./U.S.A. 107 min.

Director Danny Boyle helped jump start a new wave of popularity for the zombie narrative with his surprise breakout hit *28 Days Later* (2002). Later screenwriter Alex Garland co-wrote Sunshine with Boyle and also wrote the screenplay for the underrated *Dredd* (2012), a reasonably intelligent action movie I also wrote about in this book. In *Sunshine*, a group of scientists are heading to a safe space around the sun to set off a nuclear charge. Our big orange buddy is sputtering. The charge is meant to act as a set of jumper cables, reigniting our nearest star for use by future generations. So the world has assembled a crack team of boffins* to chuck a bomb at the sun. I'm not making fun of the idea; apparently, as with many Garland-penned narratives, there's a bit of scientific truth sewn into the premise. Theoretically, enough nuclear bombs could give the sun a much-needed boost if they were all set in place and detonated properly. The scientists in *Sunshine* have one, and as real-life scientists have pointed out, one is not enough. But I don't want to play lawyer ball with these movies. It's a neat idea. And a good movie. It really deserves the moniker of space opera as it takes us into space with the crew *Alien* (1979) style and doesn't let us go. It also keeps the *Alien* tradition by passing the Bechdel Test.

Boyle works well with an ensemble cast coping with the ins and outs of the various problems that ensue during the mission. One of the key things that happens in the beginning is they get a distress signal from the first ship that disappeared on this errand. The signal has been hidden from Earth by Mercury's position until now. As they get around Mercury, their ship is in position to pick it up. On one hand, they're risking the mission and basically the end of humanity to try to investigate the signal that surely must be on auto. They can't expect any survivors. On the other hand, it couldn't hurt to deliver a double payload either, as the number of bombs you need to lob at the sun is only academic at this point. So it might BE the mission. There's a lot of this kind of "should we or shouldn't we" at this point in the narrative, and to go too far into it gives away some of the long haul. It's a weighty story with a weighty ensemble cast and a lot of speculation that Boyle keeps alive in the hideously dangerous and exciting setting of space. The film is visually stunning. The sun is as famous a co-star as you can get in a film like this, and its role in the film is striking. Long, orange beams and a rowdy surface flow and buzz during close-ups and certain crisis modes. The use of gold, black, and orange to create the environment around the ship when it's near the sun contrasts sharply with the old-school set inside the ship. Here we have a lot of green, blue, and gray interiors. The production design is modeled on some classic sci-fi spaceships. It's a cerebral movie with a hint of horror and no long, weepy ruminations about kids, dads, etc... Some of these movies tend to devolve that way. I don't mind it per se, but Sunshine is a bit of fun amongst a hard sci-fi template.

---

* boffin is a U.K. word for a person excessively trained in complex and difficult subjects. I strongly feel we need a specific word for this in the U.S. Try it out in your everyday life and let's see if we can make it stick.

Chapter 9:
Franchiseus Interruptus

The qualities of films in even the best of franchises suffer when they become too formulaic. But they stay formulaic because, for some reason, that's what brings people to the theater: the notion they'll see the same thing they enjoyed last time. How does that work? That's a mystery as old as sequels. It's a lot easier to ask people back for more than it is to explain something new to them. Here are three movies where producers attempted to throw in a new angle to an existing series with interesting results.

Superman Returns (2006)
Directed by Bryan Singer
U.S.A. 154 min.

I won't be writing this review without engaging in a certain amount of gross nostalgia. Superman Returns is meant to continue the *Superman* (1978) storyline where the Richard Lester film *Superman II* (1980) left off. In *Superman II*, the Man of Steel, famously portrayed by Christopher Reeve, defeated General Zod (Terrence Stamp) and his crew of Krypton criminals, thus saving the Earth from a powerful fascist state. That message isn't as simple as it used to be, but it made an altogether satisfying film in the 1980s. Reeve as Superman is one of those iconic cinematic portrayals like Humphrey Bogart as Phillip Marlowe, John Hurt as Winston Smith, or Anthony Perkins as Norman Bates. Reeve was born for it. You can just see the character of the actor. A generation of people accepted him as the quintessential Man of Steel. A hero. And by all accounts, Reeve was a good guy. He took on the role with a sweetness and positivity that inspired moviegoers of all ages. It's a role you hate to see go to anyone else. But we all know movie execs won't let Superman go, especially with so much renewed interest in comic book properties. There was bound to be a new Superman movie eventually. The decision to carry on the same story line with different actors was a really a very bold one when you think of it. Dozens of angles could have been taken. Loads of good Superman narratives have been written in the interim.

So we're picking up where Reeve and Lester left off. It's a lot to put on new Superman actor Brandon Routh. Routh succeeds in playing Superman as the hero we almost certainly need now. Routh's interpretation evokes the sweetness and upstanding morals purveyed by Reeve's persona. Routh has a similar nervous grin. Similar eyebrows. He breaks off into incomplete sentences in the presence of Lois Lane (Kate Bosworth) the way Reeve did. He evokes a similar sense of humor. Routh is charming and reminiscent of Reeve without distorting the lines. He handles the movie comfortably with a knack for picking up on what made the character so great in the early movies without being boring or hacky. In the current climate of comic book movies, this sort of creativity and positivity must be immediately punished, so we were treated now to another inferior reboot.

Back to *Superman Returns*: Sam Huntington brings some of the old-style Superman flair to the movie without doing a total nostalgia job as photographer Jimmy Olsen, who acts as Superman's liaison back to the real world. Olsen has just been hanging around snapping photos between stories and has no trouble picking up on his friendship with Clark Kent. I guess Olsen lives in a solid rent control apartment. Lois Lane is now somewhat disinterested in the Superman phenomenon. We find out more about that later. Kevin Spacey does a fine Lex Luthor, although with an angrier edge than the swarthy and fun-loving Gene Hackman. It's not too bad because we understand Luthor has become more polished and sophisticated, as well as more capable of severe mood swings. But Luthor is the character that suffers the most. Spacey is good, but the spineless, fast taking Hackman version is sorely missed. Parker Posey adds character to the mix as, mostly, Parker Posey, who is welcome in almost any film as far as I'm concerned. If she showed up in a remake of *Quest for Fire* with a sun-dried tomato bagel and an oversized scarf I would be fine with it.

All you need to know in order to have a good time now is that the rest of the film is just regular Superman hooey. If you don't want to see a *Superman* movie, you won't like this. But if you want to see one, this film feels at home as number three to Lester and Reeve's two. It's much better than these more recent portrayals, and better than Lester's *Superman 3* from 1983 that starred Richard Pryor as Reeve's foil, although as stated in the film *Office Space* (1999), it is a somewhat underrated movie. And *Superman IV: The Quest for Peace* (1987) is funny for a whole 'nuther reason. For more information on that note, I highly recommend the documentary *Electric Boogaloo: The Wild, Untold Story of Cannon Films* (2014).

The Thing (2011)
Directed by Matthijs van Heijningen Jr.
U.S.A./Canada 103 min.

Like a lot of horror fans, I'm skeptical of horror remakes. I enjoyed the 2004 version of *Dawn of the Dead*. I was pleasantly surprised, as I felt the original *Dawn of the Dead* (1978) was one of those texts not to be tampered with. But the new version had fresh ideas while generally following the important rules of the original. Try thinking of it as just another chapter in the Romero canon. That first group probably wasn't the only band of misfits attempting to take over a shopping mall. *Dawn of the Dead* (2004) was also written by James Gunn, who I read about beforehand in the book: *All I Need To Know About FILMMAKING I Learned From THE TOXIC AVENGER: The Shocking True Story of Troma Studios*. Gunn wrote for Troma and has gone on to write some great horror and comic narratives since then.

The producers of the new Dawn also made a "remake" of the 1982 version of *The Thing*, which again feels like a narrative that shouldn't be tested, but itself is a remake of the 1951 classic *The Thing From Another World*. I've been a fan of these two versions since I was a kid. So let's first get into the spirit of the thing: what if John Carpenter decided not to remake the 1951 film? We'd be out one classic and beloved horror thriller. This most recent version of the story of an Antarctic outpost terrorized after discovering a malleable alien buried under ice is not a remake but a prequel. And I won't sell it as a classic. But if you're into the original films and disinclined to see this new one, give it another thought. If you don't care about any of this, you might try reading something else.

This story takes place in the Norwegian outpost Thule. Thule is the burned out Norwegian geological research station R.J. MacReady (Kurt Russell) and Dr. Cooper (Richard Dysart) investigate at the beginning of the 1982 version of *The Thing* searching for clues as to what exactly made its way across the Antarctica tundra from Thule to the American station on Antarctica. Thule isn't immediately recognizable at the beginning of the 2011 film, but as the action unfolds, fans of the 1982 version begin to get clued into the chain of events leading up to the story. Questions like "Why were there so many burned walls?" and "How did that ax get there?" come into play as we watch the plot unfold. It sounds a little cheesy, but they do a good job of not letting you see it coming all the time. The story also breaks some new ground with the rules created by the first movie and creates some interesting new paranoia for viewers. At one point, visiting paleontologist Kate Lloyd (Mary Elizabeth Winstead) figures out the creature doesn't replicate metal and decides those with fillings are safe bets as still being human. But it doesn't help the characters with obsessive dental hygiene.

The film has taken a few hits from fans due to the absence of legendary SFX guru Rick Baker's work and its subsequent replacement with CGI. My answer is that the CGI is at least faithful to the story, and the story itself is well written. It would be nice if the film was made with more analogue effects, but we all know that wasn't going to happen in a project of this scale during the time it was made. I take the position that some of the FX seem organic and those obvious digital effects are not distractingly bad. It's hard to guess whether someone who hasn't seen the 1982 film would get as much out of the reboot, but for fans of the film, it's not a part of the story to dismiss. Screenwriter Eric Heisserer said writing the film is like "creating by autopsy." I think that's a good attitude, and here, he created the best movie he could.

Wes Craven's New Nightmare (1994)
Directed by Wes Craven
U.S.A. 112 min.

When considering big-time horror franchises like *Friday the 13th* (1981), *Halloween* (1978), and *A Nightmare on Elm Street* (1984), I imagine it's easy to dismissively say to yourself: "I don't like horror," or "I don't like that type of horror." For the former, I can't help much. But if you're among the latter and find these franchises impenetrable, *Wes Craven's New Nightmare* stands out for a few reasons.

Let me start by saying I can relate a little. I'm a serious horror fan but am not as enamored by the *Friday the 13th* franchise as others. I enjoy them on a level, but I do find them formulaic and mildly boring at times. I used to see them in theaters and enjoy the experience. I've revisited a few here and there. But I don't have the endless admiration some people claim for Jason Voorhees and his sporting goods store-inspired murders. *Halloween* is a different animal to me because I find the first installment in the series to be of a slightly higher caliber of filmmaking with a focus on well-executed suspense. Also, the series canon includes the strange and wonderful *Halloween III: Season of the Witch* (1982), which diverts greatly from the slasher trope. (See the *Halloween III* entry in this book.)

Then there's the *Nightmare* franchise. Why do I prefer it over others? I find the various methods that villain Freddy Krueger uses to off his victims mildly creative and hallucinatory. Anyone can pick up a pitchfork and go to town on two people fucking. But it takes a real wise-ass to stab you with syringe fingers and yell: "What a rush!" You may die, but at least you get a good line before Krueger brings the hammer down. Try getting a gem like "How's this for a wet dream?" from Michael Meyers or the aforementioned Jason Voorhees. In reality, I guess it would be better not to be taunted by a murderer, but these are just movies after all. This is a lot of lead up to a movie I'm not likely to change your mind about if you've already decided not to like these movies, but I still encourage you to try *Wes Craven's New Nightmare* if you're interested in skimming the milk for cream.

Wes Craven's New Nightmare is a highly creative early metanarrative. The film precedes Wes Craven's huge success, *Scream* (1996), but addresses many of the same tropes his oeuvre is criticized for. *New Nightmare* stars much of the original cast of the *A Nightmare on Elm Street* portraying themselves. The story focuses on actor Heather Langenkamp, who portrayed the primary protagonist in the first film and has since made appearances in many other installments. Heather is having nightmares. She becomes aware of a new *Nightmare* script in the works and feels the new script is causing the Krueger character to come to life in her mind and the minds of those around her. Along the way, she confides with friends and co-stars like John Saxon who played her father in the first movie and has taken a fatherly role in her life, at least, within the terms of this movie. She also confides in original *Nightmare* creator Wes Craven, who informs her another sequel is being made. She confides in Krueger portrayer Robert Englund himself, with whom she has maintained a close friendship. But seeing the actual face of the killer in the real world doesn't do much for her confidence. The film follows Langenkamp throughout several phases of the film production and, as Krueger gets closer to the reality goal line, problems arise at every corner. It's a well-conceived film and especially interesting if you're a fan of Craven's *Scream* series as a lot of the ideas brought out in *New Nightmare* translate to the first Scream movie. It's an engaging movie with offerings for both the esoteric and casual horror fan.

Chapter 10: H.G. Wells

Where would science fiction be without H.G. Wells? Literature in general owes him a debt. But his stories haven't always transferred well to the silver screen. Here are two similar time travel stories that begin with a dinner party.

Time After Time (1979)
Directed by Nicholas Meyer
U.S.A. 112 min.

Time After Time is an early time travel story for me. I saw this film as a kid and sought out H.G. Wells' books as a result. He fascinated me, and in the film the inventor and sci-fi visionary is portrayed by none other than the great Malcolm McDowell who I would admire in later years. *Time After Time* is another movie I watched with my grandmother where the dark streak in it wasn't apparent until I revisited the movie as an adult. Time travel tropes have become a landmark of hard sci-fi, but this simple story holds its relevance nicely due to excellent performances and an innovative time travel plot that doesn't require extensive mapping.

The story opens at a dinner party in 1893. H.G. Wells has called some friends over to show off his new invention: a time machine. Arriving late is Dr. John Leslie Stevenson (David Warner). He claims to have been working late. After some discussion about the ins and outs of time travel, the police interrupt. Jack the Ripper has struck again. After a search of the house, the police find a bloody glove in Dr. Stevenson's medical bag. And Stevenson has lammed it. The police set out to find him and make sure the other guests get home. As the dust settles, Wells discovers that his machine is missing. The Ripper has escaped into the future. Wells gets in the machine and takes a nice psychedelic interlude similar to the end of *2001: A Space Odyssey* (1968), arriving in circa-1979 San Francisco where the machine is on display in a museum featuring an H.G. Wells exhibit. (Side note: the journey ends with a young Corey Feldman as a boy in the museum.) The befuddled Wells sets off to find Stevenson and free the future of Jack the Ripper's tyranny.

McDowell embodies the spirit of Wells' intellectualism and forward thinking. His Wells is charming, intelligent, and appalled by the violence prevalent in the future. David Warner portrays Dr. Stevenson. Warner's interpretation of the gentleman doctor gone off the rails is a prototype for smart serial killers in movies. He's intelligent. His deep voice and serious tone creates the perfect foil for McDowell's optimistic Wells. The movie also introduces an interesting gambit for the initial chase: Wells visits several banks to see if another Englishman has been changing old currency. He gets a hit when he comes across the head of foreign currency at the Bank of England, Amy Robbins (Mary Steenburgen). Robbins is a modern woman: confident, motivated, and independent. Of course, it wouldn't be a movie if she didn't get a little too close to the situation. Before long, the Ripper is after her. But Robbins is not just fodder ripe for saving. She becomes Wells' sidekick and, as the stakes grow higher, the game is afoot.

Of course '70s San Francisco looks a bit different to modern eyes, but the city serves as a terrific backdrop for the story that doesn't feel dated. The same dynamic works for the movie *Invasion of the Body Snatchers* (1978). San Francisco portrays a very modern and timeless American city. Stevenson trolls discos and hip clothing stores searching for victims while Wells and Robbins walk casually around landmarks discussing ways to break open the case and foil Stevenson. As bodies turn up, there is just enough serial killer intrigue to keep up the intensity for the horror fan. The movie doesn't spare the details of Stevenson's murders as he plagues the city's nightlife.

At the core of all this is Wells and Stevenson's relationship. The two were friends in 1893. Wells, the forever optimist, sees his utopian vision of the future has not come to pass. Stevenson rejoices in the violence and indifference in the modern era. But Wells maintains that love will conquer in the end. It's a classic face off between two mythical characters played by two legendary actors. Some will find the movie a bit corny, but the performances are worth the watch and the story is well conceived leaving itself few holes to fall through in the time travel genre.

The Time Machine (1960)
Directed by George Pal
U.S.A. 103 min.

The Time Machine has a bit more cult/academic cred than some of the films in this book. It is sometimes mentioned in textbooks due to its time-lapse special effects. Gene Warren and Tim Baar won Academy Awards for the time-lapse photography showing the world aging at an accelerated pace. Their work, which was revelatory at the time, is often remembered alongside Rick Baker and Ray Harryhausen as game changers in the field. The story begins with a New Years Eve dinner thrown by H. George Wells (Rod Taylor). At the dinner, Wells casually tells his intellectual friends he has invented a time machine. They don't believe him of course, but it wouldn't be a story if Wells didn't get in his contraption and scuttle away across the boundaries of the future. Wells sits in a fancy chair and watches as the machine barrels through time using a sort of gear shift, accelerating time as he pushes it forward and slowing time as he pulls back. This effect is achieved using time-lapse photography. Wells watches out the window from the safety of his ornate, Victorian contraption. Or perhaps not so safe. A feeling of dread creeps in, as the world grows darker and harder to understand without the scrutiny of being in it. Wells stops the machine once in a while. He first stops in 1917 and happens upon a friend's son. The now seventeen-year-old lad is off to fight in World War I. Wells is disappointed in this development. (Wells in real life was a well-known pacifist.) He stops again in 1940. Again, Wells hopes for the future are dashed when he discovers that World War II is going on. Wells goes on to speculate about a coming nuclear war, which has a devastating effect on London. Of course, don't ask yourself why the sentient machine isn't destroyed in this exploding lava melee, but all time travel stories have holes in some manner.

Wells wrote the novella the film was based on in 1895. Some great time travel narratives would follow, including the 1981 comedy *Time Bandits*, the complicated 2004 time travel stock gift *Primer*, the 2007 Spanish thriller *Timecrimes*, and the 2010 comedy *Hot Tub Time Machine*. And they all have holes somewhere. You just have to want to believe. Eventually he blasts way into the future and discovers mankind has divided into two species: the Morlocks and the crossword puzzle staple Eloi. Here the film goes a bit H.R. Pufnstuf on acid. The story is so old, you're bound to kind of know how these two species serve each other, but Wells, the Eloi, and the Morlocks reveal themselves in the film using wild costumes, scary sets, and psychedelic lighting. It's a fun ride for fans of '60s horror or people interested in sci-fi history. The album cover *Mello Jello... for Groovy Ghouls* features a Morlock on the cover. They are kind of groovy. It's a simple old cult geezer, but one that's fun to watch and seems to have been, ironically, lost a bit in the passage of time.

Chapter 11: Hi, Karate?

    Karate films are categorized into many subgenres. Most people enjoy a good karate movie. Some people enjoy a bad karate movie. I'm certain purists won't like this section. I don't think casualists will either. Purists will find the selections too obvious and American. Casualists would rather watch something they've heard of. The average Jackie Chan movie is generally better than all three of these movies. So I'll ask you to take this list with a grain of salt. These are just three movies I like. I believe *Black Belt Jones* is a generally great karate movie. I enjoy *The Octagon* because I think Chuck Norris was really great before he engaged in so many absurd action films and became so, you know, Chuck Norris. I feel similarly about Jean-Claude Van Damme. Think of these movies as a schmear of American karate films. All three go down well on a lazy Saturday afternoon.

Black Belt Jones (1974)
Directed by Robert Clouse
U.S.A. 85 min.

In the beginning of this 85-minute film, *Black Belt Jones* (played by karate champion and certainly one of the most positive characters in any of these movies Jim Kelly) is forced, for some vague reason, to kick eight to ten people's asses in a parking lot. This is no problem for Black Belt Jones. As the credits roll, the bad guys go down, often in slow motion. As the last one attempts to flee the scene, Black Belt Jones picks up a gun and shoots the man in the ass. He then hops in a sports car and drives away in front of an assembling crowd who are just amused by all this. No one bothers him. And apparently, none of this was part of the plot, just some character development.

Where is Black Belt Jones when we need him most?

The actual plot to the film concerns Black Belt Jones's mentor "Pop" Byrd (career character actor and guy you'd most like to smoke a joint with Scatman Crothers) and the dojo he owns, which is right in the center of an area where the Mafia is buying up land. The Mafia owns all the land in the area where a new civic center is going up except one building: Byrd's dojo, which is where African American youth study the tenets and discipline of karate. Byrd won't sell, so the Mafia tries to persuade him. Jones steps in with help from the rest of the gang at the dojo to stop these developers from changing the neighborhood and closing the dojo. This, of course, is the plot to a surprising number of karate movies.

Oh, where is Black Belt Jones when we need him most?

Director Robert Clouse also directed the Bruce Lee classic *Enter the Dragon* (1973), in which Kelly had a small role. Funk guitar master Dennis Coffey composed the soundtrack. Watching Jim Kelly do karate to the sounds of deep funk is the true pleasure of the film. Kelly was a master and the fight scenes are inventive. One takes place in a car wash where the suds rise alongside the action. Another takes place within the narrow confines of a train corridor, where we cut outside to see Jones' adversaries flying through windows. Along the way, he teams up with Sydney (Gloria Hendry), whose karate prowess adds chaos to the mix for the bad guys.

I won't tell you if Kelly stops the Mafia from prevailing, but you've likely seen a movie before, so you may have a solid guess. Sadly, we all know that in real life developers will likely push the neighborhood out of the way and crush the buildings needed to build a giant civic center without much effort. We can only hope for this world where Black Belt Jones saves the day and keeps an African American karate school open. I think it's now appropriate to quote Hemingway: "Isn't it pretty to think so?"

The Octagon (1980)
Directed by Eric Karson
U.S.A. 103 min.

Although Japanese folklore can only vaguely pinpoint the origins of the ninja, Scott James (Chuck Norris) can look at a roomful of corpses and easily determine the cause of death: "Ninjas!" Does it have to be ninjas? Couldn't it be disgruntled employees? Ninjas are as good a guess as aliens, I suppose. In the film, Chuck Norris plays Scott James, and James is a guy very much like Chuck Norris. The film never fully explains James' stake in the circumstances presented except he is an ex-soldier, ex-professional fighter, and he trained as a ninja, probably at one of those ninja schools you are always hearing about in the grocery store circular. As the story progresses, he acquiesces to receive a call from someone for an assignment. Who was that on the phone? Who does he work for? It doesn't matter. Scott James walks around kicking ass. Women swoon. Evil schemes fail. His entering a room is enough to stop a square dance.

The movie is mostly a series of fights with an occasional break thrown in to attempt a plot. Eventually, we are treated to the excessive martial arts expo we are all waiting for. James and all his cronies converge on his old training camp governed by his arch nemesis Seikura (Tadashi Yamashita). There, ninjas get a chance to show off their ninja training, which includes important topics such as how to hang around under leaves until an intruder happens by, and how to stop in the middle of a fight you are winning and swing your weapons around skillfully until you get kicked in the head. And throwing stars. Yes, there are throwing stars.

If the plot sounds comically vague by modern standards of action movies, *The Octagon* still stands as an excellent vehicle showcasing Norris' talent as a martial arts practitioner. Modern movies no longer seem to care about time, space, or the limitations of the human body when it comes to action sequences. *The Octagon* delivers great analogue action in the tradition of the best Bruce Lee films. Norris obviously learned something about stage fighting from the master. *The Octagon* exceeds as a full-on karate movie: too much plot would slow it down.

The Octagon contains early appearances by *Oz* and *Ghostbusters* star Ernie Hudson and character actor Tracy Walter. The movie was written well before the Internet, before people had ready access to casual information. All that people knew about ninjas in 1980 was that they are awesome. That's really all you need to know to enjoy *The Octagon*.

Timecop (1994)
Directed by Peter Hyams
U.S.A. 98 min.

Futuristic time travel madness and high-kicking action sequences come together nicely in Peter Hyams' sci-fi thriller *Timecop*. The film was produced by Dark Horse Comics co-founder Mike Richardson and penned by comic writer Mark Verheiden. Dark Horse Comics is responsible for iconic comic titles like *Hellboy, The Mask,* and Frank Miller's *Sin City*. Although *Timecop* never reached the level of cult status as some of its time-policing predecessors, the film adaptation of the comic launched a direct-to-video sequel, a short-lived television program, and a series of follow up sci-fi novels. With a time travel narrative, you can always cover a lot of ground.

Max Walker (Jean-Claude Van Damme) is a police officer in charge of monitoring criminal activity involving the new technology of time travel. He is sent to investigate instances of people going back in time in order to steal something or change events to their advantage. Some of these people just aren't thinking things through. There are predicaments like sending a guy with two knives into the future to kill Walker instead of sending a guy with a gun. Or why not catch him while he's asleep? That works in the here and now. But Walker counters these complicated measures using a lot of karate. Martial arts take center stage as Walker travels through history solving crimes by kicking people in the face. As a director, Hyams has an aptitude for sci-fi and Van Damme manages, although without the same charm that made Schwarzenegger an unlikely '80s sci-fi hero. Since this is a time travel movie, I'll include this quote from what 1994 thought 2004 would be like: "Don't tell me what I can't do. Elections are won on television. You don't need the press, you don't need endorsements, you don't need the truth, you need money." And another quote showing Van Damme not quite up to Schwarzenegger's kill-quote standards: "Have a nice day."

Timecop, which was Van Damme's top grosser, found his star reaching its zenith between the release of two of his other well-liked movies : John Woo's *Hard Target* (1993) and the popular video game adaptation *Street Fighter* (1994), which is another movie I recommend if you're in the mood for this type of action. *Street Fighter* is one of those movies that is better than it needs to be. Hyams also directed two underrated sci-fi stories from the '80s: 1981's *Outland* (mentioned in this book) and an underrated adaptation of Arthur C. Clarke's follow up of 2001, *2010: The Year We Make Contact* (1984). Hyams and Van Damme reunited again in 1995 to create another of Van Damme's more popular films, *Sudden Death* (1995). With its use of both analogue and burgeoning digital special effects and winding time travel narrative, *Timecop* is a good film from a fun era of sci-fi movies.

Chapter 12: Horror

What can I say about my beloved genre: Horror. I love it. If you're reading this, it is likely that you love it too. Of course, everyone has pet horror movies. These are just a few horror titles I love that I don't see written about often. Every horror fan has a pet list like this. I hope you find something here you like.

Body Snatchers (1993)
Directed by Abel Ferrara
U.S.A. 87 min.

Jack Finney's 1955 novel *Invasion of the Body Snatchers* has been adapted for the screen four times. The first, 1956's *Invasion of the Body Snatchers*, is a horror classic. At this time, the story was interpreted to be a commentary about the threat of the rise of communism in the 1950s. The 1978 version starred Donald Sutherland, Jeff Goldblum, and Leonard Nimoy. This movie told the story well and showed some nice shots of San Francisco from the '70s along the way. This version reached cult classic status as both a horror film and a mainstream hit. Even Pauline Kael had nice things to say about the 1978 version. Along the way, the storyline has become ensconced in American culture. People who have never heard of Jack Finney understand the tropes of his story. Surely with all this in the books, a third remake of the story would be unnecessary. It's hard to believe a simple little sci-fi story can warrant a third version and be a good movie, but I'd go as far as to strongly recommend *Body Snatchers* (1993), another remake of Finney's tale of aliens and the pods that love them. This version stars Meg Tilly, Christine Elise, Gabrielle Anwar, Forest Whitaker, Terry Kinney, and R. Lee Ermey. Here the focus is on the teenagers, adding to the American paranoia that kids are intuitive, yet no one will listen to them. Marti (Anwar) is in the car with her family moving to Alabama. Her dad Steve Malone (Kinney) moves his family around a lot as a consultant for the military. In a gas station bathroom, a man in a disheveled soldier suit accosts Marti. He makes some crazy claims while he has her trapped in, of all glorious places, the gas station bathroom, and then quickly takes off into the nearby woods. Later, while the family is getting settled, Marti's younger brother Andy (Reilly Murphy) is scared into running away from school. He gets in trouble for not wanting to take naptime. If you're familiar with these *Snatchers* tropes, you can see where this is going, so I won't spoil it. The kids soldier on trying to convince people something is amiss on base, but the uniformity of life in army barracks impedes their persuasive abilities. Besides a slightly new and refreshing take on the story, the movie has some surprising performances for such B-movie fare, including a great soliloquy by Forest Whitaker, lots of stern posturing by R. Lee Ermery, what I believe to be Meg Tilly's greatest rant, and really solid and likable young actors selling the premise that you're supposed to be rooting for them, not just humanity in general. The special effects are also top notch and include some new and unnerving visuals for the transformation sequences. It's great low-budget fare especially for the horror fan. But I think there's enjoyment outside of the genre in this. It's a fun watch.

Calvaire (2004)
Directed by Fabrice Du Welz
Belgium/France 88 min.

Calvaire is not a typical gross-out or torture porn horror film, but it does contain some genuinely strange and creative moments that can be pretty disturbing. If you're not at least casually into modern horror, you will not enjoy this movie. It's a low-budget hostage horror story with a similar "in the wrong place at the wrong time" quality as the *Texas Chainsaw Massacre* (1974). Leatherface is the face of that franchise, but horror posers and the faint-at-heart may not recall or even realize Massacre is as much about Leatherface's extended family, the Sawyers, and an evening they spend at home antagonizing someone who doesn't quite get them. *Calvaire* has a similar story arc. After spending time with Bartel (Jackie Berroyer) and the local townspeople in *Calvaire*, even the Sawyers might find themselves scratching their heads in the car on the way home.

Marc Stevens (Laurent Lucas) is a traveling lounge singer. While traveling through some remote locations between engagements, his van breaks down. He encounters Boris (Jean-Luc Couchard) looking for his dog on a remote road in the pouring rain. (Boris will continue to look for that dog for a lot of the run time of the movie.) Boris leads Marc to an inn you wouldn't stay in for any reason run by the aforementioned Bartel. Bartel is an unassuming man who poses scenarios to Marc in a matter-of-fact manner similar to how Peter Falk's detective Columbo would walk perpetrators into verbal traps by asking "just one more thing." But it's not Marc harboring secrets in this duet. Bartel convinces Marc to take a nap in one of his many vacant rooms while he tows the van back to the inn to be fixed. I don't have to tell you, but Bartel puts little effort into fixing the car, and when Marc's overnight stay becomes imminent, Bartel convinces Marc to have dinner with him. By now, you're imagining Marc is a pretty big nimrod. And yes, he sort of is. He comes across as likable, but is much too passive in this situation letting Bartel take over the planning and care of his vehicle. This part of the story is somewhat presented to make you wonder "why would he?" but it also begs the question, "would you break social conventions and potentially offend someone if you were this deep in their world?"

I'll tell you this: I hate to give this detail away, but for reasons never directly stated, Bartel convinces himself Marc is Bartel's trampy wife who walked out on him nineteen years prior. You're not missing anything; this is, of course, not possible. Somehow, the locals also go along with this premise to humor Bartel, even though Bartel is at odds with many of them. There is no reason for this except that they are also all very strange and no one ends up being much help to poor Marc. Of course Marc is not close in age or gender for this to be reasonable, but if you think I've given away the most bizarre detail of the movie, you'll still be surprised. This is where the hunt portion of the movie takes over. The whole thing is only 88 minutes long, but it's a tense 88. It's nothing if not efficient. Perhaps this piece of information will engage you to want to see it. Claustrophobic cinematography, a strange script, and solid acting come together on the screen for a bizarre and disturbing story.

Candyman (1992)
Directed by Bernard Rose
U.S.A. 101 min.

Candyman is based on a short story by Clive Barker and employs as much of the organic surrealism Barker is known for and certainly as much as the screen can handle. Helen Lyle (Virginia Madsen) is a graduate student researching urban legends at the University of Illinois. And a big ole myth exists in her own backyard. He's known as "the Candyman", and his presence is vivid in the nearby low-income Cabrini-Green neighborhood. The legend dates back to the late nineteenth century when a slave was stung to death by bees after being smeared with honey by his overseer. His ashes were spread in the area where the Cabrini-Green neighborhood now stands. According to the legend, Candyman can be summoned by saying his name five times in a mirror. Here in modern times, drug gangs run the neighborhood. Many residents believe Candyman is a real thing, or at least could be true. Candyman is taking the heat for several murders, or at least making them difficult to investigate, and the tough guys in the area are glad to keep the superstition alive. The local ruffians make Lyle's investigation difficult. One scene involves a drug dealer who even goes as far as to dress similarly and occasionally commit Candyman-style crimes against his enemies to keep people guessing. He gets the jump on Lyle during one of her exploratory visits to the neighborhood and knocks her unconscious in a public bathroom as a warning to keep away. Her friends and colleagues worry she's in over her head. Lyle has her work cut out for her, but the situation gets much worse when the actual Candyman shows up. I hope I'm not giving too much away, but it wouldn't be much of a movie without Candyman.

As Lyle gets deeper to the truth of the matter of Candyman hanging around apartment blocks, she becomes "glamoured" or hypnotized by Candyman and eventually goes on to do his bidding, or at least takes the fall for much of his reign of chaos. Along the way, the mystery unfolds. Firstly, it's a better script than it needs to be. You can watch the movie and see what's going on, but you can't always tell what's going to happen. Tony Todd takes on the role of Candyman with much mystery and aplomb. He exudes fear with a deep gravelly voice and speaks slowly in abstract terms. Like the script, he's better than he even needs to be. You'll never catch Candyman swiping any Freddie Krueger one-liners. Candyman is a smooth operator. The movie has great special effects, including a lot of abstract gore and a great use of bees. I doubt there's a time when bees have been scarier.

Christmas Evil (1980)
Directed by Lewis Jackson
U.S.A. 100 min.

I have for a long time been particularly fond of a scene in David Lynch's *Wild at Heart* where Laura Dern's character Lula describes in disturbing detail her demented cousin's obsession with Christmas. I would like to know if Mr. Lynch saw *Christmas Evil*. There are better-known Christmas themed horror movies, but to me *Evil* is a classic among classics. It's the I*t's a Wonderful Life* for horror films.

After witnessing mommy and Santa Claus in the beginnings

of having a "not-so-holy" night as a child, Harry Stadling (Brandon Maggart) becomes psychologically damaged and obsessed with Christmas. Thirty-three years later, Stadling collects Christmas ephemera, works in a toy factory, and spends his spare time skulking around his neighborhood keeping tabs on which kids are naughty and which ones are nice. His extended skulks create a sense of great unease driving the movie. What he's thinking or what he's capable of are never telegraphed. Maggart plays the neighborhood suspect as just about to unravel, but occasionally dropped into the position of being a good guy.

There is occasional gore, but the movie would not be nearly as scary without ride-alongs as we follow Harry on his various stakeouts. There is not much overt violence as there is a fear of not being able to follow his train of thought. The fun here is seeing his bizarre behavior and not knowing at any given time what he's capable of. The filmmakers know that you know Harry is going to snap at some point, but play a game of cat and mouse with the audience through various roadblocks, including Harry's noble reactions in the Christmas spirit, if you will–in several scenarios. The score consists of an extended series of ominous tones, tense music, and uneasy sound effects, some of which feel a bit ahead of their time as horror movie tropes. Some are quite strange, including an extended segment of Christmas carols warbling through a busted tape recorder. Maggart's acting carries the character nicely as he delivers a paced unraveling predating the influx of the popular trope of the quiet man psycho killer that dominates so many '80s slasher movies. Maggart broods. When the movie permits, he takes a break, and acts genuinely human. His predicaments shift him in and out of reality to the point of farce.

Stadling's younger, well-adjusted brother Philip (Jeffery DuMunn) worries from his nice home about his brother not coming over for Thanksgiving and Christmas. Philip's concern, and the ensuing phone call that leads up to the climax, are oddly convincing and add a human element often not found in horror movies. The phone call might sound a bit silly in light of the events, but Harry and Philip's conversation is thoughtful in a way that gives pause. The movie works so well as a slow burn that it's a pleasure not to see Harry go into full slasher mode. Even at his worst, he's a wild card. More than just a slasher film, *Christmas Evil* is an awesome portrayal of an already unstable man coming apart at the seams in a Santa suit.

Dead and Buried (1981)
Directed by Gary Sherman
U.S.A. 92 min.

The story opens on a photographer working on a beach in Potter's Bluff, Maine. A mysterious blonde woman named Lisa (Lisa Blount, who also appears in *Prince of Darkness*) approaches him. She finds him interesting. She asks if she's photo worthy. Before long, she takes off her shirt. The photographer figures he's hit the jackpot until he realizes that, in the process of photographing her, he's been surrounded. Now, she and everyone in town seem to know something he doesn't. She's photographing him now. They all are for some reason. Then they beat him nearly to death with little explanation, set him on fire, and fake his death in a car crash.

Dead and Buried isn't the most clever movie you'll see, but if you're expecting a typical H.P. Lovecraft or Stephen King-type cult of lost-in-time drooling monsters hanging around under a light sheet of fog are behind this ritual, you will be a little surprised. Particularly when a man resembling the photographer shows up working at the gas station later in the film. Interactions around town appear odd to Sheriff Dan Gillis (James Frentino) and the town's eccentric coroner William Dobbs (portrayed by screen veteran Jack Albertson). The two team up to figure out what, if anything, is going on. People like Gillis' wife Janet (Melody Anderson) think he's being paranoid.

There are some great special effects in this film that are satisfying in terms of early analog gore. In play are some early-modern tropes like the warbling of an antique record player that Dobb's spins his big band music on as he works late nights at the morgue. Robert Englund also makes a pre- *Nightmare on Elm Street* appearance as a citizen who hangs out at the diner making logical excuses for all the weird things happening around town.

From here, there are some guessable outcomes. But this story does take you down a few winding avenues achieved by reasonable clues and changes in the characters. Sometimes films that try to do something different with the "small town keeping a secret" trope get mired down by being too clever for their own good. Here, the story stays interesting and the conclusion stands on solid enough ground to make it fun and creepy to boot.

Def By Temptation (1990)
Directed by James Bond III
U.S.A. 94 min.

There is nothing better than a low-budget horror movie when it figures out how to fit in its own creative space. This movie is clever in how it gets all of its story and budget on the screen and has fun with it without trying to look like something it isn't. Joel Garth (James Bond III) is visiting his brother K (Kadeem Hardison) in New York City. Both are from a small town, but K has become worldlier since moving to New York and Garth is being schooled in the ways of picking up women.

Garth has lived a sheltered life; he is on his way towards a career in the clergy. Garth meets an unnamed woman (Cynthia Bond) in a bar. He doesn't know that K had drinks with her the night before. Unbeknownst to both of them, the woman is a succubus, pulling unsuspecting men from the bar scene in K's neighborhood. Cynthia Bond's character, credited as Temptress, senses that Garth is in a transitional phase and comes after him, leaving K confused and jealous. Trying to be a good sport, K encounters Dougy (Bill Nunn), a regular who hangs around telling tall tales to the ladies. But Dougy claims to have never hit on the strange woman who frequents the bar. He is the first one to notice something isn't right with Temptress. "I'm on a first name basis with pussy, you know what I'm sayin'." I can only guess what Dougy is getting at, but it's not long before he and K are putting their heads together detective style to figure out what's happening.

The cinematography in the film is excellent, especially in creating a world around a very small area of Manhattan. When they aren't at the bar or in K's apartment, the scope and look of the neighborhood create the perfect space for this neo-gothic without using contrived establishing shots. Cinematographer Ernest Dickerson is a frequent Spike Lee collaborator, and it's easy to see how his talent was recognized as he cut his teeth with this good-looking, low-budget project. Garth's back story involves spooky church imagery contrasted with flashbacks of his minister father having run-ins with a mysterious woman dressed in all black. Dickerson and Bond do a lot with simple comic book lighting and cheap but ominous sets. The special effects are often good, either simple but nice, or Troma-level over-the-top when it's time to get ill, including a strange scene where K is pulled through the television *Videodrome* (1983) style in a scene that begs to be seen. All of this is set to a fun R&B soundtrack. It's quite an accomplishment for 1990, and *Def By Temptation* holds its own against movies with bigger budgets.

Evilspeak (1981)
Directed by Eric Weston
U.S.A. 89 min.

Two things validate adding this movie to your list in a big way: First, Anton LaVey cited *Evilspeak* as an excellent movie about Satanism. Second, the film was caught up in the UK's nasty legislation that attempted to regulate video sales in the 1980s. Violent and sexually explicit videos were censored similarly to the way parental advisory stickers were placed on rock albums in the US. Like the misguided American legislation, British censorship efforts had a similar effect: the movies became notorious and more sought after by the kids. For a movie about Satanism, *Evilspeak* is actually pretty tame in the beginning. There are a lot of scenes featuring Ron Howard's brother Clint looking incredulous about things. But as with most Satanism narratives, the film comes with a guarantee of nudity and unorthodox deaths. Regularly terrorized by his military school classmates, Stanley Coopersmith (Howard) finds an ancient tome owned by a Spanish priest, and he begins dabbling in the world of the dark lord. He brings one of those awesome 1980s looking computers into the basement and begins translating the book. He essentially instant messages the devil.

The movie is foremost worth seeing for the people watching. The film contains a really strange hodgepodge of character actors. *What's Happening's* Heywood Nelson plays Coopersmith's only friend. *Night Court's* Richard Moll, no stranger to B-horror films, portrays Father Esteban. Loren Lester, who played Fritz Hansel in *Rock 'n' Roll High School*, reprises his role as a nerdy looking bully. (It's a role he was born to play.) However the weirdest cameo in Evilspeak has to be Lenny Montana, who played Luca Brasi in the *Godfather*. This movie is ripe for a game of weird actor bingo. Besides all of this, there are some cool 1980s computer-generated effects representing Satan's arrival through the screen. There are also beheadings, an Omen-esque soundtrack, exceptional blood loss, and a soccer team eaten by evil pigs. It takes a little while to get started, but once it gets going, *Evilspeak* goes bananas.

Eyes Without a Face (1960)
Directed by George Franju
France 90 min.

Eyes Without a Face is a great film by a master filmmaker. It's a neo-gothic tale that stands the test of time alongside classics of the horror genre. It's interesting to consider that Hitchcock's *Psycho* (1960) was released the same year. Although *Psycho* is its own kind of movie, images and tropes of the story of Norman Bates and his Mother will be forever reborn and remembered during the Halloween season. *Eyes Without a Face* doesn't get credit for being part of the canon in the same way. A pale girl in a smooth mask wandering into darkness holding a dove could be as iconic and scary as the goings-on at the Bates Motel, as quintessential as the noir lit Universal Monster films, or even as frightening as the Hammer Studio remakes with their shiny red vampire blood and green-tinted graveyards. However, Eyes Without a Face came along eight years before the stark edge of black-and-white film would make a strong comeback in the horror genre, via George Romero's gruesome *Night of the Living Dead* (1968). Franju was accused of working beneath his abilities on this genre piece, but the combination of elements reveals the work of the master. *Eyes Without a Face* utilizes noir lighting, fairy tale tropes, grotesque special effects, and gothic sensibilities in a unique film.

Dr. Génessier (Pierre Brasseur) is involved in a clandestine experiment. His assistant Louise (Alida Valli) tracks down pretty girls for him to experiment on. The goal is to help his daughter Christiane Génessier (Edith Scub), who is revealed 43 minutes into the film to have suffered massive scarring from an accident. Christiane spends most of the movie wearing a blank mask resembling an evil skincare device. Her mask is shaped like her face, but is smooth and expressionless. It is so robotic and unfeeling as to evoke the fear of the uncanny. Because of this, it's difficult to gauge the level of her role in these experiments. We're never sure if she approves of what they are doing for her. She is also lonely. When no one is around she phones her ex-fiancé Jacques Vernon (François Guérin) and hangs up on him. He, like many others, believes her to be dead. Jacques becomes suspicious even though Dr. Génessier and Louise faked Christiane's funeral. Dr. Génessier and Louise are keeping Christiane under wraps until they can affix a skin graph on her face and change her identity. They eventually lure a young shoplifter named Paulette (Béatrice Altariba) to the house. Paulette is in obvious trouble, but has a secret as well. The surgical segments of the film contain new levels of gore for a '60s film. Christiane's seclusion and lost love add a fairy-tale element to the story. The doctor's provincial house in the suburbs of Paris provides a gothic setting as victims make the transitional trip from modern Paris to the rural suburbs. Like *Psycho, Eyes Without a Face* combines a lot of dark elements into a short black-and-white film to create a frightening classic.

Lair of the White Worm (1988)
Directed by Ken Russell
U.K. 93 min.

Have you ever seen a movie you know you're going to enjoy in the first seconds? That's the way I felt about *Lair of the White Worm*. The opening shot reads as if Hammer Studios had filmed *Raiders of the Lost Ark*. The camera closes in on a cave dug into the side of a mountain. It gets closer. We know something crazy is going on in there. We've also presumably read the title of the movie. We then cut to archaeologist Angus Flint (Peter Capaldi). Flint is finding a big skull during a dig, the kind of discovery that almost never happens to archaeologists. We all know no good is coming from any of this. The rest of this movie should be him getting tenure and being interviewed for Archeology Magazine. But never mind that. I guess it's like Vegas: someone has to win sometime.

The film is based on the 1911 novel by Bram Stoker. It's a beautiful clash of early countryside horror in the hands of a surrealist filmmaker taking jabs at religion and folklore. Russell updates the story with a lot of nudity and bizarre dream sequences. While Flint is going about the horror movie pretext that archaeologists who find large bones frequently do, Lady Sylvia Marsh (Amanda Donohoe) arrives unexpectedly to stay at the local rockin' castle Temple House. The castle is her family's birthright complete with a bitchin' hot tub and tanning bed. I can't say much more about Lady Marsh except she is a particularly swinging host. Along the way, Flint bonds with James d'Ampton (Hugh Grant), a local Lord who subscribes to the legend that a mythical snake-like creature existed and was slain by his ancestor. The two must decide whether or not there's a snake with vampiric qualities terrorizing the area. I'm trying not to give anything away here, but the movie isn't called Two Stately Gentleman Pleasantly Roam the Countryside in Conversation. They show you the "lair" in the first few seconds of the movie. *Lair of the White Worm* is a stylishly punk movie. Touching the skull sometimes brings about hallucinations, and they are shocking but colorful in a cartoonish sort of way. They occasionally resemble what it might look like if collage artist Winston Smith's work came alive. A great monster movie, it even makes an attempt at a twist ending, although you can sort of see it coming. I'd suggest watching it in relaxed mode, perhaps from your castle's hot tub or tanning bed.

Nightmares (1983)
Directed by Joseph Sargent
U.S.A. 99 min.

The '80s were a great era for low-budget horror anthologies. *Creepshow* (1982) helped revive the horror anthology going strong in Britain in the early '70s with comic book adaptations like *Tales from the Crypt* (1972) and *Vault of Horror* (1973). While *Creepshow* had a one-two punch provided by scriptwriter Stephen King and director George Romero, 1983's *Nightmares* did not have the same caché. However, the film has a respectable cast and a few good short stories with some interesting twists.

The film opens with "Terror in Topanga," a story about an escaped psychopath terrorizing a small community. It wouldn't be a story if someone didn't go out for cigarettes. The twist in the story closely resembles an urban myth, but it's a fun story and Fear front man Lee Ving is among the players.

The most unique story in the anthology comes next: "The Bishop of Battle." This chapter finds Emilio Estevez between his success in *The Outsiders* and his eventual ascension into

cult stardom with *Repo Man*. Estevez plays J.J. Cooney, a video game hustler (I only hope there really were video game hustlers in the '80s; I never met one) who goes from arcade to arcade listening to Fear on his walkman and hustling people out of their allowances with his video game prowess. Cooney does this because he's obsessed with a video game called The Bishop of Battle. Cooney is convinced there is an unreachable thirteenth level that will inexplicably validate his existence. A clandestine moment can be had with fans of the movie with the game's opening warning: "Greetings Earthlings. I am the Bishop of Battle, master of all I survey. I have thirteen progressively harder levels. Try me... if you dare." If you consider what can go wrong here for a moment, you can probably work out the twist ending, but for a glimpse into early Estevez and a good representation of early arcade culture, the second chapter of *Nightmares* is a must see.

Story three has two things working for it: one is the ever effective Lance Henriksen playing a priest, and two, it recognizes the length of time the man vs. car plotline can remain interesting. Henriksen plays Macleod, a priest struggling with his faith until he is faced with battling a satanic car. It sounds a little trite, but Henriksen makes it work. His ability to struggle with evil is inherent and he makes the story work. There is a similar dynamic in "Night of the Rat," where professional hysteric Veronica Cartwright improves the typical giant rat narrative. Cartwright is a freak out expert bringing her pushed-over-the-edge persona to films like *Alien* (1979), *Invasion of the Body Snatchers* (1978) and *The Right Stuff* (1983). *Nightmares* won't blow your mind, but it's a great Saturday night horror anthology with good performances, punk undertones, and a few surprises. It's been released a couple of times on DVD, but it's a common dollar bin as it's usually in the throwaway section of stacks of horror videos. It's easily a dollar or two's worth of fun.

Possession (1981)
Directed by Andrzej Zulawski
France/West Germany 124 min.

I was tempted to write a one-line review of *Possession*: "A lot of yelling and piles of gross stuff… but in a good way." That's primarily what I like about it, and from what I hear, a lot of people don't much like about it. But the film does warrant a deeper look. Firstly, it stars Sam Neill as Mark. It certainly must be this performance that landed Neill some of his other completely-down-to-Earth-British-man-comes-totally-unwound roles that made his legacy and brought him into contact with some great directors. Neill worked this angle in the underrated sci-fi/half horror hybrid *Event Horizon* (1997), David Cronenberg's weird brother/surgeon tale *Dead Ringers* (1988), Wim Wenders' epic *Until the End of the World* (1991), and one of John Carpenter's more ignored and underrated offerings *In the*

Mouth of Madness (1994). Neill is great in these movies. I hate his good movies, except maybe *Jurassic Park* (1993) depending how you look at it. Neill's off-the-hook bananas persona is overshadowed by Helen Isabelle Adjani's over-the-top performance as Anna. Some hurricanes are overshadowed by Helen Isabelle Adjani's performance in *Possession*.

The story takes place in early 1980s Berlin, which is fun to look at and a perfect setting for this kind of thing. You'll be jealous of the giant, affordable apartments. The café lifestyle. This is the Berlin where David Bowie and Lou Reed recorded seminal downer albums. The plot, if it's even relevant, is this: Mark is a spy (which seems a weirdly specific and unnecessary detail for this story, but it still works. Maybe it's a German thing). Mark returns from a spy mission to find his wife insistent on getting a divorce. Mark relents and leaves her alone for a bit, only to return and find she can't take care of herself or their young son Bob. Mark meets with Bob's teacher Helen, also portrayed by Helen Isabelle Adjani for no discernible reason other than to cause confusion. I don't know if I should, or really could, give anything away at this stage, but I will say Anna is hiding something.

This is all told amongst scenes of a violent and strangely moving miscarriage, a stand off with Anna's lover Heinrich that doesn't go exactly as planned, a tense electric kitchen knife fight, and what I can only describe as a very lazy mutant octopus. By now, you already know if you'd like the movie. It's strange and creative circa 1980s horror, best compared to Roman Polanski's early oddball freak out *Repulsion* (1965). Its organic parts are hard to watch at times, but the special effects are special: compelling, rather than violence for the sake of violence. It's a story that's hard to wrap, so don't look for that. It's a fun romp for a special kind of horror fan.

Resolution (2012)
Directed by Justin Benson and
Aaron Scott Moorehead
U.S.A. 93 min.

Michael Danube (Peter Cilella) is a graphic designer living in an unnamed city. He receives a strange video via email from his ex-best friend Chris Daniels (Vinny Curran). The video is a series of rants and clips sent from deep in the woods. Chris has a history with hard drugs and his problems look to be escalating. Michael hunts Chris down to find him living in squalor: he is squatting in a half-built cabin in a rural area where he occupies himself firing a 9mm pistol randomly at birds and using explosives recklessly. Michael tries to talk to Chris about his drug use. Chris is belligerent, but convinces Michael to hang out for a bit. After the initial tension subsides, Michael's plan is revealed: he tases Chris and handcuffs him to a wall. Michael says they'll sit there for seven days while the junk leaves Chris' body. Chris is not amused. The two discuss this face off with the casualness of two friends fighting over a dinner check. They speak with the shorthand that long-term friends have. It's a somewhat reasonable plan and a fine plot: perhaps a good start to an off-Broadway play. But Chris and Mike are visited in succession by a string of strangers making the task at hand difficult. Chris' drug buddies stop by and are angered by being asked to leave. A tough group of young Native American men arrive and claim Chris is squatting on a reservation illegally and the cabin belongs to them. Some people from a local UFO cult stop in. All of this creates chaos and a stable of characters that mean Mike and Chris no good. Mike is undeterred and hunkers down for the long haul. From there, Mike has a lot of responsibilities, but also has time on his hands. He goes to the store. He wanders around against all common sense. He finds clues to a puzzle he wasn't looking to solve, including videos and stills of weird scenes shot near the property. Eventually the videos close in on the timeline of Chris and Mike's occupation. The videos are becoming impossibly close to real time. The whole rehab discussion becomes secondary. It seems they are being watched. The duo are obviously being messed with. But by whom, and to what ends?

Besides having a good premise, this low-budget film really shows what you can do with very little. Directors Justin Benson and Aaron Scott Moorehead understand the chapbook of horror tropes and how to maneuver around them without telegraphing a punch. They create a genuinely creepy environment with no safe corners for the audience to escape to. The eerie reality of the situation pumps up any nods to anything supernatural going on and keeps the movie moving with an uneasiness that fills the entire run time. Much of what I read about this film compares it favorably to Drew Goddard's 2011 meta-horror masterpiece *The Cabin in the Woods*. I hate to jump on that bandwagon, but if the comparison encourages someone to seek this terrific film out, then I would have to say fans of *Cabin* would have to appreciate this.

Severance (2006)
Directed by Christopher Smith
UK/Germany 95 min.

In the *Friday the 13th, Halloween,* and *Nightmare on Elm Street* franchises, the bad guy is generally a mythical and indestructible person: one who continues to show up for murders no matter what is thrown at them. In the mid-00s a trend snuck up in horror movies I like to call the "hunt" narrative, which is when ordinary people show up or follow someone solely for the sake of terrorizing them.

An early prototype for the "hunt" movie is *The Hitcher* (1986), in which a guy driving on a slow, West Texas highway is tormented by the robot from *Blade Runner* (1982). He's not as articulate this time around, but he is surely ruthless and twice as scary. Why? No particular reason. A pivotal and more recent example is the very effective and scary *Funny Games* (1997), a movie that veers a little too close into the torture for torture's sake arena, but is itself a stylish and creative movie. The narrative aspects of these movies took hold and ultimately suffered by way of two films I didn't enjoy as much. One was *Wolf Creek* (2005), where a rugged Australian man chases two British backpackers around Western Australia because, that's what happens in Australia. The tourism board just doesn't warn you about it. It's not even illegal there. The other film I found less interesting was *The Strangers* (2008), where a guy takes the daughter of Aerosmith's lead singer to a cabin in the middle of nowhere and is surprised when some locals want to meet her.

In the middle of all this, a sleeper called *Severance* did the concept a lot of justice. The film involves a group of British and Canadian co-workers on a work-retreat in Hungary. They are the European sales group from a military company called Palisade Defense on a bus being driven to a cabin in the woods owned by the company. Most of us know not to accept a ride to a cabin in the woods, but there are Canadians in this group. The first red flag on this journey appears: a large tree in the road, the sight of which scares the driver of the bus who refuses to take the bus the rest of the way to the cabin. There is a language barrier, but the gist is this: it's a dangerous area. No one can understand what he's afraid to encounter, but there is a side road, so the group decides to try to walk. Upon arrival, the cabin is in bad shape. Things don't work. The floors are old and rotted. The fixtures are musty, including a series of files outlining sketchy facts about the company. What had they used this cabin for in the past? Rumors abound. After a while, the group finds unsettling clues as to the origin and legacy of the original purpose of the cabin and what happened to its previous visitors. It's enough to scare everyone into making an exit plan. But en route to the main road they find the bus and the driver lying dead nearby. While the group works all this out, they are targeted by a group of militant serial murderers. Paramilitary ones as it turns out. We never get a full idea of how many people are aiding them and why this group is floating around out there, but the broad stroke answers are "several" and "they're insane." Here begins a clever "hunt" story, where the good guys are down for not knowing what they are up against, but eventually get wiser and more resourceful. There are some clever scares mixed in with office politics humor to keep the movie fun. It's a mix of *Funny Games* with a bit of *Office Space* (1999) thrown in. I also like a film called *You're Next* (2011), which brought some grindhouse class to the home invasion proceedings without concentrating on pure torture scenes. Paired with Severance, it's a good double feature for your next trip outside of cell phone range.

The Shrine (2010)
Director: Jon Knautz
Canada 95 min.

The Shrine opens on a ritualistic murder. A man has a metal mask hammered onto his face. It doesn't look entirely realistic, but it is charming as far as ritualistic murders go. It's the kind of gothic killing you'd see in an old Hammer film with the gore turned up just a notch. The story cuts to a frustrated journalist named Carmen (Cindy Sampson). She is not getting the types of assignments she feels are worthy of her skills, and so she petitions her editor to investigate a missing persons story no editor in their right mind would green light. Some tourists have disappeared from a small village in Poland. Under false pretenses, Carmen enlists an intern named Sara (Meghan Heffern) and her boyfriend Marcus (Aaron Ashmore) to fly to Poland with her in order to investigate the missing tourist. It is absurd in the information age that she could get away with all of this, but it all happens efficiently and is as enjoyable as it is in an old school "let's get the horror movie on the road" sort of way.

It should go without saying they arrive at this pastoral Polish village and are met with resistance from the locals. I can't really say more, except to say what I thought was going to happen did not in fact happen. There's a fun and clever twist to this low-budget film. This movie only has one or two strings to pull, but it pulls them nicely. This is not the typical "escape through the woods defending yourself with logs" horror film that it projects to be in the beginning. And what's going on with the villagers is clever enough to be refreshing. Carmen, Sara, and Marcus are remarkably likable considering they are not given much to be except wooden types who learn in the worst way possible their modern skill sets are not useful when stalked by angry, salt-of-the-earth Polish villagers. They are horror plot fodder that must pull from some unknown source of energy within to survive. The action scenes and special effects are well adapted to the B-movie feel of the plot. You also get the old-style histrionics of an ancient cult in the woods. The Shrine is a solid afternoon popcorn horror reminiscent of '60s-'70s era horror.

Starry Eyes (2014)
Directed by Kevin Kölsch/Dennis Widmyer
U.S.A. 98 min.

As the opening credits roll to a wonderfully foreboding and eerie keyboard score, we see a montage of the lifestyle of Sarah Walker (Alexandra Essoe). She works an awful job at a Hooters-style restaurant called "Big Taters" where her boss ogles the girls and complains about their cell phone use knowing most of them are actors waiting for auditions. Alex has a low body weight but hates her reflection. Her roommate's friends Ashley (Natalie Costillo) and Erin (Fabiene Therese) have a profound competence for passive aggression. Sarah seems nice, but slightly naive for allowing all this to get to her. She, like many would-be artists, is just looking to catch a break. She goes on a lot of auditions. We've seen and/or experienced this sort of thing on one level or another, but for young actors in Los Angeles, it's a level of scrutiny no human should be subjected to.

Sarah gets an audition for an established production house specializing in horror movies. She immediately has a nightmare about it. The reality isn't much better. The casting director (Maria Olsen) and her assistant (Marc Senter) are a disinterested and rude pair. Their bizarre behavior brings an oppressive level of awkwardness to the auditions. Sarah is so traumatized she runs off to the bathroom to cry. The casting directors discover her in the bathroom screaming and pulling her hair out. They bring her back to the audition room. They're into it. There's a big, red flag, but what would you do? You'll put up with a lot to get a break sometimes. All of this leads to a casting couch situation that is creepy and gross. If that wasn't bad enough, Sarah's journey towards getting the part quickly turns into something else entirely. To say more would give too much away. The themes of integral rot and transformation are prevalent through the rest of the film. Sarah is heading into something she doesn't understand. The film relies on Alexandra Essoe, who plays both sides of the fed-up actor and disintegrating commodity role as casting escalates. Sarah has a few non-committal allies. Her roommate Tracy (Amada Fuller) cares enough to worry about her and offers comfort and counsel. Danny (Noah Segan from the excellent 2005 movie *Brick*) is as likable a character as the film will allow: a feckless filmmaker without an apparent plan, but one who seems determined to do right by Sarah if he can get his film off the ground. He is as sincere and forthright as a Los Angeles character gets in these types of films, but he also lives in a van. *Starry Eyes* has regularly been compared to *Rosemary's Baby* (1968), but it definitely delves into enough new territory so as to be frightening yet uncontrived. The performances are good and the story is unique enough to hang some good horror on. It's a "dark side of Los Angeles" tale, so it includes nasty people in the movie business. But it is more than that and a great modern horror film.

Trick or Treat (1986)
Directed by Joseph Charles Martin Smith
U.S.A. 98 min.

Those enamored with '80s metal might enjoy this a little too much. It's as clever a story as it can be and earns a place next to *River's Edge* (1986) and *The Gate* (1987) as a snapshot of what it was like to be a certain type of heavy metal fan in the '80s. *Trick or Treat* arrived amidst Tipper Gore and the Parent's Music Resource Center heyday with their crusade against sexualized and violent music. Its timing also coincided with an incident in which two men in Nevada attempted suicide blaming backwards masking on a Judas Priest LP. And thus, the stage was set for the messages on heavy metal records narrative. In the story, heavy metal fan Eddie Weinbauer (Marc Price) discovers his hero, the recently deceased Sammi Curr (Tony Fields), has included backwards messages on his records. These messages become exponentially powerful and more specific to Weinbauer. The messages take on more substantial ghostly forms and begin aiding Weinbauer with his revenge on his schoolmates who bully him relentlessly. As Weinbauer picks up on what's happening, he becomes reluctant to stay friends with the entity, which is becoming personified through sound. But Curr's hold on the natural world becomes stronger, and as long as his last recorded track exists on a tape made during the course of all this action, Curr manages to continue to take revenge on Weinbauer's behalf whether the latter character wants it or not. This movie is so '80s, there's a scene in the middle of the film where, for no reason, Weinbauer's sidekick Roger Mockus (Glen Morgan), who seems to get along better with people for some reason, talks about the awesomeness of his new call waiting feature. I remember how awesome I thought call waiting was, too. Mockus went on to write the film *Final Destination* (2000), and also wrote for *The X-Files*. There's a scene where Weinbauer's mother Angie (Elaine Joyce) flips with reserved concern through his Exciter and Megadeth albums. As the movie progresses, Weinbauer becomes closer to one of the jocks' girlfriends Leslie Graham (Lisa Orgolini), which we all know is the most unrealistic part of the movie. They team up to work together to put an end to Curr's mischief, which culminates in attacking a school Halloween dance where the tape is unwittingly played and sets Curr loose on

the school. In the end, Weinbauer is better off for everything that has happened. Wes Craven enthusiasts will recognize this as similar to the plot of *Shocker* (1989). Shocker is probably a better movie, but besides the faux documentary *This is Spinal Tap* (1984), few movies capture the pitfalls and frustration of being a dorky metal fan than *Trick or Treat*. I was one; however, my tormentors listened to metal as well. Marc and Roger are the perfect suburban dorks. A movie had to be made about the dangers of listening to heavy metal. In the end, this one is engaging enough to justify its run time. It's good Halloween screening fare.

Chapter 13:
Just for Laughs

    Societal standards of conduct change rapidly. What people think is funny evolves over time. I love classic histrionic comedies. These films aren't comedy zeitgeists, but ones that push the envelope of convention a little. Some enjoy a cult following and some just linger a bit outside the status quo. But they all made me laugh.

Brain Candy (1996)
Directed by Kelly Makin
Canada 89 min.

Nothing highlighted the youthful derision of the 1990s like the Kids in the Hall. They were hip and fresh. They knew bands, hung out in clubs, and utilized subjects young liberal slackers could relate to when writing sketches. Towards the end of their reign, they, like many in their situation, got an opportunity to make a movie. This seems to happen to comedy troupes and bands alike. It either saves them or, more often is the case, fails and gives them some capital to move on to the next thing. John Cleese said the tension that made *Fawlty Towers* funny couldn't be effectively maintained for a 90-minute film. The Kids had a similar problem: how to turn their brand of sharp jab into a narrative movie. *Brain Candy* underperformed at the box office and still doesn't get very good rankings on review websites. The Kids in the Hall themselves were dubious about the film. It was made without much help from Dave Foley. Perhaps people expected something totally different from the Kids in the Hall when the movie came out. I don't know what. Maybe I'm just being a contrarian or a mega fan, but *Brain Candy* is a hilarious and smart film with an interesting narrative structure utilizing the group's ability to relay short subject sketches effectively. I saw it in the theater and laughed. I laugh when I re-watch it.

One main criticism accuses the plot of being a weak construct on which to hang the group's weird sense of humor. I actually think the plot of the film is terrific. Scientist Chris Cooper (Kevin McDonald) is working in the development branch of a major drug corporation. There he discovers what becomes GLeeMONEX, an effective anti-depression pill. The pill cures depression, but also brings about major problems for many of its users. Cooper doesn't have a level battleground to fight the drug company and eventually has to go underground in an attempt to save the world from happiness. It's a great sci-fi plot. I'd watch a serious movie about that. But it's a fine plot for a satirical comedy troop to insert their characters into. In some cases it seems like the Kids in the Hall characters have contributed to the story as much as the actors. There are some familiar faces, but the main characters contain a competitive amount of dry wit and absurdist logic. The sketch comedy works anecdotally, but they are also able to tie the large strokes of this film together and make a story. There's even an element of Elia Kazan's *A Face in the Crowd* (1957) in play as America falls all over itself for something it doesn't really know if it needs or not. But the most important thing about a comedy movie is whether it makes you laugh. For that, you'll have to give it a chance.

Cedar Rapids (2011)
Directed by Miguel Arteta
U.S.A. 87 min.

Cedar Rapids is a rare enough comedy nowadays. It's fun and modern, but has an old-fashioned sensibility. Most movies like this require the characters to be outrageously sly or hopelessly out of touch with modern society. *Cedar Rapids* sets up a world with a Midwestern sensibility that doesn't rely on the characters being ignorant or one-dimensional. The people in this story exercise varying philosophies in the pursuit of happiness and selling insurance. When the movie unites these people at a conference taking place in Cedar Rapids, Iowa, a reasonable world is created around the characters that might be difficult for an outsider to navigate. The story opens on Tim Lippe (Ed Helms). Lippe is a nice guy living in a small town called Brown Valley, Wisconsin. Tim is not dumb, but he's hopelessly naive. He's having an affair with his grade school teacher of yore

Macy (Sigourney Weaver). She keeps telling him they're not right for each other and they're just having fun, but Lippe is determined to win her heart. When Roger (Thomas Lennon), the biggest seller at his office, dies of autoerotic asphyxiation, Lippe is picked to go to Cedar Rapids to pinch-hit at a big insurance conference. He's not everyone's first choice. Lippe has never left Wisconsin, and Cedar Rapids, which makes a great setting as a large city, is the big time in his eyes. Lippe, armed with traveler's checks, gears up for the big trip to Cedar Rapids. His coworkers think he'll be fine. He's a good guy. He's got a good head on his shoulders. He's given one piece of advice: avoid Ziegler.

Ziegler is the wild man salesman played by John C. Reilly. Reilly is a master of wild, out-of-step comedic caricatures. He plays Ziegler as basically a good guy who just walks to the beat of a different drum. It goes without saying Ziegler and Lippe will end up being roommates. Here you may be imagining a crude buddy comedy where Ziegler learns to be more like Lippe and Lippe learns to be more like Ziegler. It is that—just a little bit. The characters are well developed during the execution of an excellent screenplay and an unnecessarily well-done subplot about the pitfalls of corruption. Other seminar cohorts Joan (Anne Heche) and Ronald (Isiah Whitlock Jr.) also evolve as characters who experience believable growth spurts. Along the way, they are all funny, but not funny because they are so crass, or acting so out of their element, but because everyone has to adjust their behaviors in these human situations where people are thrown together and learn to get along. These four navigate the "friends at summer camp" dynamic for unexpected laughs. I enjoy crude buddy comedies, but this movie is particularly fresh and unformulated. The core group puts on a great performance as you watch the annoying people you see in tourist areas become human and solve realistic problems in realistic fashion. In the end, they'll go back to their lives. But it's the sort of weekend you might find yourself wishing you had suffered through.

Four Lions (2010)
Directed by Chris Morris
U.K. 97 min.

Four Lions director Chris Morris is more of a household name in the U.K. Alongside producer Armando Iannucci, he created the TV news satire shows *On the Hour* and *The Day Today*. The latter is known for being the genesis of the character Alan Partridge, a character that launched the career of Steve Coogan. Morris went on to produce the phony news show *Brass Eye* which included interviews with politicians and celebrities regarding fake subject matter that ended up embarrassing a lot of people and got him in a lot of trouble. He also became a regular on the internationally popular TV show *The IT Crowd*. Morris is not afraid of controversy. It's no surprise his directorial debut would be a satire about a cabal of terrorists planning a bombing. The group is so westernized and ineffective, they are useless as terrorists. Omar (Riz Ahmed) is the most reasonable among them: the smartest of them led to form a cell due to his disagreement with the treatment of Arabs in the U.K. He starts the cell with his not-too-bright cousin Waj (Kayvan Novak) and the hot-headed recent convert Barry (Nigel Lindsay). Along the way, they involve their soft-spoken and least-assured friend Faisal (Adeel Akhtar) and a young, fledgling rapper named Hassan (Arsher Ali). Even under reasonable Omar's leadership, the group can't stay focused enough to divert their energy towards their terrorism. The group experimented with making videos. They mess around with explosives. None of them properly know what they're doing or really even what they want to accomplish. Eventually, they hope to bomb something. Along the way, they discuss subjects like who's more Al-Qaeda, how many bottles of bleach can you buy at one store without arousing suspicion, which parts of the car are Jewish, and if or not the Mosques have "lost it". The actors get a lot of play with the physical humor in the film. It is first-rate chaos, although I won't presume to describe these situations because they are so masterfully and playfully scattered throughout the movie. The real trick unveiled by the end for the film is slightly startling. We've been inundated by so much satire and physical comedy; we don't realize we've been put into a situation where we don't have much of a guess as to what is going to happen next. It's a solid ending of cat and mouse playing with the lives of characters you've come to care enough about.

Hamlet 2 (2008)
Directed by Andrew Fleming
U.S.A. 92 min.

On the surface, *Hamlet 2* comes across as one of those movies designed to aggravate certain people and petition others. Some of its ideas are in bad taste. But no worse than some funnier movies have succeeded in pushing. It goes without saying some people inherently won't find a musical numbers like "Raped in the Face" and "Rock Me Sexy Jesus" funny. But on the whole, there's a lot more to enjoy in this story than the film's broader shock value. One of the fun things about *Hamlet 2* is when you get past the things meant to be distressing, you're actually watching a funny movie.

Dana Marschz (Steve Coogan) is a failing actor who teaches drama at a high school in Tucson, Arizona. Marschz puts on bad plays even by high school standards. When he gets wind through the school paper's drama critic that the arts program is going to be cut next year, Marschz becomes determined to write a play so good it will save the program. The play is *Hamlet 2*, where many of Shakespeare's characters arrive in modern times through a time machine and try to redo the tragedies leading to (spoiler alert) the death of all the characters in Shakespeare's *Hamlet*.

The bulky but effective ensemble cast includes a group of talented young actors: two are teacher's pets and the rest are blasé at best about their drama class. There are also some heavy hitting comic talents including Amy Poehler as Cricket Feldstein, a zealous ACLU activist, Catherine Keener as Brie, Marschz's wife, who is beyond indifferent of him in that Catherin Keener way she is known for, the Gay Men's Chorus of Albuquerque portraying the Gay Men's Chorus of Tucson, and a selfless performance by Elisabeth Shue as Elisabeth Shue in a meta version of her life since she gave up acting. The cast brings these elements together with a bit of Wes Anderson-style karate for a big rally to let the banned play be seen. And yes, it addresses *Hamlet* interestingly. And Steve Coogan at the helm conjuring his magnificent ability to streak from dry humor to outrageous ignorance in quick jabs navigates the play from its ridiculous beginnings to a really large and compelling show.

The opening segment ends with the phrase "Where do dreams go to die?" as the camera pans to a road sign that says, "Welcome to Tucson, Arizona!" To be fair, Tucson is actually a great town for film study. They have a multi-screen, non-profit theater called The Loft Cinema screening all manner of film and often has speakers for new and repertory screenings. Casa Video in Tucson is one of the biggest and best video stores I've ever seen. There is a solid creative underground taking advantage of the space and low rents. That said, I lived in Tucson in 2008. Between the ignorant party school vibe that bleeds out into every street, not being within four hours drive to any city bigger than Phoenix, and endless (but pretty) desert, you can feel like you're living at the end of the world. I don't remember if the film offended Tucson at the time: I doubt many people bothered to see it at all. But I'll go as far as to say it's a good movie for anyone feeling like they might be approaching the end of the road. It's an oddly inspiring film. Ultimately, it's a testament to what could happen if the freaks and disenfranchised of the world get their shit together.

In a World (2013)
Directed by Lake Bell
U.S.A. 93 min.

In a World is a low-key comedy performed by some of the more unsung comics and character actors in and out of movies the past twenty years. The movie was written and directed by comedy actor Lake Bell, whose low-key dialogue is punchy and hilarious. The ensemble cast includes Rob Cordry, Ken Marino, Michaela Watkins, Tig Notaro, Nick Offerman, and Fred Melamed. The story involves the world of voiceover artists in Hollywood. Carol Solomon (Bell) is working, but struggling to make ends meet. Her father is mega-successful Sam Soto (Melamed). Soto is a step away from legendary status behind the actual Hollywood voice actor Don LaFontaine, who worked in Hollywood for decades doing the voiceover for trailers. LaFontaine is famous for his line "In a world..." Soto and his daughter and young upstart Gustav Warner (Ken Marino) are competing to take LaFontaine's place at the top by bringing back his infamous catchphrase in the voiceover for a new quadrilogy of trailers promoting a new hit series called *The Amazon Games*. It's a career maker, or a legend maker depending on how you look at it. For Carol, it signifies potential stability for her unstable career. For Sam, it means being catapulted into legend status. The plot is simple, but the minutiae of the lives of people inhabiting this little-known microcosm of Hollywood is expounded on via their relationships with each other, the studio technicians who record them, and their families and friends, all of whom mostly work close to the business. It's a male dominated arm of a male dominated industry. But the industry is changing, and this theme dominates the various plots of the film. Sam is at times a good and loving father and at times an infuriating chauvinist. His counterpart Gustav (Ken Marino) has similar leanings but is a threat due to his youth. This isn't the typical "let's root for the quirky underdog to take down the smug baddies" narrative. The characters are more complex. Side plots also exist in this world. Moe (Rob Corddry) and Dani (Michaela Watkins) reverse the roles in a "spouse being bored and ignoring spouse" narrative that has an interesting turn. Bell's dry sense of humor comes across with sharp dialogue about the meta-nature of the voiceover industry.

Kind Hearts and Coronets (1949)
Directed by Robert Hamer
U.K. 106 min.

Kind Hearts and Coronets is a charming story about murder. The film employs over-the-top characters, Twilight Zone-style intrigue, and dry humor to tell a story about Edwardian-era mass murder. There is also a mysteriously non-ambiguous second ending shot to satisfy America's Hays Code that films had to adhere to if they wanted distribution in the United States. Its humor amongst a casual death toll is a modern watermark that makes the film appear more sophisticated than other offerings from this era. The story opens on Louis D'Ascoyne (Dennis Price). D'Ascoyne is in prison writing down the events leading to his incarceration and imminent hanging. Via flashback, we discover that D'Ascoyne's mother (Audrey Fildes) was the youngest daughter of the 7th Duke of Chalfont. In an act of passion, his mother eloped with an Italian opera singer named

Mazzini. She was disowned for this act, but she led a happy life until Mazzini died suddenly in an accident. Later in life, his mother tried to reconnect with her family on behalf of Louis' education, but the D'Ascoynes treated her rudely and refused to recognize her as a member of the family. The movie begins on this storyline of a fairly typical upper-class snub. Then his mother dies, leaving Louis in the world alone to fume. Louis makes one more attempt to make up with the D'Ascoynes when he requests to bury her in the family graveyard. The D'Ascoynes once again refuse Louis, who then develops a plan to kill all the D'Ascoynes that stand between him and the title of Duke of Chalfont. Louis' plan isn't to mow them down, but to use their unique situations against them to make each death seem an accident. The end result is he would acquire his lost title.

Louis begins to work his way through the D'Ascoynes, eventually ingratiating himself with one or two and thereby gaining closer access to the family. Once his plan is in motion, the primary and most obvious element at play in this film is that Sir Alec Guinness portrays every member of the D'Ascoyne family in the path of Louis' revenge. Guinness plays nine of the D'Ascoynes, including a sleepy reverend, a determined Navy Admiral, Lady Agatha D'Ascoyne (the matriarch of the family), and many other stereotypes of the British upper class. Some meet quite shocking ends, dying of strange accidents. Some aid the process by dying of their own accords. Through extensive plotting, Louis works his way up the family lineage. Along the way, Louis forms a bond with Edith (Valarie Hobson), a D'Ascoyne widow who could make his life easier. He is also toying with Sibella (Jan Greenwood), who rejected him in the past for having no prospects. Both women represent a certain type of stability, but neither distract Louis from his murderous path. Fun commentary on class and stellar performances by Sir Alec Guiness give the film a timeless quality.

King of Hearts (1966)
Directed by Philippe de Broca
France 102 min.

The term "midnight movie" has a lot of connotations. Generally cult, horror, and transgressive movies are reserved for the "midnight" screening moniker. The idea is that the more a film should be kept from the prying eyes of the general public, the more underground cred the film needs to possess. The answer seems to be: see it late at night. If you stay up late for the theater, you're among the night owls, stoners, gigglers, and pseudo intellectuals who enjoy well done, or at least earnestly produced, cinema. An early example of an anti-authoritative narrative making a big splash in the reparatory market and an impression on the emergent hippy crowd was the 1966 comedy *King of Hearts*. The film may appear tame compared to the late night fare of modern times, but its charm beckons from an era when subtle humor was not the norm in film and anti-authorism stood out in celluloid. *King of Hearts* did not do well upon its initial release, but gained a following in repertory and midnight screenings. Its absurdist and anti-authority narrative gained strength after the film flopped in its native country of France. It ran for five years straight in New York City's Central Square Cinema. A new groovy type of film fan was emerging who were into foreign films and eschewed the stodgy sensibility of the oppressive Hays Code that began to disintegrate in America with the popularity of films like *Bonnie and Clyde* (1967) and *Easy Rider* (1969).

The film is set near the end of World War I. Charley Plumpick, played by Alan Bates, who also appears as Felix Detweiler in *Mr. Frost* (1990), portrays a communications officer sent into a small French town to report on a German evacuation. The word is the Germans have abandoned the town and set a trap wiring several buildings to explode when allied troops come through. Plumplick is a communications specialist and has little experience with munitions. Communications become confused and the town's residents evacuate before he arrives. The only people left behind are the inhabitants of the local insane asylum who escape and now are loose in town taking on roles of prominence in the small constabulary. They take over the local shops, plan parades, and pretend to run the town convincingly enough to inadvertently fool the puzzled Plumpick and all others who pass through town during the course of the film. Plumplick goes about the task of convincing them to leave. But they don't see the situation from his point of view. All their strange behavior is interpreted as normal through the eyes of a man who doesn't know he's dealing with lunatics. *King of Hearts* gained cult status in the United States traveling as a package screening with two classic animated shorts showing beforehand: the classic gag animation *Bambi Vs. Godzilla* (1969) and the Lenny Bruce diatribe set to animation *Thank You Masked Man* (1971). The shorts and the behavioral themes prevalent in *King of Hearts* provide well-rounded anti-war themes that resonated with the Summer of Love crowd and can forever be enjoyed by those seeking out this beautiful film. It's a classic comedy that holds up, but still gets lost in its role as an early cult film.

Lust in the Dust (1985)
Directed by Paul Bartel
U.S.A. 84 min.

Paul Bartel was a master of a certain style of juvenile humor prevalent in underground movies of the '70s and '80s. He was very relevant during a time when the midnight movie screening was expanding from late screenings of unusual or anti-authoritarian texts to movies that were being made for the late night consumption by the counter-culture. The shift allowed filmmakers more opportunities to use crass humor, drug jokes, and anti-authoritarian themes. Bartel wasn't afraid to be crass. He had a knack for delivering silly dialogue through a histrionic acting style that uniquely specified he knew what was hip and wasn't afraid to be corny in the face of it. He often portrayed a spineless yet well-meaning person. His actions in a role were corruptible during the course of a movie is performance as the supportive but square teacher Mr. McGree in the Ramones' *Rock 'n' Roll High School* (1979) is iconic. As a director, his first film *Death Race 2000* (1975) is iconic both as a late- night movie and also within the canon of classic Roger Corman productions. Iconic still is his made for midnight consumption *Eating Raoul* (1982), an anti-swingers tale in which a down-on-his-luck wine steward lures people to his apartment for an alleged orgy only to rob and kill them. Despite all this, Bartel doesn't get enough credit for helping set the tone for absurdist comedy and immature material at the midnight movies.

Lust in the Dust reunites an electric casting pair from John Waters' 1981 film *Polyester*: 1950s teen heartthrob Tab Hunter and Waters' regular Divine. The two made a great and unusual couple in *Polyester*, with Divine playing a bored housewife who fell under the spell of Tab Hunter's portrayal of a con man. As Abel Wood and Rosie Velez in *Lust in the Dust,* Hunter and Divine are similarly excellent foils alongside a great cast of comedy actors with a knack for the melodramatic including Lainie Kazan as Marguerita Ventura, Cesar Romero as Father Garcia, and Henry Silva as Bernardo. It's a midnight comedy that doubles as an almost competent revisionist western. Velez (Divine) is lost and dying in the desert when she encounters Wood (Hunter). Wood reluctantly helps her find Chile Verde, a small town with a saloon run by Ventura (Kazan). Abel and Wood come into conflict with some of the locals. It seems the two are both hiding the fact that they have arrived in Chile Verde to search for gold based on a long-standing legend associated with the town. Also riding into town is Hard Case Williams (Geoffrey Lewis) and his gang. Some of the locals have heard of the legend of the missing gold, but the arrival of strangers reignites their interest, and the entire cast commences to forming alliances and pacts to try to get their hands on a piece of the treasure. A good line delivered by Divine: "I know when I've had enough... I fall on the floor." *Lust in the Dust* is a surprisingly competent story and the actors keep the fun moving in a short run time. The film isn't as devious as a John Waters' picture, but if you've screened *Polyester* one too many times, *Lust in the Dust* should give you value for laughs.

Safe Men (1998)
Directed by John Hamburg
U.S.A. 88 min.

Martin Scorsese helped bring the stories and vernacular of wise guys from the Bronx and Brooklyn into the American mainstream. If you're looking for a new rabbit hole to go down, look into the lesser-known, but often as violent, history of organized crime in Providence, Rhode Island. There were some surprisingly vicious crews and colorful characters battling for control of the small New England city. Had *Safe Men* been as popular as *Goodfellas* (1990) or *Casino* (1995), Rhode Island gangsters probably wouldn't appreciate the rep.

Safe Men covers a week in the life of two delusional singers: Sam (Sam Rockwell) and Eddie (Steve Zahn). The pair work hard bringing the noise to some lame gigs, mostly retirement homes and the like. They have hopes of fame. They're not quite there yet. Eddie and Sam have a tradition of getting a sloe gin fizz after every gig whether they were successful or not. Among a series of egregious coincidences, Frank (Mark Ruffalo) and Mitchell (Josh Pais) are second story men and expert safe crackers who also end their nights toasting a job with a sloe gin fizz. Here enters the ultra-sleazy Veal Chop (Paul Giamatti). "Chop" as he's known, clocks Sam and Eddie in a bar drinking sloe gin fizzes and mistakes them for the safe men he's been charged with locating. Chop is so sleazy that even Sam and Eddie are wary of him, but after a few drinks, Chop drugs them out and delivers them to his boss: Big Fat Ernie Gayle (Michael Lerner). Gayle has put forth this kidnapping because he wants to employ the ace safe crackers. Sam and Eddie discover Gayle intends to kill them due to their mistaken identities, so they convince Gayle they are the safe men he seeks and set out to acquire the items Gayle wants stolen.

If you're hung up on plausibility, this story might not be for you. The serendipity driving the action in this film doesn't end with this case of mistaken identity. In fact, coincidence is out of control at times. To be specific: Sam and Eddie arrive at a job to crack the same safe as Frank and Mitchell, Sam and Eddie buy their gift baskets at the same shop as Frank and Mitchell, Sam falls for Frank's girlfriend Hannah (Christina Kirk), Hannah is the daughter of a rival gangster, etc… But the world created for these characters to exist within fits them well and creates irreverent comedy out of awkward encounters. The movie ultimately creates unexpectedly warm relationships you can root for as well. Giamatti steals the show among a great ensemble cast as he warmly coaches Bernie Jr. (Michael Schmidt) on his upcoming Bar Mitzvah rituals. Chop is uncultured, often wearing Zubaz, and tips from a wad of ten-dollar bills. As Big Fat Ernie Gayle's muscle, Giamatti doesn't make much of an impact on the gangster community of the film, but he is hilarious and likable. The dialogue is written for matter-of-fact delivery and the actors mine a lot of humor from their lackadaisical attitudes. In terms of dialogue, relationships, and world building, it's a film fans of Wes Anderson's *Bottle Rocket* (1996) would particularly appreciate. There's a great line about safe cracking: "Remember, the last click is always in your heart." If you're into subtle comedies with silly characters winding in and out of each other's lives, it's a good one to look up.

Three O'Clock High (1987)
Directed by Phil Joanou
U.S.A. 101 min.

Three O'Clock High is one of those films that got bad press, performed poorly at the box office, and I've never quite understood why. Maybe it looks like a typical teen-sploitation outing from the '80s. It is about a teenage quandary during a typical day in school. But it is a much smarter movie than it looks. It floats at the top of the barrel alongside better teen movies: some famous ones like *Ferris Bueller's Day Off* (1986) and some more cultish offerings like *One Crazy Summer* (1986). It's a smart film that doesn't rely on sexual hijinks and racial stereotypes, thus avoiding the pitfalls of having large strokes of racism and sexual assault lurking in place of humor.

The plot opens on Jerry Mitchell (Casey Siemaszko) getting ready for school. His parents are out of town. He has a routine. But his routine is strained this morning. He's up late and rushing to school with his sister Brei (Stacey Glick) and friend Franny (Anne Ryan) in tow. Meanwhile, people around school are gossiping about a tough new arrival: Buddy Revell (Richard Tyson). It is the kind of overblown gossip that is unlikely to be totally true, but Revell turns out to be a tough customer all the same. It may go without saying, but Mitchell quickly runs afoul of Revell, and Revell says there's going to be a fight at three o'clock. The story unfolds in near real time bursts as we follow Mitchell throughout the day trying to figure out how to get out of fighting Revell. The more he plots to wiggle out of the fight, the more trouble he gets into, bringing more eyes down on him to see if he'll show up. If you think you know the ending, it may surprise you a bit.

The cast creates irreverent humor during some blasé performances. They pass information amongst each other in a caricature of teenage agitation and indifference. Only Mitchell is nervous, forever taking hits throughout a day that already promises a pummeling from a seasoned school bully. More clever still is the use of camera swoops, canted angles, and perspective shots that make the situation appear larger than it really is: large, like when you were a teenager and close to trouble. It's similar to how *The Blues Brothers* (1980) treated the nun with the camera, making her larger than life to two grown men who still see her as an authority figure. *Three 'O Clock High* is a fun, short-term adventure with characters that change in ways you might not see coming. It's got Coen Brothers-level gags in terms of funny dialogue and interesting camera work.

Chapter 14: Loose Can[n]ons

There's nothing wrong with a good shoot-em-up. These two comic book stalwarts are inked into the panels of many stories without the aid of superpowers. They have sad origins, big guns, and a resolve to fire them. My enjoyment of these movies is sealed in the supposition that these anti-heroes are best served cold. These films lack the style and wit of a John Woo gun-fu spree, but these barrel chested nimrods' hearts are in the right place. Both had lackluster films with big advertising budgets. And then there were these two lesser-known gems.

Dredd (2012)
Directed by Pete Travis
U.K. 95 min.

Build a film with the hard situations of an action feature, the high tech of a science fiction film, and the blood and guts of a horror film and you'd think there wouldn't be room for much else. Some action films try to combat this by making the hero a basically fun guy. *Dredd*, a film based on the long-running British cult comic Judge Dredd, won't be accused of that. Those familiar with the comic, (or those who heard the Anthrax song) know Judge Dredd, a law enforcement officer in a dystopian future where police and judges are the same person, doesn't have much of a sense of humor. The law is his religion. He doesn't write it. But he enforces it.

One thing that works well within this version of the iconic comic book anti-hero is that actor Karl Urban portrays Dredd with all of the levity of a falling cinder block. He never takes off the iconic helmet. He shows no fear. His heart rate barely breaks a trot while running from a high-caliber, brick-wall-destroying machine gun cutting down an entire floor of the apartment building he's sworn to protect. He shows a bit of humanity once in a while, like when some fledgling, underage gang members find him and point guns at him. Dredd orders his high tech gun to switch to "STUN" before shooting them. He's really a great guy underneath.

And what villain do you put in the movie to vex this chiseled-in-stone, incorruptible lawman? An off-the-hook Joker type? A mobster regularly challenging his blood pressure? Dredd's nemesis in this scenario is *Game of Thrones'* Lena Headey as Madeline "Ma-Ma" Madrigal, a drug kingpin who rose in the ranks from her beginnings in the same apartment block she is now defending. Ma-Ma is a ruthless leader who sustained ghastly injuries in her fight to the top and is feared since she seems to have taken much of it in stride. Much like her new enemy, Ma-Ma never raises much of an eyebrow when she orders people skinned and thrown off the balcony. Headley sells Ma-Ma without much movement or expression, but her slight mannerisms and evil eyebrows get the message across, creating another subdued performance driving the plot through interesting turns. The two rub up against each other like sandpaper, and even though the plot is mostly escalating action sequences, you can still wonder how they are going to react when they find themselves up or down.

So what else does the film have? The action sequences are brutal and large. The movie always goes big with the gore in a strangely satisfying way. Olivia Thirlby plays Dredd's new trainee Cassandra Anderson. Anderson is under scrutiny as to if she can become a judge or not, so Dredd's assessment is going to be the final word. Thirlby plays an interestingly vulnerable character without being a damsel in distress-type, as it is with some other characters in different movies. Wood Harris plays a pragmatist of a bad guy as one of Ma-Ma's henchmen. It's as if his character retains a lot of his Avon Barksdale sensibilities from *The Wire*, but it works whenever he brings the over-the-top plot down to earth.

The film is also well shot and fun to look at in general. The enormous apartment block setting captures the dystopian stage nicely. The drug Ma-Ma has introduced to the neighborhood is called slo-mo and, true to its name, it slows down the user's action time. This creates some interesting footage when the drug is in play in the plot. Judge Dredd is a great character and this film represents the long-running comic well. The story has a plot it can handle in a reasonable run time amidst some bludgeoning action sequences. After a terrible 1995 attempt by Danny Cannon and Sylvester Stallone to adapt the character in the film *Judge Dredd*, Megacity is definitely safer in the hands of director Pete Travis.

The Punisher (1989)
Directed by Mark Goldblatt
U.S.A. 89 min.

Before the days of Marvel ruling Hollywood, there was a lot of stuff going on with Marvel movie rights. This is what Marvel had to work with. DC ruled the cinema. Christopher Reeve was America's sweetheart for his portrayal of Superman, and Tim Burton's *Batman* (1989) changed the landscape of comic movies. Later that year: *The Punisher*. It didn't change the industry, but it's an exciting film all the same. I find it was a shrewd choice of adaptation, as it didn't require too many fancy special effects. Just a lot of shooting and fighting. It is among the most comic-like interpretations of many to come. The film uses excessive color in the lighting to make certain frames resemble comic art. There is histrionic tough acting. I transition between unlikely sets. If you judge it as a karate movie, or a prototype for the emerging gun-fu market, it's actually an exceptional film. Among the number of reasons to watch this movie include:

1. Dolph Lundgren IS the Punisher.

2. Louis Gossett Jr.

3. Paper-thin Mafia bad guys.

4. Ninjas.

5. Yakuza.

6. Paper-thin Mafia bad guys vs. ninjas.

7. Ninjas vs. Dolph Lundgren

8. A gunfight at a disused carnival.

9. Dolph Lundgren vs. everybody.

It's a simple story. Frank Castle (Lundgren) is an ex-cop killing Mafioso incognito as "The Punisher" in revenge for the loss of his family. Castle wipes out so much of the Mafia that acting don Gianni Franco (Jeroen Krabbé) and his crew are weak to the point of being overtaken by "Lady" Tanaka (Kim Miyori), leader of the local Yakuza network. As a final kiss-off to the Mob, Tanaka kidnaps the children of all the Mob bosses, leaving Franco to seek Castle's help in getting them back. Krabbé and Miyori portray great ruthless bad guys. Loads of people are wounded or killed by impractical weapons like throwing stars, nunchucks, swords, switchblade shoes, etc. There's a scene in the funhouse where ninjas slide down on the slides in unison firing machine guns trying to hit one person. The movie goes on like this for 89 minutes. Is there any reason to go on about it?

Chapter 15: Michael Mann

    Michael Mann's first three movies appeared separately on the big list I started at the beginning of this project. I didn't realize they were all Michael Mann films until I started cross-referencing the initial mess, nor did I realize they were his first, second, and third in succession. It appears I'm a bigger Michael Mann fan than I initially realized. Mann was famously also a producer on the hit 80s TV show *Miami Vice* (1984-1990). *Miami Vice* changed the look and feel of television detective dramas. Longer set-up shots and modern music made Vice a hip thing to watch in the '80s. His work in film and peripheral involvement in television helped define the film look of '80s action and noir cinema. His style is inventive. Although he will be forever identified with the '80s, his style has a timeless quality. He also helped bring Tangerine Dream into the foreground as a soundtrack band for American films. He really nailed his first three features.

Thief (1981)
Directed by Michael Mann
U.S.A. 123 min.

Thief opens as seasoned criminal Frank (James Caan) drills calmly into a large wall safe. As he continues to drill, music swells: not swelling as if to create excessive drama, but gradually as if the score was somehow attached to the safe cracking process. The soundtrack is not diegetic, but scoring the action like a machine with the same escalating urgency is effective. It's a stylish sequence with practical action. Frank eventually breaks the safe. He starts rifling the contents, throwing bags of jewels and other valuables on the ground. He's looking for something specific. He's a pro. We learn this about him right away and enter his world bit by bit. Mann's feature film contains watermarks of his career to come. His use of light and shadow contributes to the language of '80s noir. The score by Tangerine Dream was nominated for a Razzie for reasons I don't understand. Maybe it was so unusual at the time they couldn't get their head around it. Tangerine Dream created an excellent score and set a new standard for '80s soundtracks. They went on to score several big budget films, and many other composers tried to copy their style.

Aside from its stylish approach, *Thief* is an interesting screenplay on its own. It takes a working class approach to big time safe cracking. These safes aren't your typical screwdriver and sledgehammer safes. These are big-time security concerns: protection via everything 1981 technology had to offer. It might not sound very foreboding compared to what today's technology offers, but remember: safe technology changes according to innovation, and therefore, safe cracking technology can only be learned by revisiting mistakes. Frank knows this. He's been in and out of prison since he was young. Besides being a technical expert, Frank is an average guy consulting with various criminal elements in his industry to acquire bigger jobs. He moves freely among fences, machinists, and metallurgists. His mentor "Okla" (Willie Nelson) has been in prison for a long time. He has a partner and friend in Barry (James Belushi) whom he trusts and knows the business. But basically, it's a lonely, working class lifestyle. Caan grabs the character with a muted version of his Corleone swagger. He doesn't back down from people, but maintains an even diplomacy. Frank can't draw too much attention to himself. Police know who he is. People who could rob him easily without consequence know who he is. The Mafia knows who he is. The story progresses as a fence named Leo (Robert Prosky) wants Frank to go into business with him. Leo says he can provide the jobs and the resources to keep him out of trouble. But it ends up being too much exposure. Frank is too much of a lone wolf for that to work for very long. Eventually he gets in trouble with his employers. Excellent performances, attention to detail, and a great story keep the movie moving tightly under Mann's tasteful direction. It goes to show that story and style don't have to be mutually exclusive.

The Keep (1983)
Directed by Michael Mann
U.K. 96 min.

The Keep is a complicated movie with a great cast. Michael Mann has largely disowned the movie for various reasons, but I not only love it, I think it fits strongly as a part of his canon. It's a thinker of a horror story, and for my money, Mann's style carries the film well. If Universal made a version of *The Golem* in the thirties, it would resemble this movie. Mann's knack for long and careful shots into darkness and another great collaboration with Tangerine Dream for the soundtrack creates a foreboding atmosphere. Mann also manages a weighty cast of big personalities, leaving thoughtful consideration for a dense myriad of characters. They don't quite work as a well-oiled ensemble, but some great actors get shining moments as the film progresses.

The story opens on a squad of German troops led by Captain Klaus Woermann (Jürgen Prochnow). Woermann's squad has taken control of a small Romanian village strategic to an upcoming German attack. Woermann tries to set up his troops in a nearby cave. The caretaker, Father Fonescu (Robert Prosky) tries to talk him out of staying there. The cave is sacred and, as you may have guessed, contains one of those scary, Romanian kind of secrets. Not a clandestine waffle bar or anything nice like that. Some evil stuff happens and Woermann's command is called into question by the SS. They send S.D. Sturmbannführer Erich Kaemphter (Gabriel Byrne) to see what's going on. Kaemphter doesn't believe anything supernatural is going on, but if there is, the Fuhrer would love to know about it. They bring in Dr. Theodore Cuza (Ian McKellin), a Jewish professor languishing in a concentration camp and tell him that if he can figure out what's up, they'll spare him and his daughter Eva

(Alberta Watson). Woermann turns out to be an okay sort as far as Nazis in these types of movies go, and tries to secure passage for the daughter to escape. If the characters and long character names aren't confusing enough, Glaeken Trismegestus (Scott Glenn) arrives and throws a wrench in all this. He and Eva become interested in each other. Undoubtedly, she is into men who can gaze mysteriously into the distance. All of these elements work to contain, control, or force a supernatural creature to anthropomorphize itself and cause more trouble. It's a mean one.

Manhunter (1986)
Directed by Michael Mann
U.S.A. 120 min.

In 1991, *The Silence of the Lambs* became a huge hit. It was nominated for seven Academy Awards and won five including Best Picture and Best Actor for Anthony Hopkins' portrayal of uber-intelligent and super evil psychiatrist Dr. Hannibal Lecter. The horror-thriller hybrid made household names of the source material's author Thomas Harris, director Jonathan Demme, and the mischievous Lecter. Hopkins' portrayal of Lecter is permanently burned into the vernacular of American culture, and his antics and dialog are still regularly parodied and impersonated to this day. It's a great film. Unfortunately, the movie eclipsed a lesser-known adaptation of Harris' first novel in the series. Michael Mann's quiet 1986 thriller *Manhunter* is an exciting film containing another great against-the-clock hunt for a psycho killer and a great interpretation of Lecter (spelled Lecktor in *Manhunter*), this time portrayed by Brian Cox, who will never get enough credit for the dimension he brought to the role during his short stint as the crazy psychiatrist.

Manhunter follows the story of the first book in Harris' series. It is a somewhat more subdued affair compared to *Lambs*. Its low-key presentation of a disturbing story probably did not sit well with '90s audiences discovering it after seeing Demme's exciting, quid pro quo execution. *Manhunter* begins with an earlier and more active version of FBI specialist Jack Crawford (Mann regular Dennis Farina). Crawford is on the hunt for a serial killer striking during the same phase of the moon every month. With the clock ticking, Crawford turns to retired protégé Will Graham (William Peterson) for help. Graham is retired due to injuries and mental strain sustained during his pursuit and capture of the now incarcerated Dr. Lecktor. This ensemble cast of lesser-known character actors adds mystery to the proceedings. Brian Cox is a great Hannibal Lecktor that will no doubt remain buried in the annals of cinema history. He has a bit of spring in his step when it comes to the sarcasm of Lecktor's overeducated jabber. William Peterson as Will Graham and Denis Farina as Jack Crawford make a believable duo as FBI agents assigned to the case. Their investigation is a slow burn, one that puts you in the mind of the killer much in the way the character Will Graham does in the first half of the movie. The killer, Francis Dollarhyde, masterfully brought to life by horror regular Tom Noonan, doesn't appear until later in the movie. His unraveling goes off the rails at a point of misunderstanding with a blind co-worker Reba (Joan Allen). Until this point, you see how the sociopathic Dollarhyde functions in the world and avoids suspicion. Noonan humanizes Dollarhyde to a point where you almost feel conflicted about rooting against him. But you will. The film is good at blurring the lines and bringing them back. Compared with *Lambs*, *Manhunter* is the other side of the coin, but it has a quiet rage that leads to a unique confrontation sequence set to Iron Butterfly's "In-A-Gadda-Da-Vita" that will forever change the way you listen to that song.

Chapter 16: Monster Mash

Who loves a monster movie? It's a special sort of escapism. There are often not as many details in play as in a typical horror story. But there is often a lot of smashing. And there are fans for every big monster in the history of film. We like to root for some of them. Godzilla certainly became a complicated monster as the films stacked up. How you feel about them might depend on the viewing context. Did you see it on a date? Did you watch it because it was on the other channel against the Super Bowl and you hate sports? Did it come on after Saturday morning cartoons? Or did you happen upon it late at night after you snuck a snack out of the freezer, watching it quietly when your parents were asleep? There are so many great ones. And so many not-great ones you love anyway. Here are just a few lesser heralded ones I enjoy.

The Blob (1988)
Directed by Chuck Russell
U.S.A. 95 min.

Both versions of *The Blob* begin in the same basic manner: an elderly transient is exposed to an unknown substance. The substance begins eating away at him in a way no known corrosive acts. The transient man is discovered by teenagers; in this film they are rebellious Brian Flagg (Kevin Dillon), local high school football star Paul Taylor (Donovan Leitch) and his date, the popular but down to earth Meg Penny (Shawnee Smith). We get to spend a little time with each of the teenagers before the action begins. All are prototypes of the small town teenagers slated to save the day. Paul has an obnoxious friend. Meg has a little brother and an understanding mom. Brian has a soft relationship with the town's mechanic and a waitress at the local diner. Sheriff Herb Geller (Jeffrey DeMunn) is a high school football fan and knows Brian from his uncouth reputation. You've guessed already these and other characters are going to need saving at various moments of the Blob's reign. If you focus on that, you will be bored.

Director Chuck Russell collaborated on the screenplay with Frank Darabont. Both were on the writing team of the screenplay for *Nightmare on Elm Street 3: Dream Warriors* (1987), arguably one of the more interesting of those sequels. This duo's writing prowess comes alive as the story unfolds. In the original *Blob*, the substance landed in a meteor from space. In this remake, the substance has another origin bringing along with it a conspiracy-tinged narrative keeping the movie from being mundane. And it really makes the film a better horror movie than it needed to be.

So you're waiting for a twist? What holds your interest up to this point? This movie is not afraid to kill off characters you've become invested in. And some of these deaths are extra gross and upsetting due to good special effects and investment in the idea that a Blob of this nature would inevitably have undigested parts floating around in it, depending on where someone is in the digestive process. Aside from the big picture, there are some fun details along the way. Kevin Dillon puts in a solid performance as the rebel on a motorcycle. The motorcycle plays a major role in a couple of callbacks creating genuine tension and giving reason to cheer. There's an entertaining movie-within-a-movie playing during the remake of the iconic movie theater scene. Character actor and David Lynch regular Jack Nance puts in an appearance. The 1958 version of the film was very popular and is remembered well as solid sci-fi monster fare. It captured the imagination of moviegoers and brought Steve McQueen into the fold of stardom. This version knew it had to push the envelope a little and did so a tasteful amount. It's a nice tribute to the original, but also stands on its own as a good sci-fi movie.

Crawl (2019)
Directed by Alexandre Aja
U.S.A. 87 min.

I love Sam Raimi as a director, I also trust his taste as a producer. Raimi Productions has brought to light some silly classics like *Timecop* (1994), *Boogeyman* (2005), *30 Days of Night* (2007), and recently *Crawl*. *Crawl* is a film about large alligators getting into the crawl space of a Florida home during a dangerous hurricane and terrorizing a father and daughter. And that's really all there is to it. And it's a way better film than it needs to be. The story follows aspiring competitive swimmer Haley Keller (Kaya Scodelario). Keller is a lifelong Floridian in the midst of a snit with her father Dave (Barry Pepper). As a Category 5 hurricane approaches, concerned calls due to Dave not showing his face for a while propel Keller into the storm to see if her dad has abandoned the old neighborhood for safety. The police warn her not to go in. It's supposed to be a quick trip for her: check on her dad and then get out. But Dave proves difficult to locate. Eventually, he is discovered injured in the crawlspace of the family's old house. It's not long before we discover Dave is also in the company of large alligators. There's a nook in the crawlspace where the overfed creatures can't reach him, but the water is rising and Dave is injured. It becomes obvious quickly they can't wait out the storm and have to get out of harm's way before they drown or become snacks.

    Directed by Alexandre Aja, *Crawl* sounds like an obvious stab at a summer formula, but the movie has a lot to offer. Firstly, the script by Michael and Shawn Rasmussen does a good job of creating real and sympathetic characters. Dave and Haley have some legitimate gripes they casually discuss while plotting to evade the relentless alligators. You might think they'd wait until they are out of the storm to discuss some of these things, but the script provides characters for the audience to root for efficiently in the 87-minute run-time. The weight these well-written characters provide gives us something to think about besides abject survival. Aja also squeezes in the most suspense the premise allows with solid underwater camera work, good point-of-view angles, and playful background focus. This is a well-done narrative about a world in a crawl space under a house in a cul-de-sac in Florida that understands how long it's supposed to be and how much the audience will pay

MONSTER

- OF THE
- BODY SNATCHERS
- INVASION
- Invasion of the Body Snatchers
- IT CAME from Outer Space
- INVASION EARTH
- Giant Gila Monster
- ゴジラ ☆ ★ ※ ◎
- GORATH
- GODzilla vs. Chicago Bears
- Godzilla vs. King Chidora
- Godzilla vs. Mothra
- Godzilla vs. Biollante
- GODZILLA
- Godzilla vs. Megalon
- GODZILL vs. Gigan
- Godzilla vs. ERNEST
- Godzilla vs. EVEREST
- 三大怪獣
- GHIDRAH
- Return of The FLY
- The FLY
- Destroy All Monsters
- Destroy All Monsters
- Destroy All Monsters
- Day of the Triffids

- Dawn of the MUMMY
- Creature from the BLACK Lagoon
- Creature from the BLACK lagoon
- Creature from the Black Lagoon
- C.H.U.D.
- The BLOB

- The THING
- Terror of Mecha Godzilla
- Son of GODZILLA
- The STUFF
- RepTiLiCUS
- Werewolf of WALL STREET
- REBIRTH of Mothra II
- Q: The Winged Serpent
- キングコング対ゴジラ
- Godzilla vs. Megalon
- モスラ
- MOTHRA
- MOTHRA III
- MONSTER SQUAD
- MAN MADE MONSTER
- BEACHES
- THEM
- TARANTULA!
- TARANTULA!
- King KONG
- King Crab Attack
- King Kong vs. GODZILLA
- Attack the BLOCK
- KING KONG II
- KING KONG
- The HOST

attention to. It's a real accomplishment for the genre and a lot of fun to watch.

Dagon (2001)
Directed by Stuart Gordon
Spain 98 min.

Gothic horror writer H.P. Lovecraft's stories have traditionally made awkward transitions to film. No one knows this more than horror director Stuart Gordon, who has adapted Lovecraft several times to the tune of mixed praise and criticism. Gordon is one of the most divisive directors in horror. I meet people who think he's especially bad and people who think he's especially adept. I like to think of him as boldly flawed. Firstly, there is a campy bone supporting his films. His best known and most iconic film *Re-Animator* (1985), also a Lovecraft adaptation, is often cited as being overacted by Jeffery Combs who portrays Herbert West as an animated and nerdy medical student experimenting on the possibility of an afterlife. It's interesting to note Gordon worked much more in live theater. You can see it in the seams of his staging and dialogue of *Re-Animator*. It reads as if it was written for the stage. If this makes the work slightly histrionic, it works for me in both *Re-Animator* and *Dagon*. The campy tone set by Godden's performance in *Dagon* as a clueless and successful tech investor deflects the dire and bleak events of the story. Secondly, the worlds Gordon creates are a perfect example of the fear of the unknown. Main characters Barbara (Raquel Meroño) and later Paul Marsh (Ezra Godden) wander around a seaside town where they have accidentally run ashore following a storm causing their boat to run afoul of some rocks. They encounter a handful of very strange people who, in spite of seeming very unfriendly, agree to take Paul back to the wreck to look for other survivors.

If you can't get into Gordon's world, it's unlikely you'll enjoy his movies. And the low budget *Dagon* is buried in his filmography. I found the DVD in a $2 bin and didn't realize it was one of Gordon's films before I got it home. But I've since come to love this movie. It's not the most technical film and relies on early, poor-looking digital effects at certain complicated moments of the plot, but the whole package includes a terrifying setting, a great and unique flashback sequence complete with pseudo religious nonsense, some gross deaths, and excellent make up and costuming of grotesque baddies struggling on the evolutionary scale. The overall plot follows what I like to call the "*Texas Chainsaw* plot" where some seemingly reasonable people are held captive by psychotically unseemly people or entities and must climb down a psychological ladder to the denouement. This film also contains a very grotesque and genuinely scary scene with Spanish actor Francisco Rebal in his final film role before his death. Based on the speech he gives in the film, he could have gone out on a worse project. The film is dedicated to this beloved actor. *Dagon* is fun if you like unusual horror. In certain lights, it's unlike anything you'll see in a film set in a seaside town.

Chapter 17:
Music be the Food of Love

For music enthusiasts, a music movie can often be a no-brainer. I've enjoyed badly executed documentaries about interesting bands. I've also enjoyed good documentaries about bands I don't like so much. And, of course, there is the canon of beloved music movies, like *Rock 'n' Roll High School* (1979) for Ramones fans or *Mama Mia!* (2008) to ABBA fans. People love *This is Spinal Tap* (1984) and *Tenacious D. in the Pick of Destiny* (2006) as if they were documentaries about real bands. And they kind of are now, aren't they? Two of the three documentaries I chose for the "Documentary" section of this book are music related, but I also find them to be excellent documentaries regardless of subject matter. For this section, I picked music films that aren't, at least conceptually, documentaries, but music films that say something about music without trying. And also ones I believe fly under the radar a bit. If you don't see the distinction, I agree it's a little vague, so just let it go.

32 Short Films About Glenn Gould (1993)
Directed by François Girard
Canada 98 min.

As the title indicates, *32 Short Films About Glenn Gould* offers 32 short glimpses into the life of the infamous concert pianist and known eccentric. Or, depending on how you think about it, 31 films and the end credits. The end credits are also a short film about Gould, of course. The film is structured to show Gould's life shaped through a series of vignettes beginning with his childhood in Canada and linearly following his career highlights via biopic segments, filmed interviews, and other short films constructed to shed light on the minutiae of his career. Peppered through the film are several segments featuring Gould portrayed by Colm Feore. Feore does a great job capturing Gould's removed interest in the world, his dry sense of humor, and his extreme hypochondria. Through the biopic segments, we see Gould give up piano concerts abruptly at the early age of 31. Gould disliked live performances and quit playing in concert to focus solely on recorded media, which he felt was the ultimate relationship between artist and audience. He was known to have a visceral approach to his piano recordings, and, in later years, he experimented with recording techniques as much as he played the piano. Gould was a perfectionist, yet he would approve of recordings where heavy breathing or furniture noise bled through the tape because that's how he saw the reality of performing.

   Aside from the segments that feature Feore as Gould, there are non-biopic segments including filmed interviews with friends and associates who knew Gould well, like master violinist Yehudi Menuhin and French filmmaker Bruno Monsaingeon. Some found him charming and easy to deal with. His local piano tuner is interviewed and mentions how Gould always gave him plenty of notice when he needed his piano tuned rather than calling at the last minute. His friends enjoyed his conversation, but many agreed he had bad phone etiquette. Non-biopic segments also include shorts like "Opus 1" which features a string quartet performing Gould's composition of the same name. "Variation in C Minor" is an interpretive animation to Gould's recorded piano. "CD318" takes a long lavish look into the inner-workings of Gould's favorite piano with no dialog. Besides being an interesting approach to a documentary, *32 Short Films* particularly suits the telling of Gould's life story as it gives a well-rounded look at his genius and the neurosis that likely drove him down the avenues he followed. *32 Short Films About Glenn Gould* should be required viewing for would-be documentarians if, for no other reason, because the film takes such a unique approach without burying the subject during the process. None of these fragmented pieces seem out of place or filler. We get a bold and rounded look at a person who we probably could never fully understand or emulate.

Get Crazy (1983)
Directed by Alan Arkush
U.S.A. 92 min.

After his failed, if not somewhat misunderstood, attempt to bring Andy Kaufman's unique humor to the screen in 1981's *Heartbeeps*, director Alan Arkush tried to rekindle some of the anarchic humor that made *Rock 'n' Roll High School* (1979) a success with 1983's *Get Crazy*. Utilizing an excellent ensemble cast, *Get Crazy* is essentially a loosely connected chain of anecdotes of rock stereotypes surrounding a converging plot line involving a New Year's Eve party at the Saturn Theater, a small Fillmore East-type venue. The converging plot lines are little more than a series of sight gags with an underlying anti-corporate message. But a load of clever rock jokes and a couple of interesting musical performances is far and above what could be expected from a music film these days. It's an excellent pull for fans of jokes about sex, drugs, and rock 'n' roll.

The main plot line surrounds Saturn Theater owner Max Wolfe (Alan Garfield). Wolfe's failing health brings him close to death hours before the yearly New Year's Eve concert where rich and famous rock stars return every year to perform out of respect for their roots. Wolfe's failing health inspires music mogul Colin Beverly (Ed Begley Jr.) to make a play for Wolfe's lease for the purposes of destroying the small venue and putting up a building of his own. Wolfe is relying on stage managers Neil Allen (Daniel Stern) and Willy Loman (Gail Edwards) to keep the show running on time and to thwart Wolfe's greedy nephew Sammy (Miles Chapin) from sabotaging the show and obtaining the lease. Stern's long underrated straight man routine plays well as the befuddled stage manager whose diplomacy bonds the eccentric rockers. Mining the rockers' outlandish behavior is what works best about the film.

One of the most intriguing bands is Nada, an over-the-top punk stereotype of the kind you have never seen outside of a Tony Basil video. Every member of Nada's fifteen piece band is a representation of an '80s caricature of a punk rocker. Nada (Lori Eastman), the vocalist for whom the band is named, is in charge of Piggy, who is portrayed by Fear front man Lee Ving. As silly as they are together, Nada and Piggy's party antics are big fun; their partnership peaks during a chaotic version of "Hoochie Coochie Man" obviously recorded by Fear. Ving begins the song with a world-class stage dive that rivals the best '80s hardcore footage and the pandemonium that ensues reflects some great, albeit staged, punk footage.

Other acts arriving or racing to get to the venue are egomaniac Reggie Wanker (Malcolm McDowell), the legendary King Blues (Bill Henderson), metaphysical folk singer Audin (Lou Reed), and Jerry Garcia-inspired commune leader Captain Cloud (Howard Kaylan of The Turtles). If you are into a certain type of silly humor, none of these characters are especially weak. McDowell plays an excellent jerk and Reed's overly laid-back recluse is oddly meta.

Arkush sadly went on to direct *Caddyshack II* (1988). *Caddyshack II* at least got a DVD release. *Get Crazy* is difficult to find as it has only been released on VHS. It's a silly film, but if you pine for the days of *Airplane!* (1980) and love a little punk attitude, *Get Crazy* is a must-see.

(A version of this review was published in Lunchmeat Magazine, Issue #8.)

Nico 1988 (2017)
Directed by Susanna Nicchiarelle
Italy 93 min.

Soon enough, there will be no moments of music history not covered by a thrown-together documentary or overdramatized biopic. Gone forever will be the mystery and word-of-mouth stories regarding our most enigmatic and interesting music idols. It's a shame telling these unique stories will be squashed into molds of formulaic drivel that "put asses in seats." This future belongs to those versed in integrated marketing. Hopefully notes will remain from director Susanna Nicchiarelle, whose focused film about model, artist, and singer Christa Päffgen, professionally known as Nico, tells a compelling story of success, loss, integrity, and the point reached when those words don't mean much. *Nico 1988* may have drummed up the drama to keep the story moving, but it's largely successful as a stark and unglamorous look at an artist who didn't give up on the elements of her life that motivated her to perform. It is surely one of the best movies about music in a long time.

The scope of the film is the last year of Nico's life, when her underground fame and residuals from the sales of Velvet Underground albums barely supported her career. The story opens on Nico being interviewed by a radio DJ in Manchester who has obviously not done any research beyond her best-known achievements. She tells him, "My life started after the Velvet Underground." And so does this movie. Her time with Andy Warhol and VU is represented in flashes of home movie-style clips of Warholian parties. Otherwise, the film is supported largely by a grand performance by Trine Dyrholm as Christa, as Nico now prefers to be called.

The film portrays Christa with many of the traits of the unpredictable storm imposed by divaship. Her manager Richard (John Gordon Sinclair) takes much of it in stride. Richard's unbelievably understanding wife Laura (Karina Fernandez), who travels on tour with the band, points out that Christa has never gotten her name correct once. It's richly ironic for someone who has trouble answering to the name for which she is most known. In one town, the promoter must house the band due to lack of funds for a hotel. Christa wakes the house at 2 a.m. searching the kitchen for soda pop. Christa gets testy when she can't find drugs. But Dyrholm also succeeds portraying a clever person who faces the adversity of waning stardom without much interest while still learning she isn't always the only person on the bus. She presents Nico with many moments of likability, explaining to one host how she went hungry as a child and starved herself as a model and now doesn't care what happens to her when she eats. Her self-awareness evolves during a Czechoslovakian show where she pulls her usual indignities only to finally realize what the promoters and fans are risking to put on the concert. The stories about her life are peppered into her final tour where she's in close quarters with a young band she sees making some of the same mistakes she has.

Phantom of the Paradise (1974)
Directed by Brian De Palma
U.S.A. 91 min.

It doesn't hurt that Rod Serling narrates the opening of this movie. The story itself plays from themes of so many classic twist-style stories that his master's voice really makes you feel as if you are about to see something special. This futuristic rock 'n' roll tale follows Winston Leach (William Finley) as a musician searching for a break. After writing a rock opera, Leach approaches Swan (Paul Williams), a super rich and powerful music producer in hopes of having the piece produced. Swan loves the music, but instead of giving Leach a break, Swan steals Leach's music and has him framed for a crime that puts him in the penitentiary. Pretty big jump. Leach breaks out of prison, but becomes disfigured in the process, which strips him of his identity. Swan fits him with a voice box, a beak-shaped helmet, a red cape, and groovy leather suit. This all leads to a Faustian pact with Swan to finish his music from a hidden room in Swan's massive amphitheater. Leach agrees to finish the piece if Swan will allow Phoenix (Jessica Harper) to sing his music. Leach is obsessed with Phoenix. When the score is finished, Swan cheats the deal by putting Phoenix in the chorus and bricking Leach up Tell-Tale Heart-style inside the special studio room. Leach escapes again only to find Phoenix on the road to becoming a star. She falls under the spell of Swan's promise of fame and fortune. This first film by De Palma also gives insight into his interest in voyeurism as a theme that pops up in many of his movies. Leach watches from a window as Swan and Phoenix lie in bed together kissing. Leach tries to commit suicide and discovers yet another element of his Faustian pact in play.

The movie does take a while to get going, but those who stick with it will be rewarded. Highlights of the beginning of the film include William Finley's histrionic acting style as he escapes prison and transforms into the Phantom. The piecing together of this scenario is amazing, especially when you watch the escape sequence and realize they must have been working with a ludicrously small budget. There is also a funny homage to the shower scene in Alfred Hitchcock's *Psycho* (1960) that defies expectations. As a solid rock opera, the tunes are more often fun than not. Some of the music in the beginning is a little cheesy, like the opener "Goodbye, Eddie Goodbye," which is meant to be a '50s period song delivered by Swans' nostalgia group the Juicy Fruits, but really doesn't quite deliver. But the dramatic performance and reprises of "Faust" are pretty great.

The Alice Cooper-style delivery of "Someone Super Like You" is a lot of fun, particularly as the band fake-dissects members of the audience to construct the lead singer Beef (Gerrit Graham). The film continues to seek revenge on Swan, unveiling more close-to-the-heart horror themes like Oscar Wilde's *Picture of Dorian Gray*. The whole "creating a star" narrative makes this feel like a more-constructed version of *The Rocky Horror Picture Show* (1975) until you realize this movie came out a year earlier. But it's that kind of fun: maybe dated but definitely weird and wild. All the heavy themes and homages make for a pretty dark narrative, but the histrionic acting and silly treatment of classic themes make it a fun watch.

Rockers (1978)
Directed by Theodoros Bafaloukos
Jamaica 100 min.

Rockers began as a documentary of an era in Jamaican music history when reggae began to grow beyond an emerging regional scene and was on its way to becoming a worldwide phenomenon in the late 1970s. The seminal *The Harder They Come* (1972) introduced Jimmy Cliff to the world and exposed some of the inner workings of the music scene and island legends that were made topical as themes in the songs. Rockers includes footage of legends like Gregory Isaacs, Robbie Shakespeare, Burning Spear, Jack Ruby, and Dillinger performing and often just hanging out with each other on the scene. It's a seamless document of how music was transforming in Jamaica and the people responsible for its transformation. But the film also tells a compelling story.

The main character in the film, Hoursemouth (Leroy "Horsemouth" Wallace), is an actual drummer for Burning Spear and other bands. The fraternity of reggae musicians interacting in the film sells the idea of a big music scene emerging from a small band of musicians, producers, and fans. There is fun and collaboration and parties. The plot of the film centers on Horsemouth's desire to buy a motorcycle that he wants to use to start a record distribution route around the island. There is a lot of urgency in the Jamaican music scene to get records from the plant out to DJs, stores, and the like. It is key in spreading the word about a song and to DJs having exclusive content. Motorcycle couriers can make a living doing this. They can also make a living transporting other things, but that's not what this movie is about. *Rockers* is a music film with a plot screwed into the middle. Horsemouth portrays a fictionalized version of himself as a struggling musician in Jamaica. He is shown in his actual home with his wife and children. The camera follows him riding his motorcycle to various neighborhoods visiting a variety of record sellers, some very organized and some run out of small ragtag buildings. It's a fascinating look into the island's music industry, which emphasizes DIY in the arena of distribution to stores, DJs, and music fans.

Footage following Horsemouth in his real life environment reflects the urgent, documentary style filming of the inception of the movie. As a narrative film, *Rockers* reflects the influence of Italian neo-realist classics like *Bicycle Thieves* (1948) directed by Vittorio De Sica. Similar to how films were shot during the Italian Neorealist movement, *Rockers* is shot in real locations crucial to Horsemouth's actual life. The director films him dealing with his actual friends and associates with the day-to-day dealings of the average Kingston citizen. And very specifically, *Bicycle Thieves* is reflected in *Rockers* as the motorcycle is eventually stolen at a party. It leads Horsemouth on an adventure to further delve into the underground to find his bike. Horsemouth discovers an entry into the network he believes is responsible. He engages a group of his friends to arrange a revenge raid in the style of Robin Hood, a popular character whose themes were prevalent in T*he Harder They Come*. In the end, the film has treated the audience to an inside look into some iconic reggae scenes, shown some great performances, and has you root for Horsemouth and his cohorts to rob the rich and give to the poor. It pays to have friends.

Round Midnight (1986)
Directed by Bertrand Tavernier
France/U.S.A. 133 min.

"They're always paying the wrong people in this world." The quote comes from fictional character Dale Turner, a bebop innovator portrayed by actual bebop innovator and jazz legend Dexter Gordon. You can tell that when he says it in the film, there's some truth behind the statement. He didn't just read the line from a page, he lived it. The style of jazz known as bebop came in and out of style like a lion in the 1950s. At first, people didn't want to hear it because you couldn't dance to it. Then it became hip, but it wasn't long before jazz experimentation changed people's tastes. Players like Charlie Parker, Lester Young, and Coleman Hawkins shaped and popularized bebop before jazz took its audience and moved on to the next thing. Bebop however remained popular in Europe, and many musicians moved to European cities in order to make a living and escape America's blatant racism and heavily enforced and racially pointed drug enforcement.

Round Midnight is a film about this very specific time in jazz history. It centers on a community of jazz players whose skills and passion have served them a speed bump due to America's waning interest. The European move was big among players at that time. The story is based on Bud Powell's biography and the end of the film proclaims Dale Turner as an amalgamation of Powell and bebop luminary Lester Young. Young had a following among tenor saxophone players. A relative of mine from Indianola, Mississippi named Aubrey "Brew" Moore was among them. He followed a similar path, except he made Amsterdam his home base. There, he was prolific both as a live player and made several records. Moore also had a string of bad luck, but I digress.

The film subtly ruminates on the role of integrity, friendship, and community in the creative process. One of Turner's problems is he's a hopeless alcoholic. His friends in Paris keep him away from alcohol for his own good. The popularity of the Blue Note nightclub is the only thing keeping many of them afloat. And sometimes just barely at that. There is a subtle side-plot where the manager of the club is noticed holding his jacket closed with a safety pin because no one knows how to sew and he can't afford a new one. Turner meets a French man named Francis Borler (François Gluzet) who is such a fan he stands outside the club in the rain to hear him play through a cracked duct. Although Turner performs as a shadow of his former self, Borler is overcome and goes to lengths to meet Turner, who initially goes for a walk with Borler hoping for a free beer (an old friend has to hold Turner's money for him so he can't get access to alcohol), but the two become close friends and Borler and his young daughter Berangere (Gabrielle Haker) inspire Turner to live without alcohol. As the story progresses, Turner cleans up his act considerably and becomes creative again. But *Round Midnight* lays off the typical tropes of a comeback story. All of these people survive and thrive with each other, creating a cramped community in their long-stay hotels and apartments, sharing food, advice, and stories and eventually finding someone who will sew the button back on the manager's jacket. Borler spends time filming the major players on an 8mm camera and eventually getting Turner back into the studio. Turner is transformed, but even a five-dollar bill can be a danger to his willpower.

The film does a service to the history of jazz by making this a fictional film. It's easier to take in the broad plot strokes without having the weight of actual names, dates, and history hampering the storyline. There are plenty of jazz biggies in the movie, but the anonymity of the story causes the film to have more resonance. Dexter Gordon is astounding in the role of Turner. Besides knowing he actually lived through the bebop era, he also has many moments of great whimsy. Gordon can make light of a situation with a short grin, or a delayed response. Refreshingly light handed yet compelling with Gordon at the helm, *Round Midnight*, which preceded *Bird* (1988) and *Straight No Chaser* (1988), two excellent jazz films that also explored the lives of icons, should be remembered for capturing the atmosphere and nihilism of the '50s into the '60s jazz era.

Tender Mercies (1983)
Directed by Bruce Beresford
U.S.A. 92 min.

Tender Mercies is a slow burn and a very sweet movie. It's a gritty story about country music, and the stark direction and excellent performances generate strong realism although many of the good things that happen plot-wise probably wouldn't work out in real life. The type of story that plays well as a soap opera for men, *Tender Mercies* follows a humble man, Mac Sledge (Robert Duvall), who people secretly admire as he makes good at a skill he's meant to be adored for having after getting sidetracked from that skill at some previous, unseen point in his life. The sidetracking in this case is due to alcoholism, but the movie only holds Sledge peripherally accountable for his sins. It might sound like a bad review, but this is one of those movies that should be seen, if for no other reason, for its stunning performances. The cast is excellent. Bruce Beresford's quiet and contemplative direction creates space and patience among the characters and allows the story time to build and stay engaging without contrived jumps. If I gave you the elements of the storyline, you could easily put together a map of where it is going. But this story is so steeped in a very fine brand of American redemption it's difficult to walk away from.

Duvall's Sledge is a down-on-his-luck country singer who wakes up one morning in a roadside hotel on a quiet highway in Texas. His traveling companion has abandoned him. He has no money. He offers to work off his debt to the hotel owner and manager Rosa Lee (Tess Harper). Lee agrees, as long as he stays sober. Weeks turn into months, and without much drama, Lee and Sledge and Lee's son from another marriage Sonny (Allan Hubbard) get to be good friends. Sledge attends church with them. He eats with them. He keeps his mouth shut with quiet dignity. This part of the story unfolds without many surprises. Harper and Duvall sell the relationship with the ancient art of reserved performances that cause an audience to want to root for them. Each appears to deserve something from each other and both seem willing to put the work in to get it. It's a nice relationship.

Only after a while does Mac's past begin to trickle in. Fortunately for him, it appears in small, manageable bits at first. A van load of young musicians pull up to pay their respects. They might as well have "Redemption" painted on the side of the van. Sledge visits his ex-wife, country star Dixie Sledge (Betty Buckley) and her manager Harry (Wilford Brimley, the master of Americana) as an act of attrition. Dixie has lost her mind a bit and wants nothing to do with Sledge. She insists he stay away from their daughter Sue Anne (Ellen Barkin). Harry says some real things to him, as a Wilford Brimley character is wont to do, but he also tries to go behind Dixie's back to help Sledge out in that comforting Wilford-Brimley-characters-have-a-deep-understanding-of-your-predicament way. Sledge eschews Harry's help for taking the hard road, like all Americans are expected to do. Americans who turn their backs on solid support always have better, more honorable opportunities waiting around the corner for them. I won't tell you whether or not Sledge runs across the van of young musicians again, but, well, anyway.

Tender Mercies is a little by the numbers when it comes to dreamy Americana stories about the virtues of being stoic and kind. The pay off as Sledge sees the light and begins writing music again is satisfying. The lesson, which in this case is that regional success might be enough if you can discover other things that make you happy in life, is a nice take away. The appeal of *Tender Mercies* really comes in the form of hope for self-realization. Not just that Mack makes it out the other side, but how he does it. Duvall won an Academy Award for his role as Mack Sledge. For a pretty typical redemption story, it's engrossing and relatable even if you don't like country music that much.

Wattstax (1973)
Directed by Mel Stuart
U.S.A. 103 min.

Someone will ask, and it's not a bad question, why is *Wattstax* not in the documentary section. I don't think of *Wattstax* as a straight documentary, particularly as many of the segments between the music performances were staged. The documentary aspect lies as much in the visuals as what is being said. Nine minutes into the film we see the Staple Singers under police escort eating ribs in a limousine on the way to Los Angeles Memorial Coliseum. We also see a montage of people living in the neighborhood of Watts contrasted with people arriving at the stadium for the concert. There we see both work clothes and disco clothes. *Wattstax* is a document of a movement in transition, a country in transition, and a film about a successful regional record label taking a step towards the world stage. Besides all of that, it is also a music film of the highest standard. The film opens on Richard Pryor comparing the vibe of *Wattstax* with the vibe of the Watts riots of seven years prior. We understand *Wattstax* isn't a celebration of an event, but a milestone of a work in progress.

The legendary Memphis soul label Stax Records organized the concert. Stax founders organized and dedicated the show to Watts, Los Angeles, where, in 1965, residents rioted for six days to protest unfair treatment by the police. 112,000 attended the *Wattstax* concert. According to the excellent book *Stax: Respect Yourself: Stax Records and the Soul Explosion*, this concert happened in the same manner that so many great things come to fruition: someone asked. Stax executive Al Bell went to the staff of Los Angeles Memorial Coliseum and said, "We want to rent the stadium." It was a weighty ask for a small business to come in to inquire about renting a coliseum: particularly one where the Los Angeles Rams were actively playing football. Arrangements had to be made around a Rams game, but the arrangements were made and Stax put on a concert. People paid a dollar to see already legendary music performers like Isaac Hayes, The Staple Singers, Rufus Thomas, Luther Ingram, The Bar-Kays, Albert King, and many others including speakers like activist Jesse Jackson and comedian Richard Pryor. Most of the footage is directly from the concert itself. Some of the music segments were staged around the neighborhood due to time running out at the show. The concert and music footage is interspersed with vérité-style street scenes of people going about their business in Watts. The speaking parts were recreated with actors so as to have control over the footage, which is still a bit vexing to me, but I wasn't there. The effect is the stories, concert, and music vignettes come together to make a passionate film. *Wattstax* gave the label two live albums and exposed people to the music and the message. And they did it independently. At the time, they were a small label from Memphis. That in itself makes for an interesting film.

Wild Style (1983)
Directed by Charlie Aheam
U.S.A. 82 min.

Wild Style works as a documentary. It contains footage of some of the earliest moments of hip hop from its origins in The Bronx. Mirroring many of the tenets of Italian Realism, Wild Style uses actual people from the neighborhood as actors and characters and actual locations such as the train yards and clubs and homes in the South Bronx neighborhood. Early groups like Cold Crush Brothers and Grandmaster Flash portray themselves. It is essential footage of early rapping and turntable mixing rising in Bronx nightclubs and parties. We see trains pass regularly with early graffiti artists' work on them. We see break-dancers working the streets and clubs. The phenomenon of early hip-hop is well represented by the film as both background and the main attraction.

The actual plot involves Raymond (graffiti artist Lee Quiñones), who goes by Zoro in the film. Zoro is a well-known train painter artist among Bronx artists and teenagers, but few know who he actually is. He'd like to keep it that way since what he does is illegal. A Manhattan journalist named Virginia (Patti Astor) heads to The Bronx to cover a group of artists getting recognition by actually getting paid to put legitimately commissioned graffiti work on buildings. Virginia slowly becomes aware of the more street level action via her guide Fab 5 Freddy (as himself). Freddy tries to convince Raymond to share his more clandestine work and the risks he takes doing it for Virginia's article. Raymond doesn't want to sacrifice his underground status supporting the commercialization of graffiti art, and yet the lure of recognition looms.

Along the way, Freddy, Raymond, and Virginia visit parties and clubs. There are long segments of footage of rappers and dancers performing. At one point they end up at a Lower East Side art party where white and moneyed art enthusiasts find them interesting. Raymond sees what he's buying into, but makes no clear decisions. It all culminates into Raymond painting a set for a LES/Bronx hip-hop showdown that is set to take place mostly on Fab 5 Freddy's enthusiasm. It's a paint job that will make him a legend.

Wild Style came out only a year before *Beat Street* (1984) and *Breakin'*(1984). This low-budget film covering the early days of hip hop culture shows how fast the sound matriculated into mainstream consciousness. Both *Beat Street* (1984) and

Breakin' (1984) were big hits. *Wild Style* is interesting historically and tells a good story. There is a lot of music footage and a tight narrative fit for an 82 minute film. As far as acting goes, most people come off as well as anyone who has had a camera shoved in their face. Fab 5 Freddy is energetic and compelling and carries the narrative with moments of competent acting. He seems the most prepared for the success this exposure will bring to the hip hop community. The rest of the people involved in this film were probably unaware of the incoming explosion. And many of the scene's originators didn't get the recognition achieved by those who came after, but we have this document to show the modest roots of a cultural phenomenon.

Wild Zero (1999)
Directed by Tetsuro Takeuchi
Japan 98 min.

Zombie narratives overran the early to mid 2000s. Anyone with a camera figured they could make a competent zombie movie. And why not? It looks easy. Something's gotta get done, right? But there were a lot of bad angles explored during the zombie boom. Zombies aren't inherently interesting, but they make good bad guys because no one much cares what happens to them. You can cut one to pieces with a razorblade or blow up a hundred of them with a propane tank bomb and feel nothing. In the age of a *Star Wars* universe where we now have to care a little about the back-story and fate of some stormtroopers, it's harder to find entities available for quick and gory fodder. Zombies were the answer, but the market for mass zombie killing became saturated quickly with a deluge of zombie movies.

If you think zombie slaughter can't still be fun, imagine a world where zombies are blown to bits by Tokyo's overdriven rock 'n' roll gods Guitar Wolf to a soundtrack of high-octane trash rock 'n' roll. Close your eyes and imagine running over zombies in a military truck to the tune of Teengenerate's "My GTO." Ace (Masashi Endô), a rock enthusiast and Guitar Wolf fan, helps the band out of a jam during a standoff with a criminal network's leader. Wolf and Ace become blood brothers and Wolf gives Ace a whistle to blow when he gets in trouble. Ace later finds himself integral to the fate of the world when aliens land on earth and begin bringing the dead back to life. Ace runs across a carload of spaceship enthusiasts driving to the sight of the landings and forms a quick bond with them when it becomes clear they must survive regular zombie attacks and a crime syndicate Ace has run afoul of. They do fine, eventually having to blow the whistle in order to be saved by the god-like appearance of Guitar Wolf, Drum Wolf, and Bass Wolf. Troma-style violence and ripping live performances by Guitar Wolf are in tow, the former set to a great punk 'n' roll soundtrack including the Phantom Surfers, Greg Oblivian and the Tip Tops, Teengenerate, and other high-octane combos. With loads of shotgun blasts, exploding heads, and guitar feedback, Wild Zero is all energy and the perfect text for fans of horror and Japanese punk. They do go well together. There is also an unexpected side plot encouraging tolerance and boundaryless love. This sci-fi classic about aliens reanimating the dead to form an army for world domination (cult hounds will find the plot familiar) is more than just a conduit for the music. If you thought *Rock 'N' Roll High School* (1979) needed more head explosions, this is the movie for you. It's a zombie massacre with hotter cars and better hair.

Chapter 18: Nostalgia-rama

A little nostalgia can be good. I think. I probably ponder that question daily. Is it? Sometimes I worry it might be in charge of my life. I don't think things were necessarily better when I was growing up, but sometimes I sure do miss the quiet.

Cooley High (1975)
Directed by Michael Schultz
U.S.A. 107 min.

The minutiae of everyday life in inner-city neighborhoods is often a platform for films that focus on tragic poverty or gangland drama. *Cooley High* is an early text showing African American teenagers dealing with more balanced problems. Screenwriter Eric Monte based the film on his experiences growing up in Chicago as an attempt to dispel myths about growing up in the projects. The film centers on a group of friends and acquaintances living in the Cabrini-Green housing projects in Chicago in 1964: primarily Leroy "Preach" Jackson (Glynn Turman) and Richard "Cochise" Morris (Lawrence Hilton-Jacobs), who, along with their peers, are about to graduate from high school. The film's opening sequences set the tone for a typical '60s nostalgia picture. But as the movie continues, Morris and Jackson find themselves coping in a series of situations not widely portrayed in film and television at the time.

The power of *Cooley High* doesn't come from a barrage of dramatic, ghetto-related scenarios that are heaved at the audience, but from the subtle unfolding of these stories. Regarding the plot scenarios that are either peripheral or directly affecting their lives, the typical teenagers here might be dealing with a little more than the average American teenager in more affluent neighborhoods. After all, they have to navigate the landscape of Cabrini-Green while dealing with the typical trials and tribulations of trying to graduate high school while also testing the loyalty and foundation of the people around them. In Monte's able hands, Morris and Jackson aren't portrayed as tragic ghetto figures. For instance, the boys are friendly with a pimp named Jimmy Lee (Steven Williams). As the story progresses, Lee often plays a positive role in their lives despite having a hideous and cruel profession. They are all neighbors. Lee's profession should not be excused, but his concern for the goings on in the neighborhood with the teenagers garners some sympathy. There are also speed bumps in Morris and Jackson's daily life that are atypical of the teenage experience. Stone (Sherman Smith) and Robert (Norman Gibson) are two guys from the neighborhood not much older than Morris and Jackson, but two characters steeped in the kind of street savvy that will get the four of them in trouble and set off a chain of events that will affect the end of the film. Morris and Jackson have each other, and when this dynamic is threatened, their system for survival unravels a bit.

Matinee (1993)
Directed by Joe Dante
U.S.A. 99 min.

I love a movie that brings you back to the experience of going to the movies. *Matinee* is a film where nostalgia for the silver screen is as relevant as the story itself. It is a period comedy set in 1961, specifically in April during the Bay of Pigs crisis. Americans in the early '60s were regularly reminded of the threat of nuclear war, whether it was kids doing "duck and cover" bomb drills in school or homeowners having shelter equipment marketed to them en masse. And American monster movies were big at the movies as another subtle reminder of the impending nuclear threat during the Cold War.

John Goodman portrays Lawrence Woolsley, a film producer who goes the extra mile traveling around the country promoting his low-budget monster films. Woolsley is visiting Key West, Florida: 94 miles from Cuba. He is promoting his latest film Mant, a film within the film about a man transformed to half-man, half-ant. Nervousness abounds in this small Florida town situated so close to Cuba, but Woolsley is a showman first and finds the unrest in Key West the perfect backdrop for his self-promoting shenanigans. Goodman's character is a thinly veiled caricature of the great film director William Castle. Castle was known to travel the country pulling pranks, hiring actors, and using magic show-type stunts to promote and scare patrons at screenings of his movies. Several of his actual techniques are parodied in *Matinee*, including hooking up army-surplus vibrating engines underneath theater seats to buzz frightened movie goers at certain points of the film to give them a fright. Castle used this specific technique in his promotion of one of his most famous films *The Tingler* (1959).

Matinee is also a coming of age story for a menagerie of kids, and some of their parents, most of which will end up at the big screening of Mant at the end of the film. Many of the characters are interconnected through local grade school student Gene Loomis (Simon Fenton). Loomis is ensconced in the dread over the missile crisis because his father is active military and has been called away on a top-secret mission. Loomis is also an ardent fan of monster movies and recognizes Woolsley in the local hardware store. Woolsley hires Loomis to do odd jobs for him as the screening gets closer. Other local kids' stories are intertwined so as to cash in and clash at the big screening everyone is looking forward to. While the film drives these school age stories with a refreshing innocence, the slightly shyster Woolsley and the complications making this particular screening of Mant memorable is its most satisfying charm. Like *Cinema Paradiso* (1988), the story gets right at the heart of what makes going to the theater fun and why you can still grab a bit of that magic at the movies well after your childhood years. Director Joe Dante, a noted fan of cinema and horror from the era, also directed the horror comedy *Gremlins* (1984), where in a scene late in the film, the tiny monsters invade a movie theater and mostly just have a good time messing around. There's a moment of downfall for the gremlins when someone turns the projector on and mesmerizes them with the magic of moving pictures. It's apparent this is a moment Dante is familiar with. His knack for detail and context is vivid and recreates a moment in time for '60s cinema in *Matinee*.

The Wanderers (1979)
Directed by Philip Kaufman
U.S.A. 117 min.

Philip Kaufman directed this sleeper film about 1950s gangs after his great 1978 adaptation of *Invasion of the Body Snatchers*. He was on a roll from there. He got co-writing credits on *Raiders of the Lost Ark* (1981) and went on to direct *The Right Stuff* (1983). Based on Bronx native Richard Price's first novel, the film covers the lives of a wide swath of Bronx high school kids whose social lives are broken by mostly racial oriented gangs. At the center of the story is Richie Gennaro (Ken Wahl) head of the Italian gang called the Wanderers. The Wanderers are on thin ice with an African American gang called the Del Bombers. A rumble is arranged and other gangs meet to decide who to back. Also in play are the Baldies, an adult gang of shaved-head leather toughies led by Terror (Erland van Lidth), the Ducky Boys, an Irish-Catholic gang whose large numbers and psychotic disposition make them a formidable enemy across the Bronx, and Richie's girlfriend's father Chubby Galasso (Dolph Sweet), a local Mafioso trying to get the gangs to put their energies to better use.

This skeleton plot is decorated with several vignettes heavy with '50s nostalgia. The book is also structured this way, although the book is a lot darker. In one scenario, the kids attend a record party where all they get dressed up and spike the punch. They get pranked by The Baldies who sloppily propose castrating Richie and his best friend Joey Capra (John Friedrich). Poignant moments are in play when the small universe of these Bronx regulars is expanded by the death of President John F. Kennedy, Richie happens past a coffee house where Bob Dylan is performing "The Times They Are a-Changin'", and all the gangs come together to celebrate a milestone in Richie's life. This movie was released the same year as the street gang classic *The Warriors* (1979), in which a Brooklyn gang attempt to make their way home from Manhattan to Coney Island after being blamed for the assassination of a radical gang leader. *The Wanderers* didn't achieve the same cult status as *The Warriors*, but the story adds a new dimension to the typical New York gang story. Although racial problems come to a head at a proposed rumble, there is a nice, if somewhat sophomoric lesson about tolerance and cooperation. The world gets bigger when you graduate. Reality starts to seep into the high school bubble.

Chapter 19: Sci-Fi

It's the genre that needs no introduction. Much has been written about science fiction. Here are just a few sleepers I was inspired to write about.

Attack the Block (2011)
Directed by Joe Cornish
U.K. 88 min.

Attack the Block opens with a mugging. A group of teenagers with pipes, bikes, and a knife surround a lone woman in her twenties and threaten her until she gives them her pocketbook and ring. It's a slightly unsettling opening. It's further unsettling considering generally when a mugging or some sort of assault happens near the beginning of a sci-fi movie, it's traditional for an alien, robot, or something unearthly to take revenge on the muggers. The mugging itself ends with an object falling from the sky and crashing into a car. The kids take great pleasure in chasing it down and killing it with fireworks and blunt instruments. They wave the creature around in the air like a trophy and then take it to a marijuana trap house for storage thinking it may be worth money to someone. This creature won't be phoning home.

These young men, of course, will redeem themselves and take on a primary battle against an alien invasion, at least for their neighborhood. Part of the story is these attacks are happening all over London, and it's every earth resident for themselves. These kids have a few revelations by the end of the film, particularly the group's de facto leader Moses, portrayed by John Boyega who went from this movie to being a major player in the latest *Star Wars* franchise. It's easy to see what the producers of those films saw in his performance. Taking into consideration homage to B-movie horror the film is seeped in, Boyega puts in a James Dean in *Rebel Without a Cause*-level performance. You might think I'm crazy, but repeated viewings make clear his subtle acting style. The unintentional leader and street-level guru type can come off as really corny with the wrong actor. Boyega communicates with blank stares. He enacts plans with shifting eye rolls. He takes criticism with seeming indifference, yet conveys mild contemplative silences. He stands mute to the cops without breaking a sweat. Towards the end, he realizes some of the errors of his ways and says them plainly.

The movie also relies on a terrific ensemble cast of mostly unknown actors including a group of female peers led by Tia (Danielle Vitalis) who surpass Moses' group in maturity, a drowsy pot customer named Brewis (Luke Treadway) who wants to be part of the group but is too posh, two younger kids out to earn the nicknames Probs (Sammy Williams) and Mayhem (Michael Ajao), the block's biggest drug dealer Hi-Hatz (Jumayn Hunter) who doesn't believe their story and is out to get them, Ron (Nick Frost) the trap house keeper, and, in an odd turn, Samantha (Jodie Whittaker) the original mugging victim. Writer and director Joe Cornish should get credit for just being able to manage this many characters in his first feature film. But Cornish also creates stunning action sequences and keeps a subtle nod to the mise-en-scène of classic sci-fi by filming the tower block where everyone lives in a way that makes it appear like a ship floating in space. The aliens are only as terrifying as they need to be because, all over London, the attacks continue. No help is coming. It's up to the group to save the block. Ultimately, it's the kids who are going to see the chinks in the armor in this scenario.

The Lawnmower Man (1992)
Directed by Brett Leonard
U.S.A. 142 min.

I've never liked sports. I was one of the kids watching terrible sci-fi movies broadcast by other networks during the Super Bowl. They were always the worst of the worst 50s B-movies and I love them to this day. Many of the plots were steeped in wild predictions about what the '50s thought the future would look like. *The Lawnmower Man*, while maybe not the best sci-fi movie ever made on the subject of virtual reality, shows us what 1992 thinks the futuristic world of the computer age and virtual reality might bring to the table. It's primitive, but why criticize a movie for having outdated concepts. Neil deGrasse Tyson might take the fun out of this movie. *The Lawnmower Man* documents the crude beginnings of our paranoid delusions about virtual reality. If the technology eventually leads to a mentally challenged lawn care professional being turned into a god-like being, you're going to feel silly you made fun of *The Lawnmower Man's* graphics.

Dr. Lawrence Angelo (Pierce Brosnan) is working on a mind-developing device using virtual reality. There is a brief interruption in his research, during which he tries some home experiments. He tries these brain-expanding games on the local lawn cutter Jobe Smith (Jeff Fahey). Smith is mentally challenged. Angelo has good intentions, and at first Smith becomes smarter and more confident. He stands up to his bullies at the gas station, church, diner, and other places where overblown bullies hang out in New England towns in horror stories. He has new appeal with the ladies. He buys new jeans. He gets a taste for what the treatments are doing for him and steals a mega dose. Now he's ready to paint the town. This bumps up his rampage and abilities to include mind control. In one scene he convinces the police a man run down by a giant lawnmower was an "accidental death." Jobe becomes unstoppable. Dr. Angelo must chase him down and find a way to not only trap him, but virtually delete him.

The special effects in *The Lawnmower Man* are so outdated as to be fascinating. Those who lived through the origins of this type of animation might remember it fondly as being used homogeneously in schools, training videos, and stoner videos. They were the new kaleidoscopes. The film presents a unique and well-conceived tech plot and documents the era before we knew computers could do everything, and imagined they'd do anything. It was also David Koresh's favorite movie, if for some reason that raises an eyebrow of curiosity. You might have to cut the film some slack, but there aren't many like it.

Miracle Mile (1988)
Directed by Steve De Jarnatt
U.S.A. 87 min.

I've never seen a movie get almost boring and pull itself out of the fire so many times. It helps that the bulk of the story essentially takes place in real time. Whenever there's a lull, the movie throws water in its face, makes an inspirational speech under its breath, and adds an interesting twist to the story. Sometimes it's directly related to the plot. Sometimes it's an interesting soliloquy. The details of the very simple storyline allow the film to introduce new characters and new challenges organically, requiring the audience to ponder what's happening before the next pitfall. There are no particularly notable characters, yet the movie finds everyone interesting. Some understand they are trying to survive the early stages of a catastrophe and some don't. It makes it all the more difficult to pass judgment. They don't give you the loudmouth or smug character you are required to hate. *Miracle Mile* is fun due to its slow burn, not because you're meant to just ruminate on who deserves to live, but also because you consider how you might react.

The story opens on Harry Washello (Anthony Edwards). Harry lucks into a late-night date with a cool girl named Mare (Julie Peters). Mare encourages Harry to pick her up for a late-night date at the diner where she works. When Harry arrives at the diner, he finds the pay telephone ringing. He picks up. On the other end is a panicky soldier. He has misdialed trying to reach his father. He's calling to warn his father a nuclear bomb is en route to Russia, and they are expecting Russia to follow suit. After some back and forth, Harry hears a door bust in, machine gun fire, and a new person picks up and asks to whom they are speaking. Was it a real call? Was it a joke? Harry can't decide and puts a lot of trust in the act of roundtabling his experience with various patrons of the late-night diner. Many stereotypes from '80s L.A are present, but don't expect them to react stereotypically. Of course at first, most of them think he is crazy. But light is shown on from an unexpected source and it's not long before everyone must make a quick decision on how to spend the next 30 to 40 minutes. Some of the patrons unite under a plan to escape L.A., but it's not an easy plan in itself. Washello has a plan, but has an errand to run first.

Miracle Mile is well executed for what it's trying to accomplish in terms of tension and character building. If all these people freak out unnecessarily or violence breaks out immediately, it would not be as interesting a film. The best parts of the movie come seeing how far people will go to make a point. It also serves as a nice time capsule for those who remember circa '50s to '80s nuclear hysteria. Some of you may remember drills ducking under grammar school desks as if that's going to somehow save you from a nuclear bomb. The film expresses the nuclear paranoia well for the generations that missed it. It's a good compliment to the 1964 film *Failsafe* starring Henry Fonda as the president of the United States. All that and some solid shots of L.A.'s Miracle Mile in the '80s makes this a fun watch.

Chapter 20: Serrated Edges

I was recently shopping in a record store where *Nightmare on Elm Street* (1984) was playing on the TV monitor in the used DVD section. I overheard a young woman tell her friend "Ugh, that blood is so fake." This made me sad. Where are we when we judge movies based on how red the blood is? Isn't this a small step on the road to stifling creativity? I don't want to live in a world where someone might be inhibited from making a horror movie because they can't get the blood right. This person's statement largely reflected my experience doing a film minor as a returning college student. I know everyone casts aspersions on the youth, particularly the youth in the arts, but I'm really worried about the state of narrative where success is judged by details like how real blood looks or whether or not one character would utter a particular line. I will always fight to defend movies with unclear endings. A real fear of the unknown can include a movie that leaves you wondering. It's one of my pet peeves when people can't see the value in a movie with a weird ending or arc.

God Told Me To (1976)
Directed by Larry Cohen
U.S.A. 91 min.

Winding plots riding precariously on the rails of reality are a lot more fun than "real" movie plots with little point. Director Larry Cohen has a penchant for the unusual. Among his best known works are cult classics like I*t's Alive* (1974) (and *It's Alive 2 & 3*), *Black Caesar* (1973), *The Stuff* (1985), *Maniac Cop* (1988) (and the *Maniac Cop* sequels), and much later, the author of *Phone Booth* (2002), a sniper story that brings us full circle to his an earlier film of his, *God Told Me To*. *God Told Me To* begins as a simple police procedural. Police detective Peter Nicholas (Tony Lo Bianco) is called out to speak to a man entrenched on top of a tower shooting pedestrians with a sniper rifle. Nicholas talks to the man as he slowly climbs towards the top of the tower. Nicholas wants him to come down, and just when it seems he might be making progress, the sniper informs Nicholas "God told me to" and abruptly jumps to his death. Nicholas goes on to investigate a series of attacks all with a similar curious ending: the assailants claim "God told me to." If you have a vague idea what might be prompting this behavior, be assured you could not accurately predict the maze of details woven to include virgin births, Catholic guilt, alien conspiracies, and a psychic cult leader hiding in an abandoned building. *God Told Me To* is a daring script with real scares and strange turns.

Lifeforce (1985)
Directed by Tobe Hooper
U.K. 116 min.

"Whoa! Did someone get the license number of that movie?"- Leonard Maltin

If you can't decide what sort of horror or sci-fi you're in the mood for, *Lifeforce* has a lot to offer. It's an ambitious film too convoluted for mainstream audiences upon its release, but gained a small cult following with sci-fi fans. The skeleton of the plot is based on the novel *The Space Vampires* by Colin Wilson, the basic plot of which is a vampire-adjacent tale of aliens coming to earth to suck the life out of people. This part of the plot follows a similar storyline to the regularly remade *Invasion of the Body Snatchers* without the pods. If it sounds straightforward, the movie has some berserk moments. There is a lot to inhale in the film.

The movie begins with the discovery of an alien life form incubating inside of Haley's Comet. The crew of the spaceship Churchill brings back the aliens, one of which is in the form of an attractive female never named in the screenplay. It's not long before she creates havoc among some slack-jawed men mesmerized by the alien's "aura," aka nudity. The film continues on to become an end of the world narrative where love among dissimilar creatures must prevail as London burns from massive explosions and zombie-like chases ensue. *Alien* (1979) screenwriter Dan O'Bannon and *Texas Chainsaw Massacre* (1974) director Tobe Hooper paired up for this extravaganza, which followed Hooper's massive directorial hit *Poltergeist*

(1982). This was also the first in a series of big budget films signaling disaster for the legendary Cannon Group, Inc. film company. Hoping to elevate their status, the Cannon Group fell headlong into an expensive flop with *Lifeforce*. It was a b-movie on an a-movie budget, going the wrong direction for the successful Cannon business model that had kept them turning a profit for so many years. Had this been an isolated misstep, the company might have survived, but they continued to throw away big money hoping for a hit that wouldn't come. But ultimately a lucky break for sci-fi fans 'cause they couldn't make a big budget misstep like this nowadays.

Session 9 (2001)
Directed by Brad Anderson
U.S.A. 100 min.

Although I regularly recommend *Session 9* to people, Rarely do they come back and tell me they enjoyed it. I don't know what it says about the movie. It's a classic labyrinthian horror set in a real life disused asylum, Danvers State Asylum in Danvers, Massachusetts, which was the inspiration for the story. Director Brad Anderson and writer Stephen Gevedon set out to write a movie about the decaying remains of Danvers before it was knocked down. Like many of its kind, these institutions were shut down en masse during the Reagan administration due to lack of funding. These mega institutions were no picnic, but they were an honest attempt to provide a home for people who had mental issues or other conditions impeding them from being able to care for themselves. With the closing of these institutions, the end result is disenfranchised people living in the street. But I'll digress from the politics of this phenomenon and return to the movie.

These buildings were big and often gothic treasures, and

Danvers was no exception. In the '90s, after sitting fallow, it became a dark, decrepit building full of spirits and props. Anderson and Gevedon wanted to make a movie about the place before it was demolished. Never mind that they had no story. It's enough inspiration. They wrote one. And it's a simple story in theory. Gordon Fleming (Peter Mullan) owns an asbestos abatement company. He's under some pressure to win the bid for the Danvers job. He needs it to save the company. His regular crew consists of Phil (David Caruso) who doesn't get along with Hank (Josh Lucas). Mike (Stephen Gevedon) is an intellectual who dropped out of law school and is treading water. Along the way, Mike discovers disturbing tapes of a series of psychological sessions from the institution's active days. Jeff (Brendan Sexton III) is Gordon's young cousin hired as a temp to help out with the big job. Jeff is nyctophobic, and yes that comes into play in this horror movie. Hank quits, or disappears; we're not sure. Phil suspects Gordon is losing his grip on reality. All of these situations create a mélange of plot firing in several directions. It sounds like a mess, but it keeps you guessing.

Despite the vastness of the asylum, the film is a claustrophobic affair. Sharp hallway shots create dread at opportune moments. P.O.V. shots from within environmental suits exemplify bleak moments. The film also utilizes excellent sound design with a minimal score, sparsely placed birds, and loud power generators. Caruso and Mullen are excellent friends turned foils as the two melt down over pressures related to the job. Caruso's histrionic acting is a great counter to Mullen's calm demeanor. As the burden of guilt regarding events on the job site escalates, Phil and Gordon suspect each other of malfeasance, but can't say for sure what kind. The conclusion of the film appears labyrinthian. It has been said the story doesn't have a satisfying conclusion, but thinking in raw terms of what is actually happening on the screen and not in their heads makes the movie a lot more interesting, especially if you're in for multiple screenings. The film is setting you up for a twist and doesn't necessarily provide one. The fact that things are on their own terms is scary enough. There are also enough dark alleys to keep you going.

Timecrimes (2007)
Directed by Nacho Vigalondo
Spain 92 min.

Héctor (Karra Elejalde) is enjoying a quiet day sitting in the backyard of his new house. His wife Clara (Candela Fernández) is assembling a table and shifting things around as you do when you move into a new place. Héctor surveys the ample property with a pair of binoculars. In the distance he sees a young woman undressing near the edge of the woods. His wife leaves on an errand and he again scans the woods to find the woman lying on the ground. She doesn't appear to be moving. Héctor investigates. Out on the street, a garbage can is overturned. A bicycle lies on the street near a path. Up the path he finds the woman. She is nude and unresponsive. He tries to wake her. Suddenly, a menacing looking man in a long coat wearing a blood soaked, pink bandage wrapped around his head stabs him in the arm. Héctor runs away. The man gives chase. In his haste to get away, Héctor breaks into a nearby laboratory and meets a scientist (Nacho Vigalondo). And here begins a chain of events where time travel creates multiple Héctors and a series of events interfering with the peace in the neighborhood.

If you're the type who tears apart every little detail of a time travel narrative, *Timecrimes* might not be for you. Héctor eventually begins to straighten out some of the events in the story, only to discover more pitfalls are around the corner. As he plays out scenarios he knows to be imminent, he becomes quite resourceful, relying on his memory to connect the details and work out his narrative of events. The bike is explained. The garbage can is explained. The naked woman is explained. But once we all arrive at these moments, there are a new series of details created to cope with. As it piles on, Héctor is worse for wear, but must soldier on in hopes of getting everything back in a straight line. It's a masterfully organized plot for how much it switches gears. For all the back and forth, you seldom question the characters' logic. Director (and actor portraying the scientist) Nacho Vigalondo has created a great low-budget feature with a smart narrative. The film utilizes the usual time travel rule; everything that is meant to happen is inexorable, but as the film progresses, we root for Héctor to throw in the right combination of wrenches to change the narrative. The small cast work well together. Karra Elejalde carries a lot of screen time as several Héctors and pulls it off with reasonable action sequences and moments of deflated humor. This and another low-budget feature called *Primer* (2004) show are still some unique stories down the avenues of time travel. It's a unique story with well-conceived consequences.

Chapter 21: Speak of the Devil

Here are four fun narratives featuring the ultimate antagonist.

Angel Heart (1987)
Directed by Alan Parker
U.S.A. 113 min.

Angel Heart has a lot of high water marks for its time. In an era where the '80s slasher movie was a banker at the box office, director Alan Parker let loose this slightly more complex horror-themed film whose hybrid status would be part of a new wave of psychological horror films and create a new avenue for more involved horror narratives from the late '80s to early '90s. It's an early example of more complex stories that take hints from other mature horror like Brian DePalma's *Sisters* (1972) and Stanley Kubrick's *The Shining* (1980). *Angel Heart* also helped break the dominant '80s template of typical slasher movies, initiating a trend of more mature scares like *Serpent and the Rainbow* (1988), *Jacob's Ladder* (1990), and *Silence of the Lambs* (1990), which ultimately created a wider market for both eclectic and mainstream horror.

Set against the backdrop of 1950s New York and New Orleans, the film has a noir style and devilish protagonist giving it a timeless quality. The production design creates a drab backdrop for New Orleans street-wise tropes and unseen societies. The look of early gangster and detective films gives the classic look of a modern American gothic. The art direction, cinematography, and costuming create a perfect dreary setting for a supernatural noir thriller. Mickey Rourke was also at the height of his first big burst of stardom.

Down-and-out New York private detective Harry Angel (Rourke) is going through a slump. Angel spends most of his time chasing down evidence for divorce proceedings and missing persons. He is hired by a socialite named Louis Cyphre (Robert DeNiro). Cyphre is an enigmatic but pleasant enough person. He wants Angel to locate a singer named Johnny Favorite who Cyphre claims disappeared under contract. Angel is suspicious that it's a dangerous case, but Cypher has the funds to wave around and assures him he only wants the singer found. Angel should have no further involvement. But locating Favorite is no picnic. Angel is chased out of New York to New Orleans, where clandestine rituals and voodoo curses hound his investigation. When the people Angel has asked about Favorite start turning up dead, detectives Deimos (Pruitt Taylor Vince) and Sterne

(Eliott Keener) become aware of Angel's snooping. Angel ends up on the run, but he doesn't know why.

It isn't hard to recognize early in the film that Cyphre isn't exactly who he says he is, but there is still a mystery in play and some great performances by Rourke, Charlotte Rampling, Lisa Bonet, DeNiro, and a host of excellent character actors. It's a solid film and deserves to be remembered for more than Bill Cosby objecting to Lisa Bonet's role portraying a voodoo priestess and Angel's lover, which might ring a bell to people of a certain age. There's a dark story in play here that is worth a watch.

Devil (2010)
Directed by M. Night Shyamalan
U.S.A. 80 min.

I have a grade I assign to certain horror/sci-fi movies called "*Twilight Zone* plot". A film might have "good Serling," i.e. an interesting storyline that encourages some thought, but the story nonetheless can't hold up the weight of a 90 minute-plus run time. Stephen King stories occasionally hit this wall while trying to make the jump to feature film. I hope it won't be too insulting to say director M. Night Shyamalan has made the list a couple of times. I don't think he's a bad director at all. People love to hate him for some reason, and I believe it's unwarranted. I admire him for taking chances and for his inventive storylines. We need more directors and writers who think along these lines. As an example, I don't think *The Village* was particularly a bad story; it just gave the audience too much time to sit around and think about what was going on. You're bound to run over enough scenarios in your head while watching *The Village* to at least imagine you've figured it out. Another good idea was the one where people kill themselves because they smell trees. What's wrong with that? That's a great plot in my opinion. These would have made an excellent *Twilight Zone* episode. A thing happens, and from nowhere a cigarette smoking Serling appears. Or Whittaker. Or Peele. I'm open.

In 2008, Shyamalan announced his intention to return to shorter form horror with *Devil*. It was supposed to be a series, but only *Devil* happened. It's a shame. I thought it was a great idea for him at the time. I was excited. *Devil* escapes into the realm of "good Serling" with a tight run time, a story as clever as it needs to be, some well-executed horror tropes, and performances rising above the material. The story opens on a clever aerial shot of Philadelphia. It's similar to the opening of *West Side Story* (1961), where you're transported across New York City in anticipation of seeing one of the millions of stories that make big city life so exciting. Only this tracking shot is of Philadelphia, and it shows the city upside down. This sets the tone for seeing one of the millions of stories in a city like Philadelphia. This one includes the Devil. And this one ain't gonna be *West Side Story*. Oh sure, this could be looked at as a sophomoric jab right from the pages of a film technique textbook, but if you're refusing to enjoy the ride, you might as well stop reading here.

In a busy office building, five seemingly random people get on an elevator. The elevator gets stuck. As horror movie stuff like flickering lights and inexplicable injuries occur, the contentious five turn on each other and suspect one another of various wrongdoings. And you suspect it because you're watching a movie. While this is going on, Detective Bowden (Chris Messina) is investigating a quickly-found-to-be-related crime and helping two security guards named Lustig (Matt Craven) and Ramirez (Jacob Vargas) get a hold of the elevator situation. See, these five random people are not as random as you think, and Bowden has been recently wronged, and Ramirez is a devout Catholic, and yadda yadda yadda.

The cast of *Devil* is solid across the board. Each elevator occupant reveals their true nature and past discrepancies efficiently and helps the story unfold over a neat 80 minute run time. The horror movie stuff is as good as it gets for a major motion picture. You're going to say the story is basically Agatha Christie's novel that goes under the revised title *And Then There Were None*. What's different about this version? C'mon! Shyamalan did it on an elevator. Don't you want to see that? Most movies wouldn't be movies without stealing from Christie or Hitchcock. This movie has enough posers and vague Catholic diatribes to keep you guessing and an ending that's largely unpredictable and vaguely satisfying. Plus the film has a cool poster. If Hammer Studios made it in the 1960s, this movie would have been a classic. If that sounds interesting, you shouldn't let your attitude keep you from watching *Devil*. And you can basically see it over a long lunch break.

Mr. Frost (1990)
Directed by Philippe Setbon
France/U.K. 104 min.

The story opens on two car thieves breaking into a garage of a wealthy estate. They want to steal an Aston Martin. They open the door of the luxury car and, to their surprise, find a dead body at the wheel. Later, detective Felix Detweiler (Alan Bates) inquires at the estate and finds it occupied by a lone mysterious man soon to be known as Mr. Frost (Jeff Goldblum). Mr. Frost is welcoming and candid, and when asked about the body in the car casually admits "I was just finishing burying it when you showed up." Twenty-four bodies are discovered in the lawn and Mr. Frost is taken into custody. On his way out he hands Detweiler a videotape. "I told you that I like trophies." We don't see the videos, but they evidently have an effect on Detweiler. Two years later, Detweiler is off the force due to mental instability and Mr. Frost is being admitted into a mental institution. In two years, no one has been able to identify Mr. Frost. He has lived as "off the grid" as any person in 1990.

The film draws the viewer in well with this subdued opening. The one-to-one between Detweiler and Mr. Frost is engagingly civilized. Bates and Goldblum play intriguing foils in the first minutes of the film. It's an indicator you won't be treated to the same old Satan narrative. Frost is taken to a mental hospital where he comes under the care of Dr. Sarah Day (Kathy Baker). Frost was placed there, but insists he chose Sarah. The two match wits with cheap psychology. He toys with her, performing little tricks around the facility. Along the way Mr. Frost makes obvious references to being the devil. At first she doesn't believe him, but strange occurrences in her life slowly change her mind.

The film is nicely shot. Utilizing long shots of the English countryside, unusual and unnatural lighting creating dread, and hokey religious imagery. It evokes the tone of the old Hammer horror pictures. Goldblum's performance is unusual, portraying the devil as smug and playfully arrogant, also striking an occasional odd tone. He can be even tedious at times, but recreating what it might be like to deal with the likes of Satan pessimistically knocking around the hospital where you work needling you to mess up is better suited for a performance of some tedium.

In the hospital with Frost is Christopher Kovac (François Négret), a young mental patient thriving at therapy until Frost's arrival. Kovac enhances the scare factor in the film with an eerie performance. Frost's presence upsets many of the patients at the hospital, but Kovac falls the hardest and adds a subplot bringing some needed unrest to the film. It could be unintentional, but it doesn't hurt that Kovac bears a strong resemblance to serial killer Richard Ramirez. As Sarah's life becomes complicated, it's apparent something must be done about Mr. Frost. He eventually offers a solution outside the typical psychological thriller realm. It's a fun movie if you enjoy psychological horror, and it has enough new alleyways so as not to be contrived.

Prince of Darkness (1987)
Directed by John Carpenter
U.S.A. 102 min.

John Carpenter doesn't need much help in either the cult movie arena or the mainstream movie category, as the legacy of his films like *Halloween* (1978), *Escape From New York* (1981), and *They Live* (1988) have exited the stratosphere of horror standards and become touchstones in mainstream filmmaking. He has a lot of great movies. If I had to say one was overlooked, it would be *Prince of Darkness*. It's a slightly complicated story with a weighty ensemble cast and Carpenter pulls it off masterfully.

The story centers on a priest played by longtime Carpenter collaborator Donald Pleasence. He contacts an old acquaintance and debate rival, the pragmatic Professor Birack (Victor Wong). The subject of their meeting is a big vat of green goo that is discovered in the basement of a monastery owned by the Brotherhood of Sleep, as if that's something you voluntarily want to mess with. And it's not the fun kind of slime like in *Ghostbusters* (1984). The goo is in a big vat labeled with some old satanic graffiti, so naturally, these guys figure they have to go in and investigate.

Professor Birack convinces his best students to assemble for a weekend of sleeping on cots and studying the phenomenon over a weekend in the monastery. The team consists of various boffins trained in computer technology, religion, language, numerology, etc... They all set up equipment and hunker in for a weekend of beers, take outs, and readouts. But the goo has a mind of its own and begins squirting the staff strategically making strange demon assistants out of the crew one person at a time. The as yet unaffected begin dreaming about the same evil things. Meanwhile, homeless people are gathering outside the building and killing anyone trying to leave. (One of the homeless is played by our beloved Alice Cooper, which is neat, but also distracting at times.) The goo works serial killer-style, picking off the students one by one until the numbers tip and there are more student demons running around the building than live students. Now they are trapped and trying to figure out how to survive and how to cope with the gross demon influx. I don't want to say too much more, but eventually a demon sees a mirror, and then the shit really hits the fan.

My description might be a bit glib, but it's really a creepy movie with good gothic and supernatural nonsense woven together by a talented cast of familiar character actors bringing good weight and delivering some of the Carpenter-style humor. Carpenter keeps the weighty cast alive as the demons close in. The special effects are fun and gross with some solid Italian and Hammer influence. Sometimes you're not sure what you're looking at, but it's scary. Carpenter calls this the second in his "Apocalypse Trilogy" the first film being *The Thing* (1982) and the third being *In the Mouth of Madness* (1994). So *Prince of Darkness* is in good company.

Chapter 22: Stepchildren

Quentin Tarantino's *Jackie Brown* inspired my thinking about the stepchild film. When I saw it in 1997, people in the theater were palpably disappointed. I heard the words "pulp" and "fiction" from every conversation as the audience filed out of the theater. Of course, this is not a new thing. Stepchild fever ruins careers and steers audiences away from great films. *Jackie Brown* has since had much re-evaluation. It's still my favorite Tarantino movie. I love the scope of the story, particularly the weighty ensemble cast that never gets lost in the telling of the story. The movies in this chapter suffered from the success of their predecessors.

After Hours (1985)
Directed by Martin Scorsese
U.S.A. 97 min.

My grandfather used to say watching *Casablanca* (1942) was like visiting with old friends. I feel similarly about *After Hours*. I fell in love with the version of New York City created in *After Hours*. I wanted to live in that New York City: a mysterious place where crazy artists hang around sparsely filled diners and nightclubs. Where the conversations take you down stranger avenues than the art. Where people dance to Bad Brains records in nightclubs. It was a place where everything cool happened late at night. No movie buff can definitively say they have a favorite movie without flopping a bit, but *After Hours* comes to mind for me when someone asks me. I've watched it dozens of times and I never get tired of it. I like showing it to people and seeing their reactions. I like to see how I've grown since I first saw it as a teenager.

Paul Hackett (Griffin Dunne) is a computer programmer working a mundane office job. The movie follows him after work to his apartment, and then for a late-night sandwich in a coffee shop. There he meets Marcy (Rosanna Arquette) who gives him the number for the loft where she is staying in the artist-centric Soho neighborhood. This was back when artistic types could afford to live in Soho. Paul calls her when he gets home and Marcy invites him over. During his cab ride, a sharp breeze catches Paul's only $20 bill and sends it out the window. Later, after a bizarre time with Marcy, Paul has no money to get a cab or take a train home. Paul is "trapped" (at least in an academic, Kafkaesque sort of way) in Soho and has bizarre encounters with the neighborhood night owls. There's a waitress obsessed with '60s culture named Julie (Teri Garr), two burglars named Neil and Pepe (Cheech Marin and Tommy Chong),

Marcy's roommate Kiki (Linda Fiorentino) and her boyfriend Horst (Will Patton), and Mister Softee truck driver Gail (Catherine O'Hara), among others who make his egress from the neighborhood difficult. Paul is so normal that people begin to suspect him of various wrongdoings in the neighborhood, culminating into a late night chase that is both bizarre and terrifying. The humor is muted and self-referential. As Paul tries over and over again to get home, the situation becomes bleak, even though in reality, he's not really that far from home. Even Paul mentions in haste at one point, "I'm gonna walk home. I'm just going to walk home." Scorsese directed this film after production funds for *The Last Temptation of Christ* were pulled. *Temptation* went on hiatus, and Scorsese has stated he was thinking of giving up on filmmaking all together before this production came along. If that's true, *After Hours* is not only a great film, but spared us the loss of some classics that would not have been made if Scorsese had given up on the industry. It's funny as and odd as a New York City story gets with the experienced eye of a great director finding new blood in a young and anarchic screenplay.

Barry Lyndon (1975)
Directed by Stanley Kubrick
U.K. 187 min.

Barry Lyndon is a prototype for the stepsister film. Kubrick's success with *A Clockwork Orange* (1971) had a lot of people wondering what he would do next. Kubrick's epic period piece took many people off-guard. And on a large scale apparently. *Barry Lyndon* was a box office failure, perceived to be dull to audiences and excessively cold to many critics. Although it performed better in Europe, American audiences were not responding to it. Based on the novel *The Luck of Barry Lyndon* published in 1844 by William Thackeray, Ryan O'Neal portrays young Redmond Barry, a young, middle-class man living with his mother in Ireland who through a series of fateful events becomes adept at devious skill sets allowing him to cut corners and obtain a the title of a rich man, Barry Lyndon. The film follows him from an incident during his teenage life in Ireland which forces him into the English Army, and then later into the service of the Prussian army during the Seven Years War. A calm and sure narrator (Michael Hordern) occasionally gives purposefully misinterpreted versions of events on the screen with a sly attitude. His blasé technique provides the audience context into the attitudes of the era, but in a way comes across as if the narrator, without being god-like, is somehow himself above the events in the film. This is most often played for humor, although at times can also punctuate sharp insights into the human condition.

Some reviews criticize O'Neal for his lack of presence in the film, but his knack for playing dumb to his own ends blends into the precision of the pace and the beautiful cinematography. He is very believable as the rogue playing naïve. Much positive praise for the film is written about cinematographer John Alcott's innovative shots using natural light, and in the case of indoor scenes, using candlelight to create a natural look for the film. His contribution to the shots go a long way to creating a pastoral world around the characters. The pacing allows for an unromantic look at 18th century lifestyles and class structure. During a scene involving Barry's fistfight with fellow soldier Corporal Toole (Pat Roach), Kubrick eschews the use of triumphant music and a tense standoff, but relies rather on filming simple boxing moves and the cheers of the other soldiers surrounding the fight. This fistfight is insignificant to the plot except to say Barry can stand up to larger challenges, but the unceremonious boxing climax is a microcosm of how the story is told. Barry barely reacts to his victory; his fellow soldiers carry him off. Even the battle scenes are shot with some sense of disengagement. It illuminates detached attention to duty required to fight in battles during the time of the Seven Years War, a time before guerrilla warfare was considered civil. The film captures a portrait of 18th century Europe while creating a relatable story showing class as a hard and bitter barrier to cross, even if you have money. This idea is relatable today as it was then. The film creates its own world out of an era of history without using tricks and shortcuts.

Trafic (1971)
Directed by Jacques Tati
France 96 min.

Trafic opens on an automobile manufacturing line. We watch a panel of a car pressed out by a machine over and over again. Scenes loosely walk the viewer through the process of assembling a car. From the viewpoint of director Jacques Tati, this is a whimsical process. The monotony of the factory work is meticulously covered so by the time the cars roll out, the act of assembling them has become humorous through repetition. The whole sequence is unmistakably Tati. He had a way of deriving humor from unappealing monotony. Afterwards, the cars are carefully parked one after the other in an endless parking lot: a sea of prosperity. Later in the film we pass an automobile graveyard. It's not that shocking. We all know this happens. But in his films commentary is betrothed to the humor of the film around the edges like an ornate picture frame. He doesn't hit you in the head with it, but it's there.

After the film gets going a bit we see an advertisement for an auto show taking place in Amsterdam and then we see a quick shot of Tati's comic alter ego Monsieur Hulot briskly walking away from the camera. He is bursting from a café and into the side streets of Paris. Hulot always has the appearance of being late for something. In *Trafic*, Hulot, as a character featured through the canon of Tati films, is moving up in the world. He's gainfully employed and charged with getting a state-of-the-art camper from Paris to the car show in Amsterdam. Details of the many of the esoteric features of the camper are being finalized in the last minutes before leaving for the show. Knowing Tati, this will be an endless bucket of gags, but alas, while the camper is being perfected, the truck meant to take it to Amsterdam turns out to have real problems. The broad strokes of the movie involve trying to get the camper to the car show in time. Meanwhile, the vehicle carrying the display, a giant log and boards painted to look fake, arrives at the show in time.

Trafic was made in the wake of *Playtime* (1967). *Playtime* is largely regarded as Tati's masterpiece, but at the time it did not do well in theaters and Tati went bankrupt finishing the production as it wrapped several times over its budget. At the time, *Trafic* was not taken seriously. It was considered the film Tati could afford to make at the time. His next film *Parade* (1974) also remains largely forgotten due to the weight and controversy of the production of *Playtime*. But *Trafic* has much of the pastoral charm of his other productions, particularly *Mon Oncle*. Watched in succession, *Mon Oncle* and *Trafic* bookend Playtime bringing this enormous production back down to earth where Hulot sadly wanders off at the end of *Trafic*. It's a sad farewell to Tati's unique view on society, but it's scary how relevant his vision remains.

Chapter 23: Threes

In the days before the Marvel Universe method where the third, fourth and fifth installments of franchises are planned out and merchandised while the first film is still in pre-production, thirds could prove to be tricky. The first film in a trilogy used to determine a need for a second. The second answers some questions. The third sometimes has issues. *Star Wars. The Godfather. Spider Man. The Naked Gun.* Thirds are often the most risky and delicate in a series. Should we do something different? What should we do differently? Are people tired of what was working in the last two movies? Here are some thirds with distinct changes in tone and structure. I love these movies, but I get why maybe they didn't float the franchise at the time. Either way, these films keep it interesting.

Alien 3 (1992)
Directed by David Fincher
U.S.A. 114 min.

Alien 3 opens on an ominous note: one violin string cleverly held over from the 20th Century Fox theme and following the shot into the sky towards black space. It's a campy little intro with a fun sense of dread. In some sense, we know what's coming. A montage during the credits tells the story of what's happened since the last picture: a story often frustrating fans of the previous film, James Cameron's *Aliens* (1986). Complaints often stem from the crash at the beginning of *Alien 3* negating the story we rooted for in the previous film. I won't say why, but I'll admit, it is frustrating. *Alien 3* slogs to square one with the alien and regularly surviving character Ellen Ripley (Sigourney Weaver) again trapped in a situation where the alien is going to go bananas and no one will believe she knows what she's talking about until people start showing up torn apart. And to be fair, yes, that happens in *Alien 3*. This is the great suspense director David Fincher's directorial debut, which he has disassociated himself from. Why should we care so much about this movie?

With all due respect to James Cameron and the legacy that is the *Alien* franchise, I posit there are more actual problems with *Aliens* than with this movie. Cameron had things going for him. Fincher didn't. For instance, the advantage of being able to turn the aliens into targets for an action movie. Like zombies or Nazis, no one is going to lament the death of an alien, so Cameron can set up as much shooting action as he wants.

Aliens has great action and great characters, but think about it: *Aliens* is 137 minutes of shooting at aliens. Also, people remember the great things about that movie. I think the last half hour of *Aliens* is sort of silly and a little boring. Ripley casually poking around looking for Newt when everyone else dies pretty quickly after confronting an alien removes some of the weight of the previous 90 minutes. Then she actually saves Newt, but as the clock runs down, she takes the time to stop and blow up resting aliens that would have blown up five minutes later? It calls into question the judgment of our regularly pragmatic Ripley.

I enjoy *Aliens*, but I find *Alien 3* much more clever and world building to the franchise. Ripley survives the last movie, only to have her escape pod crash on a lonely, mostly forgotten prison planet where a few male prisoners are keeping the facility open. Among them are some great performances: Charles Dance portrays Jonathan Clemens, one of the smarter prisoners who held a doctorate before being caught doing whatever he was doing. Charles S. Dutton as Lenard Dillon, who is sort of a religious leader to the lonely men. Superintendent Harold Andrews (Brian Glover) reiterates the story once again from the point of view of the prisoners. There are enough personalities in the cast to have some genuine moments of horror-style bloodshed, and enough plot to keep some characters to keep alliances a mystery. Ripley suspects why the pod crashed, and yes, we will be back to the formula of a handful of people being picked off by our big, acid-filled serial killer. But there are a mélange of plot points pulling from subdued action films like William Friedkin's *Sorcerer* (1977).

Exorcist III (1990)
Directed by William Peter Blatty
U.S.A. 110 min.

William Peter Blatty, author of original *The Exorcist* (1973), adapted his novel Legion for the screenplay of *The Exorcist III*. The film ignores the events of *Exorcist II: The Heretic* (1977) and replaces the bad spirit from Legion (or basically it's the same demon depending on how you approach it: it's the Devil, no reason to split hairs here). The story follows Lt. William F. Kinderman (George C. Scott) and Father Dyer (Ed Flanders). The two have a friendship forged through their connection with Father Damien Karras (spoiler alert if you haven't seen The Exorcist), the priest who died falling down the famously steep stairs in Washington D.C.'s Georgetown neighborhood performing Regan MacNeil's exorcism fifteen years earlier. These two haven't forgotten the night Father Damien saved Regan's life. Who could?

The second solid connection with the first film is actor Jason Miller, who portrayed Father Damien Karras in The Exorcist and portrays the demon in *Exorcist III*. Here, he alternately claims to be the demon and also claims to be the long-dead Gemini Killer James Venamun (Brad Dourif). The Gemini Killer is molded from the real life Zodiac Killer. It's a brilliant adaptation for many reasons. Firstly, it unfurls loose ends and allows the screenwriter to pull from two established stories. It makes for a nice dense plot that is much better than it needs to be successful. Miller and Dourif are terrifying as the demon. Miller we remember from the first film where he was nominated for an Academy Award for his portrayal of Father Karras. Dourif is one of those excellent character actors who uplifts any production he is a part of. Both put in intense performances as the demon pulling strings outside of his hospital room. Scott also puts in a great performance, or at least a performance worthy of the picture. He works as a sarcastic, no-nonsense policeman who witnessed some pretty outrageous stuff fifteen years ago.

The film should also be noted for excellent scares and strange dream sequences. The cinematography rewards patience. One such horror sequence follows a nurse up and down a hallway doing rounds to an nth degree, and then showcasing long shots of quick tension instead of concentrating on gory details. While pressure causes Kinderman to have drama sequences that are a bit ridiculous, they also follow the logic of dreams, causing unease more effectively than if they had been trying to rely exclusively on horror imagery. Here, we not only have scary shots of a Gemini victim haunting Kinderman and a crucifix opening its eyes, but also shots of Fabio sitting casually as an angel. Whether or not you think it's a good movie, *Exorcist III* pushes some envelopes. It's an interesting movie across the board. *The Exorcist* upped the stakes of what a mainstream horror movie can be. *Exorcist II: The Heretic* flopped and maintains a reputation in the canon of bad films. It should have killed the franchise. *Exorcist III* is an unlikely film, but really takes the baton and ups the stakes. It really is a must see for horror fans.

Halloween III: Season of the Witch (1982)
Directed by Tommy Lee Wallace
U.S.A. 98 min.

Halloween III has outshined the canon of the *Halloween* series to the point it may not actually belong on this list. However, when I was growing up, it was a serious stepchild film, one that, because it failed to bring back iconic killer Michael Myers, was considered a real miss for the horror genre and for the successful *Halloween* series. I'm sure that you've heard that they were going to make a yearly Halloween-related story from scratch: a sort of feature film *Creepshow* or *Tales from the Crypt*. Alas, this film did not do well, and *Halloween 4* found Michael Meyers running rampant around Illinois once more. I've always loved this film and lamented the loss of the anthology series that could have been. Think of all the crazy stories that could be out there if any of them had been on the level of *Halloween III: Season of the Witch*. Sure, III is absurd. It couldn't really happen. It's an absurd story with absurd characters. But it's an earnest little film hung on a plot I've never seen duplicated anywhere.

The film follows Dr. Dan Challis (Tom Atkins) as he helps Ellie Grimbridge (Stacey Nelkin) investigate the mysterious death of her father. Clues lead to a small town in California called Santa Mira. The main industry in Santa Mira is Silver Shamrock Novelties, a company producing this year's hot Halloween masks. But something isn't right at the factory. They telegraph that punch over and over again. The masks are dangerous. The people guarding the factory are dangerous. When you finally get to the big picture, it's held on the wall by a pretty loose nail.

Stacy Nelkin does a good job taking the reins from Jamie Lee Curtis as the girl in trouble. Nelkin has '80s energy and enough intelligence to keep her from just being a generic young woman in harm's way. She plays the role with a P.J. Soles vibe. Neikin was also in the rock 'n' roll concert movie *Get Crazy* (1983). John Carpenter regular and character actor Tom Atkins is beautifully miscast here, fumbling through this strange adventure with half a beer buzz hanging over his head. He's not your typical action hero, but he does make the movie fun to watch with a crowd. Veteran actor Dan O'Herlihy portrays novelty tycoon Conal Cochran, the head of Silver Shamrock. The film has great b-movie flair. It has a few Halloween scares and some great lore. It's not the best horror movie you'll ever watch, but you won't see this plot anywhere else either.

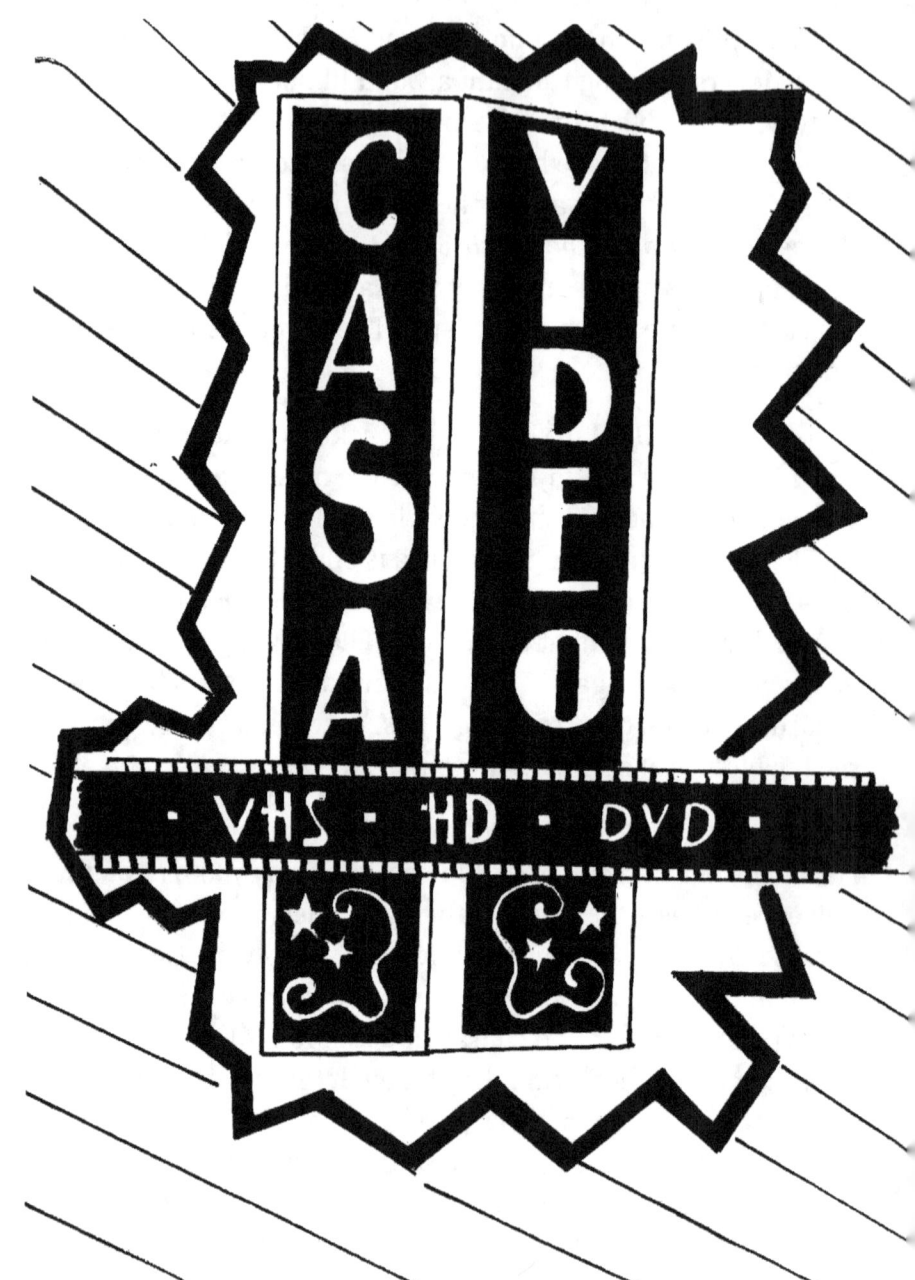

Chapter 24:
And ten more...

'Cause who doesn't like a bonus round... Let's do a bonus round. Here are ten movies I enjoy that didn't totally fit in with the other categories. You can make a case to shove them in here and there, but I feel all of these had strong crossover appeal or at least a strange point of view.

Bad Influence (1990)
Directed by Curtis Hanson
U.S.A. 100 min.

Rob Lowe is going through an interesting second act in recent years, as honed on the hit 2000s TV show *Parks and Recreation*. On the show, Lowe portrays a government pencil pusher whose reassuring advice and calm life philosophy support his alternate persona as a pious health guru in a small town in Indiana. This guise has followed Lowe in many of his appearances since. Many fans of *Parks and Rec* either didn't live through or have forgotten Lowe's wild Brat Pack party days. Fewer people still remember or got to see the film *Bad Influence*, a stark movie that came and went in 1990. It's a film that may very well have taken Lowe's adult career a different direction had things gone differently.

Here, Lowe portrays a mysterious and unrooted man named Alex who is a master of deceit, a man with all the charm and grace of a classic gigolo and con man. He is always one step ahead of his new acquaintance Michael Boll (James Spader). If you recall Spader in the '80s, you'll see here he is also playing against his standard roles. Spader as a teen actor played the baddie preppie in many high school dramas. Here he's a bit of a wimp. People are taking advantage of him at work. People in general push him around. He's engaged to a woman he's not sure about and doesn't want to get married. He buys things he thinks he needs because he can get a good deal. He's having a similar existential crisis to the "narrator" in *Fight Club* (1999). And similar to *Fight Club*, here comes a friend to solve his existential woes. Alex fixes some of his problems, but he does so in a way where he always has bigger issues to hold over his head. Before long Boll is in a position where he can't even prove "Alex" exists. He has to make some risky moves with his timid but loyal brother Pismo (Christian Clemenson) at his side.

Any parents who would name their child "Pismo" shouldn't be surprised when he turns out to be a massive stoner, but this is what Boll has to work with.

The basic plot is akin to Alfred Hitchcock's *Strangers on a Train* (1951), in which two people randomly meet and form a symbiotic relationship. Michael cannot see that Alex is way more sophisticated than he is until it is too late. Alex has his hand elbow deep in Michael's life in no time. By the time Michael realizes he is in over his head, Alex has involved him in too many situations. He can't go to the police. But that's not enough for Alex. It's obviously a game to him. He won't let up. And Rob Lowe sells this beautifully. His dubious smile and street-justice philosophy is endlessly attractive until you realize he has involved you in things you can't handle. Had he befriended me, I wouldn't have seen him coming.

The movie is set in Los Angeles in the '90s, but maintains a timeless feel as you follow the characters through street scenes populated with landmarks and club scenes which, while a bit dated, aren't far from what you might imagine a clandestine L.A. club might look like. While not as intentionally brutal as *Se7en* (1995) or as diabolically vague as *The Usual Suspects* (1995), this well-written cat-and-mouse is a precursor to these films with a dark tone that is achieved with noir and horror tropes mixing with real life.

Diamond Men (2000)
Directed by Dan Cohen
U.S.A. 100 min.

Diamond Men is a charming film about a salesman facing an abrupt end to a long and successful career. Eddie Miller (Robert Forester) is a regional jewelry salesman. He works for a big company carrying their line to jewelry stores in small towns in Pennsylvania. He has worked the same sales route for years. Week after week he drives around visiting owners and supplying their wholesale needs. His clients like him. He's suited to the lifestyle and makes a good living. But Miller has recently had a heart attack, and the company now says he is too expensive to insure as a traveling salesman. The company wants him off the road. To replace him they hire Bobby Walker (Donnie Wahlberg). Walker is a natural salesman in his own way. He's a fast talker. He's adept at picking up women. But the nuances of selling a delicate line of expensive products to small town jewelers is a little out of his skill set. The company convinces Miller to take Walker on the road with him for a few weeks to show him the ropes, essentially showing him how to do his job so they can fire him.

If you're already thinking it, yes, this is a buddy road movie about two mismatched characters forced to get along due to circumstance. Miller is good at his job because he's so mild mannered. Walker is bad at Miller's job because he's too forward. Walker gets on Miller's nerves. Forester and Wahlberg play a great team as two salesmen forced to get along and eventually gain a mutual respect for each other, almost exactly as the plot dictates. Forester is an experienced actor with a talent for the understated. Wahlberg is, well, a Wahlberg. But the two are brilliant as a comedic duo. The dialogue is well written, and as the miles pass, both actors sell their characters well. The film works as the typical indie-buddy movie where the audience warms to the eccentric characters as described.

But there is a nefarious twist in this story.

One of the other things making Miller so good at his job is his natural paranoia. There is a lot of danger inherent in being a regional diamond salesman. Professional thieves know how diamonds get into small town shops and opportunist thieves don't hesitate to rob them. They're carrying over a million dollars in jewelry at any given time traveling back roads in Pennsylvania. In the course of a day, it isn't unusual for Miller to abruptly slam on his brakes, make long detours around towns, and dart down alleys to observe if he's being followed. The sight of loiterers makes him nervous. Walker takes the situation seriously, but never fully realizes how vulnerable they are. The screenplay written by director Dan Cohen is superb. Miller and Walker's back and forth as they get to know each other is refreshing. Their unlikely friendship is entertaining and believable. Cohen also weaves the buddy road movie trope seamlessly into an interesting crime story. I won't say more for fear of giving the plot away, but this is a smart and severely underrated movie.

The Duellists (1977)
Directed by Ridley Scott
U.K. 100 min.

The Duellists is Ridley Scott's first feature film, and is a beautifully shot one. From here he went on to make his classic *Alien* (1979). Here he's more down to earth with this tale based on a Joseph Conrad short story following the life of two soldiers in Napoleon's army. These men carry on a series of duels over a period of sixteen years. The two men are Armand d'Hubert (Keith Carradine), an upstanding soldier dedicated to his role in the army, and Gabriel Feraud (Harvey Keitel), a Napoleon loyalist fighting in the army. Feraud's standards of loyalty are difficult to define, but these are two similar men fighting with slightly divergent moral compasses. One nice day in Strasbourg in 1800, d'Hubert is sent to arrest Feraud. Feraud has already been accused of dueling with another soldier. The movie presents Feraud as having quite a chip on his shoulder as part of his regular demeanor, but the movie also suggests it doesn't take much for the bravado of Napoleon's men to take the lead in their interactions. The point is, the arrest probably won't amount to much, but Feraud is incensed at the idea of being arrested by one of his own. Feraud goads d'Hubert into a brawl of a duel. The scuffle angers d'Hubert's superiors. Both would be subject to larger punishments, but Napoleon is short of men, and so instead, they are sent to fight as good soldiers in high demand. The unyielding Feraud seeks out d'Hubert for another brawl, and in this round, d'Hubert is run through with a thin dueling sword and classic crossword puzzle answer epee. Although d'Hubert will live, he can't continue the fight. Here is one of the more compelling moments in the film: Feraud's second suggests that they "Shake hands and forget it. Whatever he's done, you've paid him back now. From what I hear he's a very decent fellow." Feraud is unmoved: "Next time d'Hubert!!" he yells as he walks away.

At the time the film was released, Keitel and Carradine were criticized for their performances. Keitel and Carradine do stand out a bit among an excellent cast of character actors, most of whom could likely act circles around the American stars at that point in their careers. Some of what we expect from Keitel and Carradine does bleed into the story a bit. However Keitel's brutish posturing and Carradine's hippy reservations about fighting permeate just enough to make the characters more interesting. The pair are like the eye of the storm, swirled around by the supporting cast as they highlight the distasteful nature of dueling as compared to the very regimented lifestyle of Napoleon's army. Keitel portrays Feraud with a hint of angry Brooklyn bookmaker energy in his voice and mannerisms. He is as tough and hard to reason with as a brick wall. Feraud will return again and again, in spite of the fact that a lot of his colleagues think it's silly. Time passes and we find them, again, quite randomly dueling; this time with sabers. Their choice of weapon escalates the battle into one of ripped and bloodied clothes, heavy breathing, and brutal clanging. Those watching must intervene when the two men end up wrestling on the ground, no longer able to lift their swords. As illegal as this all is, d'Hubert manages to escape the stigma of being a duelist and continues to move up in the army. Feraud keeps his head above water, but has trouble in his career as favor shifts while Europe's borders are in transition. One primary theme in this movie is duty, whereas d'Hubert continues to fight out of honor and Feraud continues to fight out of hatred. Like two atoms, they meet and spin with each other until the situation burns itself out. They eventually forget what sets off all of this fighting, but we benefit from excellent fight sequences, consuming, and performances. Especially if you enjoy period pieces, *The Duellists* is a good one and a nice companion to Stanley Kubrick's *Barry Lyndon* (1975).

In Bruges (2008)
Directed by Martin McDonagh
U.S.A./U.K. 107 min.

Pulp Fiction (1994) popularized the archetype of two dangerous men working closely together forming a symbiotic work relationship including interesting small talk and an unlikely bond of caring for one another. *In Bruges* presents a similar dynamic with a hint of unsentimental tenderness between professional killers Ray (Colin Farrell) and Ken (Brendan Gleeson). They aren't super buddies, but generally they are both on the same page professionally. The duo are sent to spend two weeks in Bruges, Belgium due to a botched assassination in London. Their employer Harry (Ralph Fiennes) arranges the trip to keep them out of the way until things cool off. Quickly, the two get on each other's nerves. They have trouble keeping their heads down. When they arrive, they find only one hotel reservation. It's near Christmas, and Bruges is booked solid, so there's no hope for another room; they have to share. Ken is a bit older, and embraces the opportunity to sightsee, hang around the historic town, and await instructions. Ray is younger and impatient. He can't sit still. Ray manages to get into regular trouble in the historic Belgian town. He can't even sit outside and wait for Ken to climb the Belfort tower without getting into a fight. As the two try to maintain a low profile, they trade activities. But while Ken takes in local sights, Ray further exposes their precarious situation when he comes across a movie being filmed in town and meets Chloé (Clémence Poésy). The two get involved in partying with members of the eclectic cast, foreign prostitutes, and eccentric locals. Ray commits a few misdemeanors in town and scuffles with tourists. Then Ken receives a call from Harry with instructions for the trip. Their attempts to lay low become strained and Harry is forced to come to Bruges and intervene. When Harry enters the story, everyone's loyalties are tested.

The movie works on a lot of levels, but none more charming than the rapport between Ray and Ken as no-nonsense hard men out of water. While visiting the Grotius Museum Ray comments: "They all have funny names, don't they?" to which Ken replies: "Yea, Flemish." It's not all push and pull between the two. McDonagh really strikes gold with the dynamic with the two actors working for comedy. In Bruges is far from just a comedy. Ray's mistake on the London job appears in flashback and we soon learn we're dealing with a darker secret than expected. There is a compelling action movie brewing as it turns out Bruges was not entirely an arbitrary city for them to hide in. An excellent and mysterious score by Coen Brothers regular Carter Burwell also furthers the ominous proceedings. McDonagh as writer and director brings all the elements together for one of the most unforgettable and unpredictable endings these men could bring on each other. It's an absolute must-see for fans of Coen-style action.

The Last Days of Disco (1998)
Directed by Will Stillman
U.S.A. 113 min.

It's easy to be drawn to the fables of the American disco scene in the 1970s. Sex, drugs, and costumes make great background for stories. Will Stillman's *The Last Days of Disco* takes an interesting approach, removing the story from the typical underworld characters and leaving it to be told by the fringe players of the New York City nightclub scene. The club they frequent is never named, but it's a large one resembling the legendary Studio 54. Like 54, the average patrons wait and grovel behind velvet ropes set up on the street for a chance to get past a small group of decisive bouncers. From here the story is told from the point of view of the regulars with day jobs: recent college graduates working entry-level office positions in finance and publishing. Besides being church for the disenchanted, these clubs were playgrounds for the emerging "yuppie" movement. The characters here sometimes don't realize their roles. Des (Chris Eigman), who works at the club as a low-level door manager, talks about his situation: "I wish we were yuppies. Young, upwardly mobile, professional. Those are good things, not bad things." The characters often don't see the flaws in their logic.

Other members of this group of friends are Alice (Chloë Sevigny), who lives with her workmate, the excessively narcissistic Charlotte (Kate Beckinsale). Both work in publishing and go clubbing on the weekends. Charlotte and Alice have entire conversations about the minutiae of getting in the club. They are the subsidies in a way: the club can't let everyone in, but they have to let someone in, and often it's young women. But they are convinced of weird lore like people getting out of cabs get in more often, so they walk up to a block or two away to save money and then pay taxis to take them the rest of the way.

Director and writer Will Stillman's stylized dialogue and dry humor is astoundingly thought provoking. He makes the inane appear perceptive, particularly in the blasé fashion characters blurt out inane ideas. That said, occasionally the desperation of youth causes the dialog to be poignant. Charlotte verbally beats on Alice endlessly throughout the film, although Charlotte's passive-aggressive voice is so sharp it often ends with Alice just slumping and blowing it off. Charlotte has one moment where she tries to fix their dynamic during an argument with Alice: "Anything I did that was wrong, I apologize for. But anything I did that was not wrong, I don't apologize for." Isn't this thinking the commerce of youth? Stillman's dialogue and insight into the banal philosophy of the upper-middle class is excellent. The most unrealistic thing here is this group hearing one other over the music. But one must overlook this to enjoy the film, because they are in the disco a lot and this is a dialogue-heavy film. The story is contextualized by a news clip of scenes from the Disco Demolition night at Comiskey Park where fans at a Chicago Cubs game got out of hand while trying to blow up a pile of disco records. We're also reminded of how the spread of sexual diseases became more relevant in the '80s. Towards the end, a few of the characters meet outside the unemployment office where they discuss having lived through a period that's ended. Then Josh Neff (Matt Keeslar) makes an impassioned speech about how disco mattered and will go through a period where it is derided, but will eventually make a return. It's a good rant about how disco has been perceived. The movie plays as a solid period piece, but also really captures something about being in your twenties, whether you lived this lifestyle or not. If you think you were smarter than the people in this movie, you probably weren't.

One False Move (1992)
Directed by Carl Franklin
U.S.A. 105 min.

One False Move is a surprising low-budget movie utilizing the tropes of a typical '90s indie crime drama while simultaneously pulling the characters in directions you wouldn't necessarily expect. The film leads the audience cleverly down a few dark alleys while interweaving a brutal crime story with an uncertain ending. The main story follows criminals Ray Malcolm (Billy Bob Thornton), "Fantasia" Walker (Cynda Williams), and Pluto (Michael Beach). The trio pulls off a drug robbery ending with several brutal and unnecessary deaths. Ray and Pluto are ex prison mates. Both are clear sociopaths, but not in that fun way like in Quentin Tarantino movies where sociopathic behavior inspires witty banter. These guys have a lobe loose. They can't agree with each other about anything and always look as if they have their guard up, even around each other. Their opening crime spree ends brutally with notes of the real-time video feel of *Henry: Portrait of a Serial Killer* (1986) in its violence and horrific portrayal of an apathetic crime. It's a raw, grainy, and somewhat unnecessary chain of events. It's kind of a bummer, actually, but it gets your attention quickly. Flush with cocaine and cash, the trio head out on a road trip to Philadelphia to sell the cocaine. Not to give too much away, but circumstances dictate there will be a stop in Star City, Arkansas, Walker's hometown. After this is established, we cut to Star City, Sheriff Dale "Hurricane" Dixon (Bill Paxton) getting ready for work. We discover Dixon is a simple man in a town with a police force of about three to five officers. Dixon is well-respected by his constituents, but does not possess much of the small town wisdom and ingrained country knowledge that could play a major role in solving the big city case. Dixon talks fast and kicks up dust everywhere he goes. The character is steeped in a lot of the magical Bill Paxton energy the movie needs to stay interesting. The investigation is led by cynical homicide detectives McFeely (Earl Billings) and Cole (Jim Metzler). McFeely and Cole believe the suspects are heading to Star City and ask for Dixon's help in showing them around. Yes, they come out to Star City on a hunch, which seems a little far-fetched, but the three strike up a friendship and you tend not to mind as you realize some sort of stand off is on the way. Some of the movie is just a waiting game to see if the bad guys show, but this doesn't get dull as the characters are developed juxtaposed against the criminal's movements. As the movie progresses, the baddies do more terrible things and take steps towards turning on each other. Meanwhile, the police wait hoping the bad guys are heading that way. Dixon also has a secret that will complicate the proceedings, but there is no way to get into that here. This low-budget picture is better than it needs to be to entertain: well written, well acted, and has a realistic feel that at times is genuinely eerie.

Take Shelter (2011)
Directed by Jeff Nichols
U.S.A. 121 min.

Take Shelter opens on Curtis LaForche (Michael Shannon) staring at the clouds. It's a quiet moment in the life of a quiet man. LaForche lives in LaGrange, Ohio with his wife Samantha (Jessica Chastain) and his deaf daughter Hannah (Tova Stewart). LaForche has a good life. He works regular hours. He has beers with friends after work. He gets along with his wife and daughter. He's not without life's tribulations. His daughter is due for surgery that could help her regain her hearing. He is sleeping. He's having apocalyptic dreams; intriguing George

Romero-type end-of-the-world style vignettes with zombie attacks and visions of general human pallor. He notices birds flying in strange patterns and stops to examine the rain on his fingers. The rain has a strange viscosity. Or does it? His hallucinations weave in and out of reality in the film. We see what he sees. The world looks like it's in trouble through his eyes, but not enough for him to be able to produce any evidence. His best friend. His brother. His boss. His mother. His dog. They all seem likable and genuinely care about him. But they slowly decide he's crazy. LaForche knows if he's right, they will all be lost. We also find out his mother Sarah (Kathy Baker) suffers from paranoid schizophrenia. And boy does she, according to the story. Halfway through the movie we see him driving home from a nighttime ASL session. He pulls the car over with his wife and daughter asleep in the back seat to observe a distant storm. He again stares blankly for a while and then says to himself, "Is anyone else seeing this?" He is talking to nobody in the story, but is he talking to us?

The special effects in the film are minimal, but impressive. As the dreams escalate and the rain continues, we as the audience notice there is something unusual, but again, there isn't much evidence. Michael Shannon has enjoyed a bit of a meteoric rise in the last decade. And rightfully so, as he's put in some great performances, particularly a favorite of mine from John Waters' *Cecil B. Demented* (2000) where Shannon has the best line in the film, and perhaps all films, where he excitedly shouts out: "Tell me about Mel Gibson's dick and balls!" *Take Shelter* requires a slightly more nuanced performance, but Shannon gets a chance to show crazy as a slow burn in the tradition of when Sam Neill is off the leash. Shannon's ability to channel small town paranoia serves in both gears. It's also akin to *Close Encounters of the Third Kind* (1977) where Richard Dreyfuss builds a model of a mountain in his mashed potatoes as his hysterical wife played by the great Teri Garr looks on with quiet panic. Here Shannon sticks to the quiet side of lunacy and shines as a fanatic eschewing all societies normalcy to work on an old storm shed behind the house. It would be criminal if *Take Shelter* fell into obscurity. It is one of those great roles where one person's treatment of the character makes the movie.

Vanya on 42nd Street (1994)
Directed by Louis Malle
U.S.A. 119 min.

I was once laughed at in line renting *My Dinner With Andre* (1981). The person in line making fun of me was renting, I kid you not, T*he Bourne Identity* (2002). I don't care what some lunk head thinks of my rental, but I was sad because I see no problems with things blowing up in movies. If André Gregory set off a bomb in *My Dinner With Andre* I'd have been fine with it. But seriously. How cliché? Making fun of me for *My Dinner With Andre*? It's called an education, fuck face.

Vanya on 42nd Street reunites Louis Malle, Wallace Shawn, and André Gregory along with a cast of sharp actors creating a voluntary performance workshop studying Anton Chekhov's work. Chekhov was known for being an early example of a modernist, and his play *Uncle Vanya*, first published in 1899, is a humorous narrative from its time. It's the story of a wealthy professor and landowner named Aleksandr Vladimirovich Serebryakov and his much younger wife Helena Andreyevna Serebryakova. Serebryakov wants to sell the estate to elevate his class status. Vanya, brother of the professor's late wife, and Astor, the local doctor both help manage the estate and do not support the sale.

The film of the play takes place in the then disused New

Amsterdam Theatre at 214 West 42nd Street. The material is presented without costumes, sets, or soundtrack. At the time, the theater was in such terrible disrepair parts of the stage could not be used. Rats had chewed through much of the wiring. The actors set scenes arbitrarily around the theater using minimalist chairs and tables, the sort of thing you might find lying around. The movie is a compelling read of *Vanya* from an interesting swath of actors. Julianne Moore, Larry Pine, Brooke Smith, George Gaynes, Phoebe Brand, Jerry Mayer, and Lynn Cohen join Wallace Shawn in the cast and use the space of the theater beautifully. What struck me so much about this movie is how entertaining it is to see fine actors chew on this material. These are serious professionals who have collectively gone on to act in movies like *Police Academy* (1984), *Silence of the Lambs* (1991), *The Ladies Man* (2000), and, of course, The *Princess Bride* (1987). Yeah, it pays to have an education and a real sense of humor about yourself, doesn't it, Mr. Bourne Identity Man!

Here is the perfect opportunity for a costume drama, and this group proves there is no better costume than acting by eschewing all accoutrement and relying on your own abilities. Occasionally the players insert their own affectations, perhaps on purpose, but sometimes perhaps not. It's hard to tell. You see them watching each other. What is obvious is they have spent time on this material together and are having fun doing it. Jazz from the Joshua Redman Trio plays during scene changes that warrant a quick distraction. The Joshua Redman Trio also play during the intermission, during which Malle filmed leaves the cameras on showing the players having lunch and interacting with each other. It's an interesting look into the process and an insightful look into a classic piece of work. And Matt Damon does not ONCE appear in it.

The White Ribbon (2009)
Directed by Michael Haneke
Germany 144 min.

Michael Haneke's enigmatic style of interweaving convoluted plot lines paints an ominous portrait of a small German village shortly before the beginning of World War I. The town is experiencing a string of bizarre occurrences stretching the boundaries of bad luck. As the citizenry attempts to decipher this run of misfortune, bad light is cast on each of the primary characters. The genesis of these bad incidents appears solvable, but answers don't come easy.

The plot centers around the memories of an unnamed elderly schoolteacher. The schoolteacher's narration is voiced by Ernst Jacobi. The teacher is portrayed at the time of the events by Christian Friedel. The schoolteacher recounts a distant memory of strange events transpiring in the year of his courtship and engagement to his wife Eva (Leonie Benesch). The story begins as the town doctor (Rainer Bock) is knocked off of his horse by a nefariously placed wire. The doctor is taken to a hospital out of town and an investigation begins. The police cannot figure out who tied the wire, nor can they figure out who took it down. Meanwhile, the town's land Baron (Ulrich Tukur) becomes the target of vandalism. Children disappear. Adults disappear. As accidents become commonplace, no one is above suspicion. Even the town Pastor (Burghart Klaussner) is discovered to be so hard on his children he could be unraveling. As the plot progresses, theories about the source of all this trouble arrive and fade almost as quickly.

The film is masterfully shot in black and white using stark contrasts creating an ominous backdrop for this bleak narrative. Haneke knows his audience and elements of German expressionism are prevalent with regards to the lighting and contrast to the point near satire. The film's moves at a calculated pace: as characters drop in and out of favor, red herrings are slid in to drive the story. Slow pacing and a convoluted plot may turn a few people off, but fans of his 2005 film *Caché* will enjoy the evolution in Heneke's style. Heneke creates a convoluted maze in the tradition of Picnic at *Hanging Rock* (1975) and *Lost Highway* (1997). The film forces the audience's best guess right up until the end. It's not for everyone, but if you're up for a well-constructed thinker, the labyrinth of *The White Ribbon* will resonate.

World's Greatest Dad (2009)
Directed by Bobcat Goldthwait
U.S.A. 99 min.

"I don't find the creative process rewarding. I have to be honest, I want to reach an audience." It's a simple line from a simple character in a movie rigorously challenging the ethics of its main character. In the course of the story only nebulous rules are broken. One particular rule is a favor you might do for someone to spare some embarrassment. It's easy to say you wouldn't, but could you be persuaded? Lance Clayton (Robin Williams) makes a decision in the heat of a moment. He didn't do it nefariously. But boy things get out of hand quickly. The story is driven by a tragedy, but I strongly feel the story plays better if you go in fresh. Bobcat Goldthwait has a knack for pushing the edges of good taste. *World's Greatest Dad* does as well, but also creates a quandary that is a fun ride and a thinker of a situation.

Clayton is an English teacher who dreams of becoming a famous writer. He's never had much luck with the process, and it's led him to a divorce and a low-tiered job at a private school where his son Kyle (Daryl Sabara) is attending high school. Funny enough, Williams has reprised his role as poetry teacher at a private school, much like a movie he got great notoriety for that I can't stand called *Dead Poets Society* (1989). In that film he was the beloved poetry teacher who told his students with great aplomb that they could do anything. Here the poetry teacher is a bit weathered. Clayton seems not to have the same faith in this crew of students. The students don't give a shit about poetry, or much else for that matter. Clayton is also sending out manuscripts of his latest novel. He has typical feelings of someone going through that creative process. Meanwhile his co-worker Mike Lane (Henry Simmons), the younger and more popular English teacher, gets a story published in The New Yorker on his first attempt. The tropes of this sort of comedy might dictate these two become fast enemies, but the script gets a slower burn out of Lane's performance as the nice guy who exhibits some genuine friendship for Clayton. Kyle is a disagreeable kid testing his father by annoying him regularly and calling him names until he gets what he wants. Generally what he wants is more access to pornography.

The brightest light in Clayton's life is the alternately saccharine walking and filthy talking girlfriend Claire Reed (Alexie Gilmore). Claire also seems to care for Clayton a lot, and their relationship appears to be pretty strong and fun until Clayton's insecurities seep in. There are some great side performances in the movie as well. The no-nonsense character actor Geoff Pierson portrays school principal Wyatt Anderson. Anderson's blaise disposition and side comments let Clayton know he's on thin ice at the school. Evan Martin, an excellent young actor with a flat delivery, portrays Kyle's friend Andrew Troutman. Martin creates a likable character that gets several solid laughs throughout the movie. As Troutman, he is loyal to Kyle although Kyle often proves he's not worthy of much loyalty. Goldthwait, like Williams, is not afraid to go histrionic to make an uncomfortable laugh work, but here they both have the reins pulled back just enough to make a truly unusual comedy. The film has shock value, but is carved in comedy fundamentals enough to evoke real laughs and make you think a bit. The end wraps beautifully with a callback from Clayton's youth set to the best use of Queen since *Wayne's World* (1992).

Three Interviews

I have never felt interviews were my forte. There's something to be said for the notion: you shouldn't meet your heroes. I can't help giving off a "fan boy" vibe people either don't respond to or just manage to tolerate. But I like the research and historical context involved in doing interviews. And it makes sense some people don't want to sit and talk about themselves so much, especially if they're discussing things they did years and years ago. I like to move forward as well, but I find people and their accomplishments interesting, and I do still pursue interviews. I decided to include three interviews that first appeared in print magazines I was proud of in this book. These are three of my favorite interviews from the fringe of the film industry. Two of the interviews first appeared in Razorcake Magazine and one appeared in Lunchmeat Magazine.

I included an interview with Pleasant Gehman who has worn many hats in the L.A. punk scene and is a great interview. Besides being a big fan of the Found Footage Festival, video collectors play an interesting role in film preservation. I also had a chance to interview character actor Mary Woronov. Woronov was my white whale. I am a fan of so many films she's been in. I was nervous from the start of the interview because I could tell she didn't really want to talk to me and I watched all those movies again and had tons of fan questions. She eventually warmed up to me. Perhaps she recognized I had done my homework. These are three unique views from the fringe of the film industry. I was glad to have had a chance to learn from them when I had the chance. For me, writing is learning, and it's what I most enjoy about writing. I hope you enjoy these interviews.

Interview with Pleasant Gehman

This interview first appeared in Lunchmeat Magazine, issue #9.

There was a long stretch of time before DVD and the Internet when a canonical list of punk films was hard to compile. A late-night TV show in the 80s called *Night Flight* introduced me to "cult" movies and art videos, some of which would follow me through life. Included in the shows programming were some of the more legendary punk films: *Another State of Mind, Rude Boy,* and *Ladies and Gentlemen, the Fabulous Stains*. It was the coolest thing around in the '80s before the great VHS dump when punk and horror titles could be found in thrift stores and piled by the doors of bookstores for a dollar or less. *The Runnin' Kind* came to me through my friend Matt who is equally obsessed with punks in movies. The film distinguished itself with a deep look into the early Los Angeles punk scene and a scene in the film where a party is launched with a guy ollieing on to an old couch. As I get older, opportunities to start a party that way wane, but other opportunities arise like speaking to *The Runnin' Kind's* co-writer Pleasant Gehman over the phone from L.A. where she still lives and writes.

Lunchmeat: How did you get involved with writing *The Runnin' Kind?*

Pleasant Gehman: Max Tash, the director and co-writer, wanted to do a story about an all-girl band. He contacted the Go-Gos, the Bangles, and me. He wanted to get interviews for the sake of realism. He didn't really know much about what it was like to be in a band. He picked bands that were at different stages of development. I'm not sure how much he interviewed from the Go-Gos or the Bangles, but after a while he started asking me: If I was going to do this, is this realistic? And I'd say no or not. I started taking him around to clubs to see what the rock scene was like. He started coming around a lot to see what people wore or how they acted, stuff like that. After a while he asked if I'd co-write the script. When he first approached me, I don't think he knew I was a writer. I said yes. He had a little office off of Hollywood Boulevard and we started writing there. And we started figuring out the structure of it. The structure was going to be a little different at first.

Lunchmeat: Was it initially a narrative story?

Pleasant Gehman: It was gonna be a fictional story about an all-girl band. The interviews were to get the details right so it wasn't a dumb, movie-of-the-week-type movie. It wound up being a process of months and months, he started going to the Roxy every night. So by the time we actually started filming, we were filming at my house Disgraceland and in the clubs, most of the roles were played by people who were really at the

Roxy. A lot of it wasn't actors.

Lunchmeat: Could you talk a bit about Disgraceland?

Pleasant Gehman: Kid Congo and I found Disgraceland in 1978. I lived there 'till 1988. 'Till right around after The Runnin' Kind was shot. It was owned by Mickey Hartigay, Jane Mansfield's ex husband, the bodybuilder who was in *The Girl Can't Help It* (1956) with her. It was a duplex with four apartments in what was really a slummy area of Hollywood. Just south of Frederick's of Hollywood on Selma Avenue. Right in the heart of Hollywood Boulevard. There had been no urban renewal then. Anyone living in that area was older people, people who had come in the '40s or '50s to make it in Hollywood and ended up living in a one-room apartment. Or houses that had been in people's families. There were hellish apartments. It wasn't really crime ridden, but it was a very sleepy part of Hollywood. Because of its proximity to Hollywood Boulevard, it was sandwiched between Hollywood and Sunset, right near Club Lingerie, right near The Masque, near all the bars on Hollywood Boulevard and all the after hours places like The Zero which was in the movie, it was within walking distance of all this and none of us had cars, it wound up being the biggest punk crash pad in Hollywood.

Lunchmeat: You're working on a book about it now, aren't you?

Pleasant Gehman: Yeah.

Lunchmeat: What's the structure of the book going to be?

Pleasant Gehman: We got stories from people who were there constantly. We've got flyers and photos. We want it to be done right and not just about us. There's going to be other people's memories, some of them are famous and some not. Disgraceland was in Rolling Stone. It was on a documentary on

MTV. It was a famous punk house. People would just show up there. Someone from the record company brought the Split Enz over when they were visiting from Australia just because they wanted to see Disgraceland. Madness came when they got to L.A. because they had heard of it. Screaming Jay Hawkins used to party there all the time with us.

Lunchmeat: That's amazing.

Pleasant Gehman: Any traveling band you could think of stayed there. And we were always behind on the rent. There was always psychotic shit going on that was fun. There was a plaster, Tijuana bust of Elvis on the mantle with painted-on Alice Cooper makeup surrounded by empty fifths of booze. My boyfriend at the time was a bail bondsman and he started calling it Disgraceland and it stuck.

Lunchmeat: Sounds like a punk house.

Pleasant Gehman: It was in a James Woods movie called *The Boost* (1988). It was picked as the crack house in the movie and they didn't change anything. They put a work out mattress on the lawn. That was all the art director did.

Lunchmeat: So it played a crack house in a movie.

Pleasant Gehman: Yeah. Character acting. None of us were into crack, but that's what the outside looked like.

Lunchmeat: Did you feel like a lot of your band experiences wound up in the movie?

Pleasant Gehman: Yeah. It all developed as we went along. The Screamin' Sirens weren't going to be in it. I wasn't going to be in the movie. It all kind of happened. A lot of it was filmed as it was happening. We'd really be doing a gig somewhere and there'd be crowd footage.

Lunchmeat: I wondered how much of the film was just people

you knew who were just around.

Pleasant Gehman: So much of it.

Lunchmeat: I tried to pick faces out. I didn't recognize a lot of people. El Duce from The Mentors is kind of prevalent.

Pleasant Gehman: That's a good example. He wasn't even supposed to be in it. He was an extra, but he didn't have a speaking part. But he got so drunk and woke up and started yelling and Max (Tash) said: "This needs to go in the movie." Like the guy skateboarding through the house...

Lunchmeat: I'm glad you mentioned that because my friend and I are really into the party that begins with a guy ollieing on the couch. I wanted to ask about that.

Pleasant Gehman: Do you know Chuck Treece?

Lunchmeat: No. My friend might; he is a really good skateboarder and is really into it. I wanted to know because we've never successfully started a party with a guy ollieing on a couch. That's more my interest in the scene.

Pleasant Gehman: That shit used to happen a lot. I had a lot of pro-skateboarder boyfriends. I went out with Tony Alva. Steve Olson. I was involved with the guy who did that in the movie: Chuck Treece.

Lunchmeat: I still hope to be a part of a party that begins with someone ollies on to a couch.

Pleasant Gehman: Well, it seriously happened.

Lunchmeat: That gives me hope. Does that count as improv?

Pleasant Gehman: It was a complete improv. That's just what used to happen. Everyone was ollieing off everything.

Lunchmeat: With so many friends and acquaintances around,

there must have been a lot of improv. Or was the script pretty tight?

Pleasant Gehman: All the party scenes. A lot of the conversations, even though there were markers, were improved.

Lunchmeat. Did that seem unusual at the time? Improv in film is such a normal thing now, but did you notice that being unusual at the time? I don't know, maybe it was more prevalent than I know.

Pleasant Gehman: It's kind of just how it came together. This is just my assumption, but I don't think that's what Max had in mind at first. He started realizing that you can't make this shit up. Even though it's sort of b-movie-ish, I think it's very authentic. Almost everyone on the set knows each other through rock 'n' roll. The few actors hung out with us.

Lunchmeat: It seems very real.

Pleasant Gehman: We didn't do much. The scene where I woke up in my room: That was my room. The only thing that was done was a loft bed that had to be moved for the camera equipment. Otherwise nothing changed.

Lunchmeat: The realism is there. I feel like there is a canon of punk films I watched when I was younger that I tried to get insight about what it was like to be in a band. Lives of musicians. That sort of thing.

Pleasant Gehman: A lot of our lives were in it. Like Playmates of Hollywood (represented in the film). I worked there. It was a store that sold lingerie that was our day job. A place where we found employment. It was an institution. It was a place to buy stripper clothes. The whole staff was punk rock girls.

Lunchmeat: Has there ever been talk of a DVD release of *The Runnin' Kind*?

Pleasant Gehman: No. I wish there was. I would bootleg it. I get so many crazy messages or emails from random people all the time wanting to know about it. To me it was shocking that MGM picked it up for distribution. Even when that happened, at the moment that that happened, I knew they were marketing it all wrong. The posters were fine, but they should have opened it as a midnight movie. They thought it was going to fly in the mainstream.

Lunchmeat: This is probably a stupid comparison, but the story and tone was similar to *Valley Girl* (1983). Do you think they were trying to recreate that success?

Pleasant Gehman: Definitely. *I was in Valley Girl.*

Lunchmeat: Yea? I didn't know that.

Pleasant Gehman: I didn't have a speaking role, but I was in all the club scenes. A lot of us did stuff like that. Besides Playmates, the only employment we could get was being movie extras and TV show extras. There was an agency run by Janet Cunningham called Cash. The office was right next to the Zero Zero, which was a club in TRK. Janet was in the music scene and she was working in film and got the idea to start an agency that booked real people who were fringy. Like punks or people into heavy metal or bikers or tattooed people. It took off because Central Casting would send over clean-cut people to be in *Rock 'n' Roll High School* or whatever. A lot of the people in TRK already worked in almost any '80s movie you can think of. I can't even count.

Lunchmeat: Did you happen to be in a movie called *Get Crazy*?

Pleasant Gehman: I was in *Get Crazy*. That was our employment. I worked for Cannon (Films). If you weren't doing extra work or working at Cannon or the art department at L.A. Weekly you couldn't get a job. I wrote taglines. I wrote the tag line for *Bill and Ted's Excellent Adventure*. Someone recommended me for the job. Cannon was close to Disgraceland too.

Lunchmeat: Sounds like a fun time to be in L.A. Has there ever been any talk of rereleasing *The Runnin' Kind*?

Pleasant Gehman: No. I haven't seen the movie in 15 years. You can print this, if someone wants to make a DVD of it and send it to me, I'd love that.

Interview with Nick Prueher and Joe Pickett by Billups Allen

This interview first appeared in Razorcake Magazine, issue #63.

Before the days of YouTube, unusual video footage was generally acquired by either tape trading or ordering mix tapes from people who collected videos. Sources such as these were a peephole into a bizarre world where obsessed Steve Vai fans blow out candles with their vaginas, politicians commit suicide in front of news cameras, and men air drum to Metallica. On the front lines of tape trading and third generation film copies are VHS hunters like Joe Pickett and Nick Prueher. Pickett and Prueher are VHS enthusiasts who have turned the act of video sharing into a full-blown program that has filled independent movie houses across the country for years. The Found Footage Festival has produced five videos of shows where the two present a cornucopia of strange footage found in thrift stores and acquired by occasionally dubious methods.

Interview with Nick Prueher and Joe Pickett by Billups Allen

Billups: I am really pleased at how the show has grown. When you watch the first DVD, it seems like a respectable — but small — crowd. Now you are doing two shows a night in some cities.

Nick: We did about 75 dates last year and we have about a hundred this year. It started out fairly modest and now we're on the road nine months out of the year.

Billups: You have mentioned in the show that the two of you grew up together.

Nick: Joe and I met in sixth grade. We met in middle school in Stoughton, a small town in Wisconsin outside of Madison. We quickly bonded over our appreciation of things that are so bad they are good.

Billups: Were you involved or interested in any other DIY pursuits? Was there a punk scene in Stoughton or a group of people you hung out with who had similar or collector-centric interests?

Joe: Stoughton is a small town, so it was important to find ways to entertain myself instead of succumbing to the booze and drugs that typically satisfy boredom in small towns. Nick and I started a humor magazine in sixth grade called The Daily Chimp; the word "humor" might be a little strong. Then in high school, we got obsessed with making prank phone calls and started recording and selling the cassettes to classmates. I remember we actually made around forty dollars on them, which was when we realized that we could actually make money doing fun stuff.

Billups: Do either of you collect anything besides videos?

Joe: I've always loved collecting shit. When I was a kid it was the usual stuff—baseball cards, Garbage Pail Kids, etcetera. As a frequenter of thrift stores now, I find myself collecting answering machine tapes and old remote controls. Both of those things are nearly obsolete. Plus answering machine tapes can be pretty awesome.

Billups: Was thrift shopping a significant activity before your interest in videos?

Joe: I've always loved thrift stores. I used to go to garage sales with my mom all the time. She always liked old, weird stuff and I guess she passed that onto me.

Nick: We had been thrift store junkies already, so we thought we'd watch out for videotapes as well. The collection just grew and grew. Garage sales. Thrift stores. Work places. We had fourteen years of material to choose from when we did our first show. When we began touring, we started stopping in thrift stores in other places and people started bringing videos and it grew. Like all good things, it grew out of being bored.

Billups: Was Stoughton a good place to shop? Lots of thrift stores, perhaps?

Joe: Yeah. We had a great store there called Wayne's Bargain Store. The owner, Wayne, was this mean old man who hated kids, but he had the coolest shit that kids loved. Whips, nunchucks, ninja boots, rugs with naked ladies on them. I think it was at Wayne's where Nick and I realized we shared a common bond.

Nick: In terms of us realizing we had similar sensibilities was in sixth grade when everybody loved this syndicated TV show called *Small Wonder* and we couldn't believe how bad the show was. We would watch it and make fun of it. We realized we didn't excel at anything in school except having an advanced sense of irony.

Billups: What are some other sources you have explored to acquire a video?

Nick: When I was a freshman in high school I worked at a McDonald's, I found a video there called *Inside and Outside Custodial Duties*. It was a training video for janitors at McDonald's. They make you sit through this video where they try to be cute and funny and try to entertain you. It's like, "Just give me the information. Don't try to patronize me with plots." My jaw dropped. My first thought was, "You know who would appreciate this? Joe." So I put it in my backpack that night and showed it to Joe. We fell in love with the tape. We had friends over—there isn't much to do in our town—and we didn't have our driver's licenses yet. We'd watch the tape and make short films around the video and say what we wanted them to say. It basically became the blueprint for what we do now. It sparked our interest in the idea that videos can be entertaining in ways they were never intended to be.

Joe: About ten years ago, I got a tip from someone that the training videos at Suncoast Video (a chain that sold videos and movie paraphernalia) had a training video where Wayne and Garth impersonators taught you the finer points of customer service. So I filled out an application, interviewed, got the job, worked a four-hour shift at a mall in suburban Minneapolis, found the stack of training videos on top of the break room TV, and tossed them in my duffle bag. I went home that night, duped them, returned the next day with them, and told some random employee I couldn't work there any more. The bad news is that the Wayne and Garth video wasn't in the stack. The good news is that there was a Siskel and Ebert impersonator who gave "thumbs up" or "thumbs down" for good or bad customer service. It was wonderfully stupid.

Billups: When you first decided to do the live show in front of people, were you at all nervous as to whether or not people would get what you were doing?

Joe: A little. But we knew we had some gems in our collection that were undeniably funny. Plus, we started the show pre-YouTube, so the charm of weird videos wasn't as ubiquitous as it is now. I think we were most surprised to find that people really liked watching these videos with a group. There must be something cathartic about watching videos that are typically relegated to a break room.

Nick: It was such an insular thing. It was a crash course in ironic enjoyment of things. We found there was a larger audience really tapped into that sensibility. We were nervous; we didn't know if this was something we just found funny.

Billups: What do you think is so appealing about watching and showing eclectic videos to other people?

Joe: A few things. First of all, everything is better on the big screen. Most of the videos we show were intended for the small screen, so something magical happens when you project them on a big screen. Second, it's fun to watch these with other people. Most of these videos weren't intended for a mass audience.

Nick: You're watching these things that were not meant to be shown in public: exercise videos and training videos and home movies. You're sort of giving people permission to laugh at it. The laughter is contagious the more people are in the room. That's something that I think is missing from Internet sharing.

Billups: Do you think there is an element of mass psychology in presenting videos to people in public?

Nick: I think there is. You feel a bit subversive watching stuff that was not meant for someone else to see. If it's a training video you had to watch at a job or an exercise video you had to watch your mom use after school, it's not only nostalgic, but also it's being able to laugh at those things.

Billups: It's apparent to me that you guys have fun hosting the shows. What is your favorite part of the process? Is it searching for videos, editing, or the public sharing?

Joe: Probably the search. There's nothing better than finding some random Salvation Army in rural Alabama and finding boxes and boxes of old videos. It makes the drudgery of travel between shows totally worth it.

Billups: There is a sparse but significant history of hosting when it comes to presenting movies. Horror hosts like Vampira and Elvira. *Mystery Science Theater 3000.* I wondered if that sort of thing was an inspiration in any capacity.

Nick: I don't think it was a conscious thing, but I'm certain those things were influential. For us, the footage is so weird it needs to be grounded in some reality. We thought playing the straight man to the footage would help take people on a guided tour of this very weird place. A lot of times—what sort of turned us off about compilations or people manipulating the sounds and whatnot—it becomes weirdness on top of weirdness. There is definitely a place for that. There are people like TV Carnage who do that very well. For us, we came to it very much the same way we do it in our living room for friends. "Here's our latest find. Here's where we found it. Here's some background" and we make some jokes along the way.

Billups: One thing I like about your show is that it, overall, seems fairly good-natured. The climate for video sharing on the Internet seems to be leaning on the nastier side, in my opinion. Do you think your reverence for strange videos comes across to the audience during your shows?

Joe: I hope so. We're certainly not a mean-spirited show. It's not really our style. There's really no reason to disparage videos that, for the most part, have already disparaged themselves. Badness speaks for itself. It usually doesn't need any help from us.

Billups: The rash of Internet video sharing these days seems mean spirited to me.

Nick: I certainly can appreciate having any footage you want at your fingertips, but I do feel that something is lost, like the charm and innocence when you are trading videos. That is something that we try to sort of rekindle—the antiquated practice of gathering in a living room and showing off your latest finds. It's too easy to leave a snarky comment on the Internet when you're anonymous. We certainly lavish these videos with more attention than they probably deserve. I think the fact that we found them getting our hands dirty rummaging through VHS tapes certainly creates appreciation.

Billups: Sometimes in your shows, you include bits about meeting people who make videos you've shown. Many of the people you have met seem to have a sense of humor about what you're doing. Were you ever nervous to approach someone?

Nick: We've had some close calls. Sometimes we'll get an email from someone in a video and our first thought is, "Holy crap. They're pissed." But, without fail, so far, people have been flattered by the attention. I think people seeing that it is not a mean-spirited show helps. They might think we are snarky jackasses — maybe we are to a certain extent — but I think it comes from a good place. We genuinely love this footage. It is close to our hearts since we found it ourselves.

Billups: What sort of finds get you excited?

Nick: What really gets us excited are home movies. Those are the most difficult to find because, generally, people don't give those up on purpose. Sometimes they just end up in a box with other VHS tapes that go off to the Salvation Army. Lately, we've been going to estate sales and buying camcorders. A lot of times there is a tape of a home movie still inside. Or if there is a camcorder for sale at a thrift store, we'll look inside for a video. That's solid gold for us.

Joe: My wife and I were at an estate sale in Queens, NY where I purchased a camcorder for four dollars. I brought it home and out popped a VHS tape! We tossed it in and our jaws hit the floor. It felt like we were watching Crispin Glover's home movie. It began with a woman with Down's Syndrome and a glittery vest dancing in a living room to *Phantom of the Opera*, while a freshly sheared poodle wandered in the background. Then, after a couple minutes, it cuts to a topless old man, wearing a long blond wig, also dancing to *Phantom of the Opera*. Then he put on the glittery vest and danced ominously at the camera, kinda like that guy in *Silence of the Lambs*. Then, just when you think it can't get better, it cuts to a house being destroyed by a bulldozer in a Queens neighborhood. The videographer—who I assume is the dancing old man from earlier—got into a vicious argument with the foreman of the construction crew who was questioning why he's "taking pictures" of the house being destroyed. It was the strangest, most unpredictable home movie we ever found. That video is featured in *Volume 2* of *FFF*. It's called *Queens Home Movie*.

Billups: Often, when watching videos you present, there is at least a pretense to understanding the context of what is going on, be it people screwing around or some sort of misguided information being conveyed. Do you ever get videos that are completely dumbfounding?

Nick: One example we found is a video called *Rent-A-Friend*. We have seen a lot of stupid concepts put on to VHS: interactive video board games and aquariums and fireplaces you are supposed to put on your TV, videos designed to entertain your dog or cat by having squirrels running around the yard. Any dumb concept that you can think of has been committed to home video. This one probably takes the cake. 1986. It opens with the guy sitting in an armchair saying: "Hi. My name is Sam. I wanna be your friend. What's your name?" and then you are supposed to answer to the screen, apparently. Then he asks you stuff like, "What do you do?" and "Can I look around your place?" You are supposed to suspend your disbelief and answer the screen. The only thing we could figure was that this was for extremely lonely people who have VCRs who needed a friend for an hour. So for an hour this guy talks to you and tells you things about himself. Then he runs out of things to say about himself and starts revealing more about his personal life than he should have. You sort of watch this guy unravel in front of your eyes. I'm still not sure of the full story, but we have tracked down the guy. We're going to meet him in Chicago.

Billups: There is one video in one of your shows that I want to know more about. Do you mind if I ask about *Dancing with Frank Pacholski*? I know it must be a public access show, but I don't understand the concept.

Nick: It's all elderly people sitting in a semicircle watching this portly, balding man in an American flag Speedo slap his ass and dance around to John Philip Sousa marches. It's just another day in the life of a Los Angeles public access channel. I don't know if it's art or insanity, but it's one of the most entertaining things we have found. This one was taped from TV and given to us by a friend. Apparently, Frank Pacholski had this regular show that he did every week. We've tried to contact him but he hasn't returned any emails. I'm afraid it's still a mystery, but maybe it's better that way.

Billups: Is it always John Philip Sousa marches?

Nick: Well, we have a whole tape of him. He mostly dances to marches and classical music. Sometimes it's patriotic music. In one episode he has this tray out and he is serving hors devours wearing the bikini, asking people if they want dressing on their salad. It's very strange. The best part about it is the people watching seem like they were just told to come to the studio, having no idea what they are getting into. They seem as if they want to be anywhere but watching this guy prance around in an American flag Speedo.

Billups: I can't imagine what those people were told. It works on a lot of levels for me.

Nick: That's why I feel as if the mystery behind it might be more interesting than what it actually is.

Billups: Do you feel as if VHS and Public Access Television document a time and place in media?

Joe: Definitely. VHS is officially a dead format. The last VHS factory closed its doors in 2008. It concerns us a little because we're seeing thrift stores reducing their VHS prices to almost nothing. They can't get rid of them. I spoke to one thrift store employee who told me they turn away a lot of VHS now. I have a feeling that within a couple years, VHS tapes will be relegated to landfills. Because, honestly, who's going to buy a used VHS copy of *Air Force One* at a thrift store? Public access is a dying breed, too. The funding isn't what it used to be and several of these channels are drying up. I don't know the numbers, but I hear from public access people who come to our shows that it's not looking good. Lucky for us, people are sending us stuff we would never otherwise see, so at least a tiny fraction of it will be preserved. As for us, we have a pretty good stockpile right now, so we'll be fine for a while.

Nick: We definitely are nostalgic about VHS being the format we grew up with. More and more we see ourselves as preservationists of VHS: a format that has seen no love, compared to vinyl. The whole video store movement is almost extinct. What's worse yet is the mom and pop video stores—with their special interest sections—was a place where you would go to browse exclusive videos and free rentals, free anti-drug rentals, things like that. I miss that. We are trying to stage a storefront art installation in New York called Special Interest, which will be a mom and pop video store, but just special interest. A good portion of our collection will be on display and available to watch at stations. I think what the American Film Institute is preserving is the greatest one hundred films of the last century in a temperature-controlled vault. Nobody is doing that for Alan Thicke's say no to strangers video. Nobody is doing that for the Zsa Zsa Gabor exercise video so we do see it as our duty. These are videotape moments that most people would rather forget about. For us, there is a lot more truth and innocence than, say, in a polished film. The "warts and all" nature of these videos say more about us as a culture than some of our greatest intentional works of art.

Billups: YouTube and Internet video sharing has made strange videos a self-conscious pursuit, in my opinion. Do you think there is a quality in amateur production that is being lost or is changing in some manner?

Joe: Absolutely. Cameras aren't as novel as they were twenty years ago. Look at something like *Heavy Metal Parking Lot*. The people in that video are genuinely excited to see the camera. Everybody clambered for the microphone because it was rare to be on TV. That genuine excitement is gone now. With a few exceptions, quirky amateur videos feel really calculated to me now. We don't seek them out. Our rule is that videos have to be physically found. We don't take anything from the Internet.

Billups: Do you think that people's wider access to video cameras is a hindrance or an asset? Could it turn into anything as magical as a mountain of strange videotapes?

Joe: The thing we've realized is that formats may change, but bad ideas are here to stay. So, yeah, I think it's a good thing that more people are producing crappy stuff. But I don't think hard drives are quite as charming as VHS tapes.

Billups: I hate to see VHS go. My wife told me that the local Blockbuster was closing and I was sad. Then I thought, you know, I've traditionally hated Blockbuster but I hate to see this part of the culture die.

Nick: I used to work as a manager of a Blockbuster for a while. One of the first video finds I had in their two-dollar video bin was *Mr. T's Be Somebody or Be Somebody's Fool*. That was among my first finds along with the McDonald's video. It was in the bargain bin for $1.99. Even Blockbuster had its value, even with its corporate ugliness. There were so many videos on the wall you could find that were true gems. Now that those videos are in thrift stores or in garbage cans, the frustrating part for us is that there are so many tapes out there and there's a timeline for when they need to be found. That's why we keep doing ambitious tours. It gives us a chance to hit thrift stores and make sure these videos are rescued and not lost to the ages.

Interview with Mary Woronov

This interview first appeared in Razorcake Magazine, issue #59.

Mary Woronov is an actor with an impressive filmography. Yet, even after working with a variety of well-known directors over forty-plus years, only a loyal following of cult film buffs know her by name. She is also dynamic, often portraying characters traveling up the ladder of empowerment or disintegrating into madness.

Her deep voice and stern disposition make her stand out in films of varying quality. She has put in several lead performances, but more often she is relegated to small roles in which she shines brightly. When she is on the screen, Woronov exudes a uniquely vicious female presence that is devoid of the tomboyish charm often associated with harder female character actors. Her steadfast ability to command authority on screen is tough, yet unmistakably feminine. A sinister glare from Woronov can evoke primal fear in male characters, often reducing them to a wormlike state.

Woronov has had a long-standing connection with rock' n' roll throughout her career, including, on-stage performances with the Velvet Underground, a key role in the Ramones vehicle *Rock 'n' Roll High School*, and an appearance as a demented 1950s housewife in the music video for Suicidal Tendencies' "Institutionalized."

But her music associations only scratch the surface of her extensive work in movies and television. Mrs. Woronov spoke to Razorcake about the triumphs and frustrations of negotiating her vastly eclectic catalog of roles in the midst of her involvement in a documentary currently titled *Confessions of a Cult Queen*: a film that may finally lavish credit on a largely overlooked career.

Billups: What sort of films influenced you early on?

Mary Woronov: My early interest in film was very American. It was kind of average for what a child likes. I liked Hitchcock and things like that. It wasn't until my first marriage that I was introduced to Truffaut, the French guys, and it wasn't until I moved to Los Angeles that I was influenced by people who I had never heard of.

Billups: It seems that music must also be significant.

Mary: I am into Brooklyn rock'n'roll, sort of like the Shirelles and stuff like that. The Shangri Las. I met Lou Reed and I loved their music, but I didn't know many bands like them. They tremendously influenced me, of course, and I danced for them. Blues and New Orleans blues after that. There was nothing after Lou Reed. It wasn't until punk rock in Los Angeles that my music experience came alive. I was really, really dedicated to a lot of bands here. Then I went into heavy metal when that ended. I loved some of those bands. But I went immediately from heavy metal into Wagner. Now I'm just an opera freak, I guess.

Billups: I have read the descriptions of your performances with Exploding Plastic Inevitable in Legs McNeil's book *Please Kill Me*. The book describes the performance as dressing in S&M-type clothes. I wondered if you could elaborate a bit on what it meant to be a member of the EPI?

Mary: My connections with the Velvet Underground were through Warhol, of course. I never even heard of them until Warhol. I don't think anyone had heard of them because they came to his studio unknown and he decided to back them. The radio wouldn't even play them. So, they did the banana album (The Velvet Underground and Nico) and started the Exploding Plastic Inevitable, not just for the band, but also so that people could see his movies the way they were intended to be seen: as tapestries on a wall. Or, you know, large paintings. They played on the walls around us, on the ceiling. We loved the movies playing in the background and the Velvets would stand in front. There would be two movies on either side of this little stage and then a movie behind the stage. And then in front, dwarfed by the movies, would be the Velvets, who were not very showy. The Velvets were very hardcore. They just stood there and played the music and as the audience disliked them, the band became more antagonistic, often turning their backs on the audience or just leaving their instruments near the sound box so it made this horrible screeching noise. But if the audience did like them—like when they played in the village the audience loved them—they wouldn't do much else but stand there and play.

Billups: So the Exploding Plastic Inevitable fit in making their performances more visual?

Mary: I don't know how it went, but Warhol told (poet and Warhol regular) Gerard (Malanga), "Go up there and perform.

Do something. Dance." Gerard was tremendously sexy. I had been discovered by Gerard at Cornell and was brought to Warhol to do a screen test. I did a couple of movies. Gerard took me as his dance partner. It wasn't enough just to dance. He would think up things to do. For "Heroine," all of the sudden he appeared with a giant, neon pink plastic hypodermic needle and he would mime shooting up and dance with this needle and I would dance around him. At one point, this guy ran up on stage and shot up in front of us. It was very alluring. He danced with strobe lights at one point.

He had me, in "Waiting for the Man," lift weights. I just stood there lifting weights. But our biggest and probably most sexy dance was for "Venus in Furs." He put us in leather pants and then a bullwhip appears and he gives me the bullwhip. I didn't really know about dominatrix. Gerard did a movie where he did nothing but lick my boot and I just stood there and worried about what I had stepped in recently. We did another movie, which was taken from *A Clockwork Orange*, where Gerard was tortured by me. So I understood the sexuality between us, which was not real in life, but was what he wanted to portray. I took my whip as the domineering force.

Billups: Is this where your—would it be fair of me to say "severe"—persona started?

Mary: I had done plays at the Theater of the Ridiculous and they always cast me as some domineering force. I was in *Conquest of the Universe* once. Even Warhol would cast me as such. In *Chelsea Girls* (1966), I am the raving lunatic bitch. In order to distance myself from the other superstars—who I found extremely annoying, most of whom were talentless—I decided not to portray a sexy girl but to play the male counterpart to these drag queens. In *Hedy* (1966), I played the policeman who was in love with this drag queen. The drag queen was playing Hedy Lamarr, who was a shoplifter. So I arrest her, become enamored of her, and I am supposed to kiss her, only she spent like 9,000 hours putting her makeup on, so it was like ruining a painting. But I embrace her. And I was so good at this. That was my role, but it came so naturally to me because they were portraying women. I liked working with them. They were the thing that Warhol was interested in. Most people had never seen a drag queen in their life. It was the dangerous area. I assumed this role more and more with Warhol, this strong and dark girl. I was nothing like that in real life.

Billups: You did the Warhol films and a few projects in New York, and then around the time of *Death Race 2000* (1975) you relocated to Los Angeles to pursue film more seriously.

Mary: I was told if I came to L.A. I could be in that movie. I wanted to be in movies because I did a play at Lincoln Center and it was a hell of a lot of work for very little money. My agent then got me a soap where I did make a lot of money, but it was hideous. I hated it. I was an artist, a painter. I wanted to make money, but I didn't want to work. One thing I could do, which I did, was to get married to someone who would support me. But the other thing I could do was make movies. I only had to do a little tiny bit of work, only a little bit of your life was taken up by it, but you made a lot of money to live on. That's why I was in L.A. And I did support myself.

Billups: Was it (*Death Race 2000* director) Paul Bartel who first asked you to come out?

Mary: Paul saw me in the theater and loved what I did. And he desperately wanted to work with me, but doing what? Then he got this movie for Roger Corman. He said: "Come to Los Angeles. Corman will definitely hire you and I want you to be in this movie I'm doing called *Death Race 2000*." Paul understood the Theater of the Ridiculous and camp acting. He loved to work with me and he loved to act with me also, so we did *Hollywood*

Boulevard (1976). Everybody wanted us to do our thing in all these other movies, so we did. We became a team. Finally Paul said: "This is ridiculous. I'm gonna make a movie and you and I are gonna star in it because I don't wanna do these bit parts all the time," like acting in *Rock'n'Roll High School* (1979). He had a small part and I had a relatively small part.

Billups: I watched *Hollywood Boulevard* the other day and I thought it was really funny. It struck me how it precedes a lot of films with meta-narrative themes.

Mary: Well, it was a take off on making a Corman movie. Not that Corman fucked all the starlets, which was added in. Corman had no humor. He wanted to do grade-b movies and his movies were fabulous. They played in drive-ins for a certain set of people. If you went to a motorcycle movie of Corman's, you got what you wanted. You got the motorcycles. You got the tits and ass. That wasn't dangerous like in a Warhol movie. It wasn't weird. There wasn't even any fucking. It was sort of homey. People go to the drive-ins and had a good time and weren't surprised. When Paul came, he was interested in humor. That's why he brought me. He understood my sense of humor, or at least the way I acted. I'm not your normal actor who tries to be someone. Paul and Roger fought all the time.

For *Death Race 2000* Roger said, "More blood," and Paul would say "No! No blood. Everything has to be a game. These killings, they can't be real. There has to be more humor." Roger would take it out. Paul would put it back in. Finally, Alan Arkush, who was just an editor back then, said, "We can do a movie in one week using outtakes." Paul and I put humor back in. I was almost insane about it. I was like, "This is what I want to do." That is why Paul wanted to do a movie of just us. We brought that kind of humor to Corman's movies.

Billups: You mentioned *Rock 'n' Roll High School*. Principal

Togar is obviously a role people remember you for.

Mary: I told Alan (Arkush) I would act like a principal and it was bullshit. I got out there and I was acting like some insane, lethal, bizarre woman that is totally screwed up that doesn't exist in real life but is really funny. From then on, he called me Mrs. Togar. I didn't have to say the lines. I could do whatever I wanted because they couldn't believe it.

Billups: I read that you had once said that Mrs. Togar affected your career in a negative way. Do you still feel that way?

Mary: It did have a bad effect on the idea that I could not play Lassie's mom. They would never think of hiring me for that. I might have been very good at that, and that's what makes money. I didn't do one or the other. If I needed money, I tried to do what they wanted. If I didn't need money, I would do what I wanted in very low-budget films where they weren't paying me at all and then I would get a big-budget film and I would have to do exactly what they wanted. So I was always on the fence. I should have stood on one or the other side. I should not have done Mrs. Togar and done things like Lassie's mom and eventually I would have gotten a role or two that made me famous. Or I should have stayed with the wacky Mrs. Togar. If I had just stayed with it and stayed with it, I would have made a place for myself. People would have gotten used to me and wanted me. I would have been more than just a cult queen.

Billups: I think it's a shame there is not more of a mainstream need for that: the severe persona.

Mary: Directors want what they want. They don't want what you bring. Although, if you insist on doing what you want, you end up being like a Joan Crawford, and then they want you.

Billups: I would say another film you are known for is Paul Bartel's *Eating Raoul* (1982). Here, your character comes across as uncharacteristically naive.

Mary: There, the script was so wacky that it was better to undercut the script and it worked well. It was a great movie and then he did four other movies and he didn't hire me anymore because he wanted to work with real actors. I was pissed off at him. Any time someone would interview him they would ask "Where's Mary?" and he would say, "Oh, Mary? You know, we're married," and that ticked me off, too.

Billups: You weren't, were you?

Mary: No! He's gay. One time we were being interviewed and I said, "Look, I'm not going to interview with you anymore. You always tell everyone we're married and I'm sick of it." He said, "Okay. I won't do that anymore." And so the woman interviewing us asked, "So you're married, aren't you?" and you know what he said? He said, "No, we're divorced."

Billups: That's a strange thing to do.

Mary: I don't know why he did it. It certainly put a real dent in my career. People don't want to hire someone's wife.

Billups: Something I particularly enjoy about Eating Raoul is that it seems to be sort of a reaction to overt sexuality. Is that part of what the film is about?

Mary: It was the fucking lame times of the 1980s where everyone was [with mocking in her voice] going to S and M clubs.

Billups: I feel like I'm having a similar reaction to the overt sexuality of the current times.

Mary: It's so bizarre. It's too sexy now. In L.A., the girls look like whores all the time.

Billups: Another film you were in around this time was *Night of the Comet* (1984). There is a scene where you tell (*Eating*

Raoul co-star) Robert Beltran's character that his friends were abducted. I only noted the scene because it seems incongruous from the rest of the script. I thought it might be an example of improvisation on your part.

Mary: I did write that. The whole movie was upsetting, but he let me write the scene where I kill myself and he let me go and it was so great.

Billups: That scene does stand out. I like scenes from that movie, even though the film itself is sort of nominal.

Mary: The other movie that people know, I mean punk rockers love it, not like Richard Nixon was watching it or anything, the punk favorite, I found out much later was *Terrorvision* (1986).

Billups: I'm not familiar with that one.

Mary: It's hard to get a hold of. It is about a monster inside a TV and I play this insanely hideous 1950s wife with Garrit Graham who is my insane husband. There is this hideous monster inside the television eating everybody. The punkers aren't afraid of it and they take it out of the TV and train it to be nice and have dinner with it. It's hysterical.

Billups: I wasn't sure whether or not this would be significant because you were not in it much, but another movie I liked that you were involved with was *Get Crazy* (1983).

Mary: That movie was terrible. Because Alan (Arkush) did *Rock 'n' Roll High School* they said, "We want you to do this other rock 'n' roll movie." It turned out not to be as good. It wasn't fair to him.

Billups: You did a lot of TV in the late 1980s to early 1990s.

Mary: Just trying to make money.

Billups: Roger Corman's book describes this period in time as one when small budget studios were going out of business fast and regularly. Do you feel the climate for acting in smaller films changed around this time?

Mary: I loved doing small budget movies. I could act how I wanted. Back then, I could not even explain what I was doing, I just did it. And the TV stuff, you have to do exactly what they want. "Let's have her be the bad guy. She'll actually be a lesbian." But that can't be in the script. So they hire me, and they sort of get what they want. Then they'll do stupid things like, "Hey Mary, will you hold this whip?" And it was so bad and so behind. Pathetic.

Billups: A film you were in that I liked because it reunited the cast of *Eating Raoul* was Scenes from the *Class Struggle in Beverly Hills* (1989).

Mary: No, I found the script to be really terrible. Not that it was terrible, but very Hollywood. It wasn't like *Eating Raul*, which was very wacky. It was a well-done Hollywood script, so it was kind of boring. Sort of strained in places. But the other thing is Paul, once again, hired me and Robert Beltran to bring back the glory that he had and really failed because he miscast Ray Sharkey. He was the butler. He was terrible. (Bartel) wanted to do it with Frank Langella. He would have been fabulous. And Jacqueline Bisset.

Billups: She seemed out of place in that crew to me.

Mary: She was. And so was Ray Sharkey. Why do you have a butler with a motorcycle? I worked with Ray Sharkey in *Hellhole* (1985). He's a great actor. He's brilliant in a certain kind of role.

Billups: Are you ever surprised with what sticks and what doesn't when it comes to movies you are working on?

Mary: I can tell when something is going south for me, but maybe the rest of the movie is going great. You can never really tell. I don't pay attention to the whole movie. I'm not the director. I've been in movies that people have claimed are stupid and going south and I've actually liked them.

Billups: I can imagine.

Mary: Like in *Hellhole*, there is one scene that I think is really hysterical.

Billups: I enjoyed a movie you recently appeared in called *House of the Devil* (2009).

Mary: Yes. People like it.

Billups: There have been a lot of positive reviews.

Mary: He is really ecstatic about the '80s. He loved making it so typically 1980s.

Billups: Was there anything that drew you to the project particularly?

Mary: What drew me to it was the director, actually. I like working with young guys who are not entrenched in Hollywood-ism. He was very excited and determined. He was so determined; the kind of guy who starts talking to you and doesn't look at you because he is so wrapped up in what he is saying. That kind of fascinates me. I like going on someone else's ride and see what happens.

Billups: Are you painting regularly?

Mary: I am concentrating on it more now. I write for Artillery magazine. I write this retrospective column. And I have finished a series of seven paintings that are about the history of the reclining nude. Of course she ends up in a porno pose. My painting is the main thing that I do.

Billups: Do you feel your experiences as an actor have informed your approach, like for instance, you are painting bodies?

Mary: No, I don't. No, not at all. Two entirely different ballparks.

Billups: Have you painted for long?

Mary: I've painted since I was six. Mom gave me crayons and told me to shut up.

Billups: You studied art at Cornell.

Mary: Yes.

Billups: Did you find it difficult when you were acting to keep it up?

Mary: The only time it's difficult is when I don't have a place to do it. There are times when I don't have any money. Finally, I rented a studio in Los Angeles. The other thing is writing novels. That didn't happen until I stopped taking drugs, which I didn't do until I was fifty.

Billups: Wow.

Mary: When you take drugs, your mind gets anesthetized, which was good for me for a while. When I stopped, because I had this terrible operation, I almost died. My mind woke up. I wrote those books.

Billups: And there is a documentary on the horizon, I noticed.

Mary: Yes. It's two girls, not girls, women. I always think all women are girls because I'm so old. And they approached me. One is a fantastic photographer. The other, I have seen her work, she is a great editor and director. They are Minx Films and they are doing a documentary about me. I have written a book called *Confessions of a Cult Queen* and that is sort of the backbone of the documentary. It is only about my film career and it is about the fact that I am not a Stanislavsky-type of actress. I'm a bizarre actress. I took it from the Theatre of the Ridiculous to Corman and I have stuck with it.

Billups: Do you have plans to release the book in congress with the documentary?

Mary: They are working together.

Billups: How is it being the subject of a documentary?

Mary: I've noticed something: I used to hate people asking me about Warhol. It was so annoying, but when I go over and over, it is interesting how my mind changes about it and I realize how it fit in and where it fit in. I don't mind anymore.

Acknowledgments:

Thanks for this project go to my parents, who got me out of a lot of jams over the years.

Thanks to Eric Friedl and Zac Ives for taking a chance on this book.

This project would not have been possible without the diligent work and supportive efforts of Jen House and Andria Lisle.

Thanks also to Kathleen Murray for being on hand to answer questions and reading segments of this book over and over again in the wake of neurotic fogs.

Thanks to the Goner staff for maintaining a space where art and music can develop.

Thank you Todd Taylor, Daryl Gussin, and the staff and writers at Razorcake Magazine for allowing me my first writing opportunities and basically providing the equivalent of a Masters over the years. And I'd also like to thank Mike and Anja Stax and Ugly Things for their continued editorial shaping and support.

Thanks to Bobby Polsky, Matt Moffatt, and the present and past staff of Smash! Records in Washington D.C. for years of support selling zines and allowing me to use the shop as a home and occasional forum.

I am forever indebted to Ben Tankersley for his years of camaraderie, collaboration, and general support of my efforts.

I would also like to thank Andy Gale, Charlie Post, Nancy Dolina, Sara Moseley, Mike and Tora Estep, Daisy Lacy, Katie Zubeck, Mikey T. (whose last name I still don't know after all these years), Hanna Mangold, Crystal Bradley, Yung-En Chen, Travis Spillers, and Joao Da Silva, for setting standards of integrity in my life and for a consistent interest in and commitment to general dumb-assery.

Photo by Kathleen Murray

About the Author

Billups Allen spent his formative years in and around the Washington D.C. punk scene. He graduated from the University of Arizona with a creative writing major and a film minor. He has worked in seven different record stores around the country and currently lives in Memphis, Tennessee where he works for Goner Records, publishes Cramhole zine, contributes music and movie writing regularly to Razorcake, Ugly Things, and Lunchmeat magazines, and writes fiction.

– cramholezine.com